PHONOLOG

FOR LISTENI

Teaching the stream of speech

This is just the book I've been waiting for – an original, inventive and above all useful approach.

Mark Hancock, author of *English Pronunciation in Use Intermediate*.

This innovative publication should be on every EFL teacher's bookshelf.

Martin Hewings co-author of *Cambridge Academic English*.

This is a great leap forward that really brings listening into the 21st Century.

Jenny Jenkins, Professor of Global Englishes, University of Southampton.

Three decades of research and teacher training come together in this key book.

Ron Carter, Research Professor of Modern English Language University of Nottingham.

Phonology for Listening can be enjoyed by the gadget-lover or low-tech teacher alike.

Lucy Pickering, Associate Professor of Applied Linguistics, Texas A&M-Commerce.

This book combines solid research with practical outcomes that teachers will find invaluable.

Mike McCarthy, Emeritus Professor, University of Nottingham.

This is a book for students and teachers worldwide. Highly recommended.

Winnie Cheng, Professor of English, Hong Kong Polytechnic University.

Listening teaching has long needed a book like this.

John M. Levis, Associate Professor of English, Iowa State University.

PHONOLOGY
FOR LISTENING

Teaching the stream of speech

RICHARD CAULDWELL

A Streaming Speech publication from Speech in Action.

Speech in Action
Birmingham, UK

www.speechinaction.com

Consultant editors: Geraldine Mark, Jane Walsh

Edited by Sheila Thorn, The Listening Business

Page design and layout by CreateSpace, an Amazon Company
Printed on demand by Amazon
Cover design by Jane Bromham

First published 2013

ISBN: 0954344723
ISBN-13: 978-0954344726

A Streaming Speech publication, from Speech in Action.

Contents

Acknowledgements

Dedicated to:
My parents, Peter and Betty Cauldwell.

Thanks to:
My wife and children – Estella, Dominic, Richard, Matthew.

Thanks also to:
Linda Shockey, Richard Stibbard, Robin Walker, Jane Hadcock, Anna Linthe, Mike Beilby, Martin Hewings, Suzanne Hewings, Geraldine Mark, Martin Warren, Dorota Pacek, Sheila Thorn, Almut Koester, Dave Coniam, Liz Samson, Judy Dendy, Lawrence Schourup, Anna Mauranen, Beth Zielinski; Hiroshi Kuwabara, Iwao Yamashita, and all the teachers on the Japanese Secondary Teachers' programme at the University of Birmingham 1990-2012; former colleagues in the English Department of the University of Birmingham, Malcolm Coulthard, and the late John Sinclair and Tim Johns.

Special thanks to:
Don Weed, founder of ITM Alexander Technique.

Inspired by:
David Brazil.

Thanks also to the speakers:
Corony, Toby, Dan, Silvia, Hector, Maggie, Geoff, Rachel, Andrzej, Gail, Jess, Bob, Terry, Philip, Patrick, Kim, Jackie, Travis, Karam, Ellen, Jane, Helen, Catherine, Bruce, Jeffrey and Ashley.

Thanks for permission to:
Cambridge University Press for extracts from David Brazil's *Pronunciation for Advanced Learners of English*. Cambridge University Press, Professor Ronald Carter and Professor Michael McCarthy for an extract from *Exploring Spoken English*. Pearson Education for an extract from the app of *Longman Dictionary of Contemporary English*. Sonocent for screenshots of *Audio Notetaker*.

Symbols and notation

The symbols for vowels and consonants are shown in the table below.

Vowels				Consonants			
ɪ	pit	iː	bee	p	people	b	boy
e	pet	ɜː	bird	t	tea	d	done
æ	pat	ɑː	bar	k	cat	g	girl
ʌ	putt	ɔː	bore	f	four	v	vat
ɒ	pot	uː	boo	θ	thing	ð	that
ʊ	put			s	sing	z	zoo
eɪ	bay	əʊ	go	ʃ	ship	ʒ	Asia
aɪ	buy	aʊ	now	h	hip	l	light
ɔɪ	boy	i	cit_y_	m	man	r	red
ɪə	here	u	thank-_you_	n	nine	j	yet
eə	fair	ə	_about_	ŋ	sing	w	wet
ʊə	poor			tʃ	church	ʤ	gem

Symbols in the text
The symbols for vowels and consonants in the text are shown between single vertical lines: |t|. The context should make it clear whether they are to be interpreted as 'phonemic' – broad categories of sound – or 'phonetic' – fine details of sounds.

Word stress and syllable divisions
The stress marks for citation forms are shown thus |ˌfʌn.dəˈmen.təl.i| _fundamentally_

- the syllable preceded by a superscript stroke |ˈmen| has primary stress
- the syllable preceded by a subscript stroke |ˌfʌn| has secondary stress
- the three other syllables, |də| |təl| |i| are unstressed
- the full stop, or period, marks other syllable boundaries

Glottal stop

Very often, syllable final |t| and |d| are heard as glottal stops |ʔ|: e.g. *a little bit of metal* (cf. Chapter 11.4) becomes |ə lɪʔḷ bɪʔ əv meʔḷ|

The alveolar tap

Many people who speak American English have what sounds like a |d| instead of a |t| in words such as *writer,* which therefore sounds close to *rider*. The symbol we will use for this sound (an alveolar tap) is |ɾ|.

Diacritics

We occasionally need some smaller symbols – known as diacritics – to add to symbols for 'nasalisation' and 'no audible release'.

- Often when a final consonant |n| is dropped (and even when it isn't) the preceding vowel is nasalised, so that |ten| becomes |tẽ|. The symbol above 'e' is a diacritic, called a 'tilde', which means that the vowel is nasalised.
- Often, at the end of syllables and in consonant clusters, plosive consonants |p t k b d g| sound incomplete. Thus in making the consonant |p| in the word *slept* you might bring your lips together, but because the following sound |t| overlaps with it, the final part of the |p| sound (known as the 'release') is not audible. The symbol for 'no audible release' is a diacritic, a 'left angle': p˺ .

Notation

Double vertical lines || signify a speech unit boundary; upper case letters show that a syllable is **prominent**; lower case letters show that a syllable is **non-prominent**.

```
|| i WASn't sure what to DO about it ||
```

In this speech unit there are two prominences on *was* and *do*. The other eight syllables *i –n't sure what to a.bout it* are non-prominent.

Symbols for the tones are placed at the beginning of the speech unit, but start on the last prominence. This means that, in the speech unit below, the falling tone starts on *do* and continues over *about it*.

```
|| ↘ i WASn't sure what to DO about it ||
```

Tones:

↘	fall
↗↘	rise-fall
→	level
↗	rise
↘↗	fall-rise

Symbols for high key (a marked step up in pitch) and low key (a marked step down in pitch) are placed immediately in front of the syllables to which they apply:

```
|| ↗ i ↑WASn't SURE || ↘ ↓WHAT to DO about it ||
```

In these speech units, the first syllable of *wasn't* has high key, and *what* has low key. The symbols for the tones occur at the beginning of the speech unit, but apply to the last prominence: a rising tone starts on *sure* and a falling tone starts on *do*.

Introduction

Phonology for Listening: Teaching the Stream of Speech is for both experienced teachers of English and those teachers who are at the beginning of their ELT careers. It provides a framework – the *Phonology* of the title – for the description of spontaneous speech, and then uses this framework to help capture the realities of spontaneous speech. This framework also makes it easier to teach these realities to students so they become better at listening.

Thus the aim of *Phonology for Listening* is to improve the teaching and learning of listening in English.

We will focus on perception and decoding. This focus is needed because current listening methodology relies too much on the testing and the practising of understanding, and focuses too little on teaching learners to decode the **sound substance** of the stream of speech.

What is this sound substance? The answer starts with the fact that we tend to teach our students one soundshape for each word: the citation form. This is an isolated soundshape in which all the vowels, consonants, syllables and stresses of the word are very clearly heard. This is the soundshape that is given in dictionaries. But the language that learners have to cope with as listeners comes at them as a stream. In this stream words are squeezed into soundshapes which differ greatly from the citation form, and they vary greatly according to the way speakers say them. They also combine with other words to form fast bursts of the stream, which adds to the number of soundshapes that learners have to decode and understand. The sum total of all the soundshapes of words, and word groups, make up the **sound substance of English**. It is this sound substance – the stream of speech – that *Phonology for Listening* will enable you to grasp, teach and use to help your students become better listeners.

It is my experience, and it is probably your experience too, that listening is the language skill which lags behind the other skills. Many language learners have higher levels of competence in reading, writing and speaking than they do in listening. Rost (2001: 13) writes that listening '...is still often considered a mysterious *black box* for which the best approach seems to be *more practice...*' and he adds 'Much work needs to be done to modernise the teaching of listening.' *Phonology for Listening* aims to open up the 'black box' that Rost refers to, and to modernise the teaching of listening using both new ideas, and the digital tools which are now at our disposal. *Phonology for Listening* provides tools for you to describe the stream of speech: its speeds, rhythms, accents, and the different sound-shapes which words have in the stream of speech.

The subtitle – *Teaching the stream of speech* – refers to the fact that we need to teach our students to cope with what comes at them as a continuous stream of sound substance which they are not in control of. It does not come at them in the traditional units of language teaching: not word-by-word, nor phrase-by-phrase, nor sentence-by-sentence, but as a stream of speech. We will take the plight of the learner listener as our standpoint, and address the following questions:

- What is the sound substance of the stream of speech that learners have to cope with?
- How can we describe it?
- How can we teach it?

Phonology for Listening is in four parts. Part 1 contains an easy-to-learn framework – the window on speech. In the remaining three parts we will use this framework both to illuminate the stream of speech, and teach it. In Part 2 we will learn how words are squeezed into different soundshapes by the forces of speaker choices, rhythm and speed. In Part 3 we will learn about accents and emotion in speech. In Part 4 we will apply what we have learned to the teaching of listening.

0.1   Spontaneous speech

To teach listening more effectively we need to focus on the realities of spontaneous speech. Such speech is unscripted; it is constructed piece-by-piece in real time. It is made up as the speakers go along, while they are pursuing their own particular communicative purposes – informing, asking, persuading, promising, telling an anecdote, making a complaint and maintaining social relationships.

Rapid informal spontaneous speech is the most difficult form of the language as far as listening is concerned. It is therefore appropriate to focus on it as the goal for learning listening. However, much of the analysis and description contained in *Phonology for Listening* will also apply to naturally-occurring or well-acted speech of all kinds – including scripted speech. Thus, by focusing on the problem of decoding rapid informal spontaneous speech – the most extreme form of the stream of speech – we will be in the best possible position to help learners cope with listening of all types.

0.2   The plight of the listener

Our focus will be on the listeners' experiences of the sounds that come at them in ways they cannot control – the acoustic blur, the speeds, the accents, the 'extremely messy products' (Lass, 1980: 298) of spontaneous speech. Language teaching has largely avoided tackling the extremely messy aspects of spontaneous speech. *Phonology for Listening* aims to improve this situation by offering both a description of the extremely messy features of spontaneous speech, and a means of teaching it, while recognising that such speech is absolutely normal, and not a deviant form.

0.3   Experiences of learners: Ying's dilemma and Anna's anger

We will use the experiences of learners as landmarks in *Phonology for Listening*. In Chapter 1 we will read a diary entry from Ying, a Singaporean learner who wonders if the soundshapes of words change when used in the middle of a sentence, because *she cannot catch words that she knows*. We will refer to her situation as **Ying's dilemma**, and we will refer to those moments in speech when words are squeezed into the unfamiliar soundshapes that cause her dilemma as **Ying moments**. *Phonology for Listening* sets itself the task of helping learners avoid Ying's dilemma. We will see that in order to do so, we have to use something other than the notion of a sentence. Instead we will use the notion of **speech units**, which are defined below in 0.5, and explained in detail in Chapters 2-3.

In Chapter 16 we will read comments of another (former) learner, Anna from Finland, whose memories of listening comprehension classes make her angry. She is angry because her teachers would play recordings and get her to answer questions, but then they would *not* take what might seem the obvious next step of using the recording to teach her about the language. The recording was underused: it was used for testing understanding, but not for teaching the realities of the stream of speech.

Phonology for Listening provides tools to help learners like Ying and Anna. It will help identify where words have become unrecognisable for learners – the Ying moments – and it will give us the confidence and the ability to explain the realities of the stream of speech contained in recordings, and particularly those of unscripted spontaneous speech.

0.4   What type of phonology textbook?

Conventionally, information about the sound substance of English comes from pronunciation sylla-buses. These syllabuses largely teach the spoken language 'as it ought to be' – a correct, tidy, steady-speed, rule-governed phenomenon. There is a list of speech sounds (vowels, consonants), a set of rules on how to say sentences of different types and lengths (statements, questions, lists, etc.), and there are exercises which practise linking, assimilation, elision, stress-timing, nuclear stress and other connected speech phenomena. Taken together these elements comprise a model of speech which is optimised for clear pronunciation. We will refer to this model as the **careful speech model.**

The careful speech model is relatively easy to teach and learn – and it is very useful in promoting intelli-gible pronunciation. But its resemblance to spontaneous speech is inadequate for the task of preparing learners to cope with the rough-and-tumble, the speeds, the accents and the lack of clarity of the sound substance of spontaneous speech.

Phonology for Listening goes beyond, but complements, the careful speech model. It does this by making extensive use of the evidence of recordings of spontaneous speech which are presented in both transcription (using the window on speech) and in recordings. The window on speech pre-sented in Part 1, together with the evidence of spontaneous speech presented in Part 2, comprise a **spontaneous speech model** – a model of speech which is optimised for the teaching of listening.

The careful speech model would encourage a pronunciation of the words *It keeps me fit* in which the vowel of *keeps* |iː| is clearly different from the vowel in *fit* |ɪ|, and the two consonants at the end of *keeps* are clearly articulated. But in the spontaneous speech model there are a large number ways in which these words might occur in the stream of speech, one of which is *It kiss me fit*, in which *keeps* has become *kiss*. Learners have to be able to cope with varying soundshapes like this which come at them at speeds and levels of clarity over which they have no control. The differ-ences between the careful speech model and the spontaneous speech model are summarised in Appendix 1.

Phonology for Listening contains twenty chapters, divided into four parts:

- Part 1: The window on speech framework
- Part 2: Describing spontaneous speech

- Part 3: Accents, identity and emotion in speech
- Part 4: Teaching listening

There are a number of ways in which you can read this book. I recommend that you read this introduction and Chapters 1 and 2. Thereafter you can read the parts in any order. Each part is self contained: it begins with a one-page summary, followed by five chapters. There is then an answer key for the activities in that part.

0.5   Part 1: The window on speech framework

Part 1 (Chapters 1-5) presents the **window on speech** – a descriptive framework which provides the conceptual tools we need to hear and describe the realities of the stream of speech. This will enable us to help our students decode the sound substance of speech more effectively. This framework has its origins in the work of Brazil (1975, 1978, 1997), as developed and used by Bradford (1988), Hewings (1993), Cauldwell (2002) and others.

The principle components of the framework are five types of speech unit: these are rhythmic chunks of speech which are speaker-defined (not grammar-defined), containing between one and twenty syllables. They are up to about three seconds in length, and consist of a rhythmic alternation of prominent and non-prominent syllables, and just one tone.

Speech units are used, rather than syntactic units such as clauses, because they give a clearer picture of the moment-by-moment choices that speakers make as they communicate. Chapters 1 and 2 give a general introduction to speech units and the squeezing effects which they have on words. Chapters 3-5 give preliminary training in transcribing recordings of spontaneous speech into speech units of different sizes. After reading Chapter 2 you may prefer to delay reading Chapters 3-5 until after you have seen the value of applying, observing, and using the window on speech in the later parts of *Phonology for Listening*. You can come back to these chapters at any time if you feel the need to do so.

0.6   Part 2: Describing spontaneous speech

In Part 2 (Chapters 6-10) we use the window on speech framework to describe the sound substance of the stream of speech. The description will focus on the differences between *the spontaneous speech model* and *the careful speech model*. These differences include the placement of pauses, filled pauses, repetitions, restarts and other phenomena which are often regarded as disfluencies, but which are a natural feature of spontaneous speech. Speed and rhythm are also covered, but central to this section are Chapters 8 and 9 where we look in detail at the forces which create the unfamiliar soundshapes which cause Ying's dilemma.

0.7 Part 3: Accents, identity, and emotion in speech

In Part 3 we use the window on speech framework as an observational tool to look at other aspects of the sound substance of speech: the way it varies with a person's accent and the role it plays in communicating emotion and attitudes. Whereas Part 2 is mainly about soundshapes in the stream of speech, Part 3 is mainly about the flavours and colouring that voices have. We look at the differences between British and American English, accents of Britain and Ireland, accents of North America (Canada and the USA) and accents of Global English. We see (and hear) that many people have more than one accent, and that their accents can change from moment to moment. We also cover the notion of prejudice, and look at the relationship between how people say things, and the emotional or attitudinal meanings that they convey.

0.8 Part 4: Teaching listening

In Part 4 we see how we can incorporate the realities of spontaneous speech into classroom activities which will improve the learning of listening. First of all we look at problems with some current approaches to teaching listening. These include the over-reliance on osmosis ('listen to lots, and your listening skills will improve automatically'), inappropriate use of the careful speech model and confusion about the relationship between goals and activities. We then look at low-tech and hi-tech activities that we can use inside and outside the classroom. These activities include using our own and our students' voices to create vocal gymnastic exercises which serve the goal of listening by replicating the squeezing effects of speech units. We also look at how computer software and tablet and smartphone apps can be used both in the classroom and in student projects. We will also consider how the traditional listening comprehension exercise can be can be adapted to maximise the learning opportunities that recordings present.

0.9 Recordings

The recordings are an essential component of *Phonology for Listening*. If you are reading the printed version, you will need to download the soundfiles from the Speech in Action website and put them in your iTunes library, or other media playing application. If you are reading the electronic version on an appropriate device, then the soundfile is available on screen, next to the relevant text.

Extensive use is made of recordings to illustrate the points being made. The recorded evidence consists of people talking without a script, as themselves, on topics which matter to them. They are speaking to someone who is listening and interacting by asking occasional questions. The extracts we will use are mostly of two kinds: first, where the speaker is in mid-story or mid-anecdote; second, at moments of dialogue where the speakers are exchanging or sharing information and ideas, or prompting each other to speak further. All the recordings have been specifically chosen because they illustrate the patterns of spontaneous speech.

0.10 Symbols and notation

The window on speech requires a simple form of notation, which is explained in the list of **Symbols and notation**. The notation uses upper and lower-case letters for prominences and non-prominences, arrow symbols for tones, and double vertical lines for speech unit boundaries. We will also make use of symbols. The standard range of phonemic symbols that are found in dictionaries, plus a few diacritics (e.g. for 'nasalisation', and for 'no audible release') whose significance will be explained when they occur. The symbols are given between single vertical lines, and for those who might ask 'Are these symbols meant to be interpreted as phonemic or phonetic?' – the answer is that the context should make it clear to you whether they are to be interpreted as one or the other.

The symbols and notation are used to give you some guidance as to what to listen for in the recording. It might be helpful to consider them as signposts, pointing you in the direction of what to listen for, rather than as authoritative analyses of what the speakers have produced with lips, tongue, teeth, etc. They are used to help you to hear the realities of the recorded evidence. As well as symbols, we will use expressions such as 'sounds close to' and 'sounds between...' to guide you towards hearing the sound-shapes of words in each particular extract.

0.11 Terminology

We will need to use terms which refer to groups of people who have different relationships to the English language. In particular we need to make a distinction between those people who were born into an English-language environment and for whom English is or has become the most-used and most-at-home-with language, and those speakers who have learned English as a second, extra or auxiliary language, or for whom it is a lingua franca. Early drafts of *Phonology for Listening* used the terms **native speaker** and **non-native speaker,** but readers of these drafts have informed me that these terms are unacceptable in some quarters. I realise that whatever choice I make in this controversial area is likely to annoy – perhaps enrage – some people. The choice I have made to differentiate the two groups is to use the terms **L1 speakers** of English and **L2 speakers** of English, where L1 stands for 'first language' and L2 'stands for second or additional language'.

Occasionally we will use terms which may be new to you, or used in a new way. These will usually be defined on their first appearance and will appear in the **Glossary**.

0.12   Activities

At the end of each chapter there are two activities for you to do on your own, with a friend, a colleague or a fellow teacher. The types of activity vary with the content of the chapter. They include:

- reflecting on your experiences as a language learner and as a teacher
- observing the language around you: friends chatting, videos on YouTube
- listening to and analysing recordings
- working with a short script to perform speech units in a certain way
- experimenting with activities in your own teaching.

You will need to keep a record of your observations, reflections and feelings about learning and teaching listening. You will also need two pieces of equipment: a recording device and a computer. The recording device can be your smartphone or a device such as an Olympus, Sony, or other brand voice recorder. You will also need to be able to transfer recordings from your device to your computer, and to edit those recordings in software called a digital audio editor – *Audacity* is an example of free (at the time of writing) software that would be appropriate to use.

You should *always* get permission to record people – everyone whose voice you capture on the recording. If you use other people's recordings, you must make sure that you get their permission, and respect their legal rights.

Some activities have an answer key, and these answers appear at the end of the Part in which the activity is set. Thus the answer key for activities in Chapter 3 will appear at the end of Part 1 and for Chapter 7 will appear at the end of Part 2, etc. There is no answer key for Part 4, as the activities are all open-ended.

0.13   Website

Additional materials to accompany *Phonology for Listening* are available from the Speech in Action website, www.speechinaction.com. If you are a lecturer running a course where you and your students are using this book, you will find resources there to help you.

0.14   Finally...

I have really enjoyed creating and writing *Phonology for Listening*. Both because I have finally addressed issues in the teaching of listening that have bugged me for years (actually decades), and for the opportunity it has given me to discuss issues with the many people who have given me comments and advice.

I hope you get as much enjoyment out of reading and working with *Phonology for Listening* as I have in the writing of it.

References

Bradford, B. (1988) *Intonation in Context*. Cambridge: Cambridge University Press.

Brazil, D. (1975) *Discourse Intonation*. Discourse analysis monographs no. 1. English Language Research: University of Birmingham.

Brazil, D. (1978) *Discourse Intonation II*. Discourse analysis monographs no. 2. English Language Research: University of Birmingham.

Brazil, D. (1997) *The Communicative Value of Intonation in English*. Cambridge: Cambridge University Press.

Cauldwell, R. (2002) *Streaming Speech: Listening and Pronunciation for Advanced Learners of English*. [CD-Rom]. Birmingham: Speech in Action.

Hewings, M. (1993) *Pronunciation Tasks*. Cambridge: Cambridge University Press.

Lass, R. (1984) *Phonology: An Introduction to Basic Concepts*. Cambridge: Cambridge University Press.

Rost, M. (2001) *Listening*. In Carter, R. and Nunan, D. (eds.) *The Cambridge Guide to Teaching English to Speakers of Other Languages*. Cambridge: Cambridge University Press.

PART 1

The window on speech framework

Part 1: The window on speech framework

The **window on speech framework** is a way of representing, in writing, the rhythmic and intonation features of speech. Using orthodox spelling and a few symbols, it provides transcriptions which throw light on (hence *window*) the streamlike characteristics of spontaneous speech. This window helps us describe the sound substance of the stream of speech and it helps us identify those parts of it which are likely to cause problems for learners. The transcription works alongside the recording to which it relates: it directs our attention to features of the recording, so that we can hear the effects of the speakers' choices on the sound substance of speech. Each chapter ends with two language awareness activities: the majority encourage you to listen to the language that you encounter every day, to record and comment on some of that language, or to analyse a recording using the tools presented in the chapter concerned. There is an answer key after Chapter 5.

Chapter 1 *Phonology, listening and Ying's dilemma* explains why current models of speech are inadequate in helping to prepare teachers to teach listening. It also explains why the window on speech is necessary, by describing the experiences of Ying, a learner whose dilemma is central to the purpose of *Phonology for Listening*.

Chapter 2 *Prominence, speech units and squeeze zones* introduces the concepts of prominent and non-prominent syllables. Prominences are the building blocks of speech units: they are the syllables that speakers choose to highlight as they speak. Squeeze zones are those parts of a speech unit which contain non-prominent syllables, where words are squeezed into a wide variety of soundshapes which are very unlike their citation forms.

After Chapter 2, you have a choice: to read Chapters 3-5 or to read Parts 2, 3 or 4.

The remaining chapters in Part 1 are more technical, and aim to give you preliminary training in the skill of transcribing. You can go to any of the other parts of *Phonology for Listening* before reading these chapters.

Chapter 3 *Transcription I: Speech units* describes the five sizes of speech unit which make up the window on speech framework.

Chapter 4 *Transcription II: Tones, contours, and key* continues the description of the window on speech by looking at the tunes of speech – three levels of key (steps up and down in pitch) and five types of tone (fall, rise, fall-rise, level, rise-fall).

Chapter 5 *Transcription III: Reliability and meaning* examines whether there is a relationship between speech units and grammatical and other categories of meaning. It also discusses the extent to which different transcribers will agree on their respective transcriptions.

Remember you need the recordings. Download them from www.speechinaction.com.

1 Phonology, listening and Ying's dilemma

In English language teaching the skill of listening is poorly learned: it tends to lag behind the other skills. One Singaporean learner, Ying, commented on her experiences as a learner listener and, in doing so, describes the problem that we address in *Phonology for Listening*:

> I believe I need to learn what the word sounds like when it is used in the sentence. Because sometimes when a familiar word is used in a sentence, I couldn't catch it. Maybe *it changes somewhere when it is used in a sentence.* (Goh, 1997: 366) [Emphasis added]

This is *Ying's dilemma* – she believes that she knows a word, but this knowledge is inadequate because she cannot *catch* the word when it occurs in speech. Ying wonders whether there is something about the position of the word in a sentence that results in her not being able to recognise it. Her thinking is that it changes somewhere when it is used in a sentence.

The purpose of *Phonology for Listening* is to help us prepare our students for their encounters with real speech, and thus help them avoid Ying's dilemma. We will see that in order to do this we have to investigate what Ying means by the words *somewhere ... in a sentence*, and to do so we have to introduce the concept of the **speech unit.**

1.1   Definitions

Speech units are sections of the stream of speech, usually multi-word, with a distinct rhythm and a tune which is assigned by the speaker at the moment of speaking. They feature alternations of **prominent** and **non-prominent** syllables, steps up and down in pitch and the glides (up, down and level) of tones. They range in size from one to twenty syllables. We will see that words change their soundshape in different positions in speech units – in some positions the word remains easily recognisable, but in others they are squeezed into shapes which can be unrecognisable to someone who only knows soundshapes that are close to the citation form. This approach to speech units derives from that of Brazil (1997), although the term he used was *tone unit.*

Spoken words have a wide variety of **soundshapes**, depending on accent, speed, volume and their position in speech units. The **citation form** of a word is the soundshape that is given in pronunciation dictionaries in both phonemic symbols and, in recently published dictionaries, a soundfile. It is the form of the word that is given in answer to the question 'How do you pronounce this?' It is a slow, isolated form of the word in which the vowels, consonants, syllables and word stress are given explicit and careful treatment. But words have a wide variety of different soundshapes, many of which can be sufficiently different from the citation form as to cause Ying's dilemma. We will see this illustrated in Section 1.2 below, and more fully explained in Part 2, Chapters 8 & 9.

The **phonology** of the title of this book refers to the five types of speech unit (roughly equivalent to the *tone units* and *tone groups* of other publications) which together comprise the window on speech framework. The usual concerns of phonology are **segmental** – the study of how a language makes use of combinations of vowels and consonants to build syllables and words. *Phonology for Listening* is not a segmental phonology, it is a **suprasegmental** phonology, one that is concerned with how speakers divide up their speech into rhythmic bursts of between a quarter of a second and three seconds in length – from one to about twenty syllables. In this approach to phonology we will see that it is the speakers who are the creators of the sound shape of the stream of speech, not the language system itself.

Listening in its most general sense means the process of understanding everything that comes a person's way in the form of speech. But there are three components to listening: **preparation**, **perception** and **understanding**. The *preparation* component involves activating contextual knowledge and strategies, and directing your attention to what is being said; the *perception* component involves decoding the sound substance of speech and identifying the words that are said; the *understanding* component involves deriving meaning from what has been said. *Phonology for Listening* deals with the second of these components, perception. We thus focus on decoding (in Ying's terms *catching*) the words that are contained in the **sound substance** of speech. The *sound substance* is the acoustic blur of the stream of speech which exits the mouth of the speaker and travels through space before entering the ear of the listener. It is the substance that a computer programme or a recording device captures. The process of picking out the words that the sound substance contains is known as **lexical segmentation**. In essence, our object of study is the acoustic blur of the stream of speech – the raw material which arrives at the learner listener's ears. An additional focus is on how we teach the relationship between this sound substance and what the learner knows already – the citation forms of the words.

1.2   Ying's dilemma

Ying speculated that 'the words change somewhere ... in a sentence'. We will now see and hear what she means by this. We will listen to four speech units of scripted speech from Brazil (1994: Chapter 1), all of which contain the word *where*. In Extract 1.1, prominent syllables are shown in upper case (prominences will be defined fully in Chapter 2; but for the purpose of Extract 1.1 you can consider them as 'stresses'), non-prominent ('unstressed') syllables are shown in lower case. You will notice that *where* is prominent in 01 and 02, and non-prominent in 03 and 04. Extract 1 contains the four speech units and ends with the four occurrences of *where* placed side-by-side.

Extract 1.1 Examples of *where* (Brazil, 1994)

```
01 || but i WASn't sure WHERE ||
02 || WHERE MARket street was ||
03 || where she'd SAID ||
04 || where there were STREET LIGHTS ||
      WHERE ... WHERE ...where ... where
```

These four speech units are from different parts of the recording. At the end of the recording, the four occurrences of *where* are placed side-by-side so that you can hear the differences clearly.

In unit 01 *where* is close to the citation form: it is slow and clear, and it occurs before a pause. In 02 *where* is again prominent, but it is shorter because it comes before the word *market* and not before a pause. The soundshape is different, but its close resemblance to the citation form makes it easily recognisable. However, in both 03 and 04 *where* is reduced to a short sound rather like the sharp bleat of a lamb. The two non-prominent soundshapes in 03 and 04 are much less easy to relate to the citation form than the prominent ones in 01 and 02. Another factor is that the two non-prominent versions are part of groups of words which are streamed together in fast bursts: *where she'd* goes at 360 words per minute or 6 syllables per second and *where there were* goes at 750 words per minute or 12.5 syllables per second (we will deal with speed in Chapter 7). Being streamed together with other words makes their relationship to the citation form even more distant and makes them – in Ying's terms – less catchable.

1.3   The blur gap

L1 speakers and expert L2 speakers of English are generally not aware of the variety of soundshapes that spoken words have. L1 speakers understand meanings without realising that there is very often a big difference between the soundshapes that occur in the **acoustic blur** of speech and the citation sound-shapes that words have. The *acoustic blur* refers to the way in which words, in the stream of speech, do not have clearly defined beginnings and endings. Their edges are blurred, syllables are dropped and vowels and consonants disappear or change their nature. L1 speakers often hear mere traces of words in the acoustic blur and yet they believe they have heard citation forms in these traces. For example (as we heard in the previous section) the acoustic blur may contain a rush of three syllables going at 750 words per minute – *weatherwuh* – but L1 speakers will believe that they hear *where* followed by *there* followed by *were* in soundshapes which are close to the citation form. L1 speakers are deaf in this special way – deaf to the fact that we decode traces. We do not hear the acoustic blur of the sound substance that reaches our ears. Instead we hear the results of an extremely rapid, automatic, internal decoding process which has already, in a split second, matched the traces that are heard to the citation form soundshapes of words. It is an expert skill which operates subliminally, below the level of awareness and attention. The gap between what L1 speakers believe they hear and what is actually in the acoustic blur of speech is what I call the **blur gap**. It is another purpose of *Phonology for Listening* to raise awareness of the blur gap, and to ensure that allowances are made for it in the teaching of listening.

1.4   Careful speech: the wrong model for listening

The model of speech which dominates language teaching is one that is designed for clear intelligible pronunciation. We will refer to it as the **careful speech model**. It is a model in the sense of being something to aim at, to copy and to emulate. Indeed we can also think of it as an **emulation model**. Its components include the citation forms of words, the rules given for the relationship between clause and speech unit, the tunes of statements and questions (falling and rising tones) where to place stresses (on content words such as *street,* not on function words such as *where*) and the nuclear syllable (on the last lexical item in a sentence or clause). It is an orderly model of speech, optimised for clear pronunciation and for the delivery of planned speech. It has two main advantages: it is teaching and learning friendly, and it is easy to describe in terms of rules and advice.

However, as we shall see and hear, this careful speech model is inadequate for the purposes of describing spontaneous speech and teaching listening. It is inadequate because spontaneous speech is not as orderly as the careful speech model would have us believe, and because its rules, whilst excellent as guidelines for pronunciation, are often misinterpreted as facts which are accurate descriptions of spontaneous speech. The careful speech model is mistakenly treated as if it were a descriptive model – a model based on the collection and analysis of the evidence of speech of all kinds – whereas it is, in fact, an emulation model. For example, the rule that *yes-no* questions rise, which is reasonable advice for careful speech, is not warranted by experimental findings. The most common tone for English is the falling tone, and it is the most common for questions, just as it is for statements.

Language teaching is so attached to the rules of the careful speech model that even when experts such as Wells (2006: 91–92) warn that their guidelines are not to be taken as evidence of the facts of language use, the warning is ignored, and the guidelines of the careful speech model are said to be true for all types of speech. The pedagogical usefulness of the careful speech model for pronunciation has led to the mistaken belief that it is the outcome of descriptive research.

To improve the teaching of listening, and help with Ying's dilemma, we need a model of speech which will complement the careful speech model and add a descriptive dimension to the teaching of listening. The window on speech framework, and what it reveals about spontaneous speech, can provide us with this complentary model – optimised for the teaching of spontaneous speech – which we will refer to as the **spontaneous speech model.**

1.5   Spontaneous speech: the right model for listening

The sound substance of speech has many features which make it difficult to teach. Most of them are shared by speech of all kinds, but informal spontaneous speech often has extreme versions of these features which it is our aim to identify and describe. It is the job of the window on speech framework to help us describe both the features which differentiate speech of all kinds from writing, and the 'extreme', non-careful speech features of spontaneous speech.

The facts are that speech is:

- invisible
- transient
- speedy (often very fast)
- plastic (it can be squeezed into different shapes)
- shaped by speaker choices
- context related (both situational and psychological)
- of varying clarity
- never accent-free

To this list we can add that spontaneous speech is made up moment-by-moment in real time in pursuit of a communicative purpose (cf. Section 1.10 below).

The sound substance of speech – particularly unscripted spontaneous speech – is far less easy to describe for the purposes of teaching and learning language than the careful speech model would have us believe. This is not least because the spontaneous speech model cannot be taught by rule and example: none of its features are under the control of the listener, the learner, the teacher or the textbook writer. It is however a model that we need to get used to, and become familiar and comfortable with, for the purposes of learning and teaching listening.

1.6   Invisible, transient, speedy

The substance of speech is invisible – it comes to us through our ears, not through our eyes. We can study speech by translating it into a graphic substance – writing – but at that point it becomes something else. It is re-substanced into a metaphor, something which stands in the place of the original. Once that translation has been made we have de-natured the stream of speech – taken away those essential elements that differentiate it from writing.

The substance of speech is transient – it comes into existence briefly and then disappears. It does not remain present so that it can be studied. There is a perpetual appearing, disappearing and replenishing act as patches of sound substance follow other patches into and out of existence. Short extracts of the substance may survive briefly in the listener's short-term memory, but they are then quickly replaced by new input.

Much of language learning can happen at the learner's pace. When working with the written language they can re-read passages that they do not immediately understand, and look up words in a dictionary. The written words remain visible, findable and learnable-from. But the spoken language is different – speech comes at a speed which is dictated by the speaker. This speed varies all the time, and is not under the direct control of the listener. The listener can control the speed indirectly by asking the speakers either to slow down, or to repeat what they said, but this very quickly tires the patience of those involved.

1.7   Plasticity: soundshapes

Words have the property of **plasticity** – the capacity to change shape. Although it is possible to list some of the shapes that a word can have, it is not possible to list them all because the soundshape will vary according to factors such as the neighbouring words, whether or not the speaker has highlighted the word, the speed of speech and the accent of the speaker. The metaphor of the car crash is sometimes used to describe what happens to words in speech. Words are described as being crushed in front and crushed from behind as word bumps into word as in a multiple-car crash where a long line of cars collide head to tail. It is a useful metaphor, but it is misleading. A traffic accident is a visible event – it remains in place so the damage to vehicles can be analysed and described. But in the stream of speech all evidence of shape-change disappears, and because of the blur gap (explained in 1.3) most L1 speakers have no idea that the squeezing of words happens in this way. It happens fast, invisibly and transiently, and when a listener or speaker is asked to reflect on what they heard or said, words bounce back to their full shape and assert 'I was not involved in a traffic accident! Here I am – fully formed, and in great shape!'

1.8   Varying clarity

The stream of speech is spoken with variations in clarity in two senses. In the first sense, the stream of speech comes to the hearer against a background of **ambient noise.** Out of doors, there might be traffic noise, or the noise of people and announcements in an airport departure hall, or the noise of people chatting in a café. In the second sense the stream of speech varies in **levels of realisation**. At a high level of realisation most sounds will be clearly pronounced, the rhythm of words and phrases will be clearly heard and the ups and downs and tunes of intonation will have the peaks and valleys of a mountainous area such as the Alps. Language learning materials promoting the careful speech model are often composed of such high-realisation speech. However, most spontaneous speech is delivered at lower levels of realisation – the sounds of words are much more likely to dissolve into each other, or even disappear entirely, and the peaks and valleys of intonation are reduced to low and shallow undulations.

1.9   A clash of models

Most of the examples of speech that are used in language teaching are acted speech which is scripted for the purpose of exemplification of the language system, or for showing the language at work in social situations such as 'at the doctor's surgery'. Even where recordings of spontaneous speech are used, the explanations which are given are based on the expectations and rules of the careful speech model. This often results in a clash between the explanation and the realities of recordings of spontaneous speech. It is not the case that what is true for acted speech is also true for spontaneous speech. So we need the spontaneous speech model to help us describe what has happened in the recordings (of spontaneous speech) that we use, and to help us more generally to compile a description of the wide range of phenomena that can happen in spontaneous speech.

1.10   Spontaneous speech is unscripted

Spontaneous speech is unscripted. It is constructed piece-by-piece in real time. It is made up as the speakers go along, while they are pursuing their communicative purposes - informing, asking, persuading, promising, telling an anecdote, making a complaint and maintaining social relationships. Although such speech contains pre-packaged elements such as idioms ('He can turn his hand to anything') and other ready-made formulae ('and that kind of thing'), its distinctive characteristics come from the fact that it is created at the moment of speaking and therefore all the changes of mind, errors, repetitions and pauses remain present in the sound substance. It is spoken, and has to be understood, in real-time – at the first and only time of hearing.

1.11   Listening is a private process

Listening is a private process. It happens inside the listener's brain in ways which are not directly observable. There may be evidence of successful understanding (they may have 'the right answers'), but this is not evidence that they have successfully matched the sound substance against what they already know. Successful understanding might be due the successful use of compensatory strategies such as guesswork or applying contextual knowledge. My training as a teacher (and I suspect, the training of many other teachers of the Communicative Language Teaching generation) focused on the generation of observable behaviour on the part of our students. We like to see them happy, we like to see them speaking, we like to see them reading and writing enthusiastically. We are much less comfortable with their frowning silences as they try to process the stream of speech. We will return to this aspect of teaching listening in Part 4.

1.12   Summary and what's next

In this chapter we have seen that the careful speech model is not suitable for teaching listening because it is an emulation model optimised for teaching careful rehearsed scripted speech. We have seen that there is a need for a spontaneous speech model, and using the window on speech framework, presented in Chapters 2-4 and used in Chapters 6-10, we can now make a start on constructing this model. The framework is a way of attending to the stream of speech which foregrounds the speaker's choices. It helps us identify parts of the stream of speech where Ying's dilemma is most likely to occur.

1.13   Further reading

Brazil (1995, chapters 1 & 2) provides an excellent account of the nature of spontaneous speech. Field (2008) writes eloquently about the problems of teaching listening and is critical of contemporary approaches to the teaching of listening, particularly the traditional listening comprehension approach. Parts 1 and 2 of *Phonology for Listening* can be viewed as a much extended version of Field's (2008) Chapter 9, and his Appendix 1. Brown (1990) is the classic text on the re-shaping effects that the stream of speech has on the soundshapes of words. Again, *Phonology for Listening* can be viewed as an extension – into the domain of 'private' spontaneous speech – of her work, which featured examples of 'public' English … 'spoken to be understood by many listeners'.

1.14   Language awareness activities

Activity 1.1: Consider and discuss Ying's dilemma

In your own experience of learning a language, have you ever experienced Ying's dilemma? Either make notes about your own experiences, or discuss your experiences with a friend, colleague or fellow teacher.

Activity 1.2: Record and observe

Choose a recording of spontaneous speech, or make your own, and identify words that occur both before a pause and in the middle of the stream of speech (i.e. the same word in two different positions). Using a digital audio editor such as Audacity, copy the individual words, and paste them side-by-side in a separate file. How closely do they resemble the citation form? Play this soundfile to a friend, colleague or fellow teacher, and ask them for their opinions.

2   Prominence, the speech unit and squeeze zones

This is the first of four chapters which present the **window on speech**, our framework for the analysis, observation and teaching of spontaneous speech. This framework, in combination with the findings which emerge from it, constitutes the **spontaneous speech model** – a model of speech for the teaching of listening. It is designed to cope with the unruliness of the speech which learner listeners have to cope with. It places no prior restriction, nor expectation, on what can happen. Any feature can happen anywhere, within the limits of physical possibility. The usefulness of the framework will become apparent in Part 2 (Chapters 6–10) where we will use it to explore the nature of spontaneous speech. This is the only chapter on the window on speech that you need to read before you embark on the other Parts of *Phonology for Listening*. Chapters 3-5 give preliminary training in learning to transcribe recordings according to the window on speech, and you can revisit these chapters at any time.

In this chapter we introduce three concepts: **prominence,** the **speech unit** and **squeeze zones**. **Prominent** syllables are those syllables which the speaker has chosen to highlight by making them longer, louder or at a different pitch (or all three) than neighbouring syllables. These prominences interact with the stress and syllable structure of words to form the characteristic rhythmic patterns of the stream of speech. **Speech units** are (usually) multi-word rhythmic sections of the stream of speech, which feature alternations of prominent and non-prominent syllables, steps up and down in pitch, and the glides (up, down and level) of tones. They range in size from one syllable to twenty syllables. **Squeeze zones** are those parts of a speech unit which contain non-prominent syllables, where words (content words as well as frequent forms and weak forms) are squeezed into soundshapes that can vary dramatically from the citation form.

2.1   The citation form

The citation form is the basic building block of the careful speech model, but it is useful for the window on speech for two reasons. First, it provides a reference point for discussion of the variety of soundshapes that a word has. Second, the pattern of stressed and unstressed syllables of the citation form of a word can be used as a starting point to show the relationship of prominence and non-prominence in multi-word speech units. In what follows we will focus on the citation form of the five-syllable word *association* and see how its soundshape may vary when it occurs together with other words.

In pronunciation dictionaries, information about the word *association* is given in two forms: in symbols and in a soundfile.

Extract 2.1 Citation form of *association*

| ə͵səʊ.siˈeɪ.ʃᵊn |

The symbols gives us three different kinds of information about the pronunciation of this word: phonemes, syllables and word-stress:

- the syllable preceded by a superscript vertical stroke |ˈeɪ| has primary stress
- the syllable preceded by a subscript vertical stroke |͵səʊ| has secondary stress
- the three other syllables |ə| |si| |ʃᵊn| are unstressed

Using these symbols, readers have to create the pronunciation for themselves, interpreting each symbol as an instruction. For example the symbol |ʃ| means 'make a voiceless post-alveolar fricative', and the vertical strokes mean 'make this syllable stressed by making it louder, longer or at a different pitch (or all three) than its neighbours'. Alternatively, people can listen to the soundfile, which introduces additional factors such as speed and intonation – in this case a falling tone starting on the penultimate syllable |ˈeɪ| and continuing over the last syllable |ʃᵊn|.

We take our next step in explaining the relationship between citation forms and speech units by placing *association* in Table 2.1, which shows the five syllables in five columns. The columns are numbered in reverse order, starting with 5 on the left and 1 on the right. The reason for the reverse order is that it enables us to make generalisations (about **squeeze zones** and **tones**) which cover all sizes of speech unit, as we will see later.

Table 2.1: Extract 2.2 Citation form of *association*

5	4	3	2	1
a	sso	ci	a	tion
ə	səʊ	si	eɪ	ʃᵊn

The secondary stress on |͵səʊ| occurs in column 4, the primary stress |ˈeɪ| occurs in column 2, and the unstressed syllables go in columns 5, 3, and 1. From this point onwards we will refer to the syllables in columns 4 and 2 as being **prominent** syllables. In the particular case of the citation form of this five-syllable word, prominences and word-stress coincide in the way shown in the table. However, as we shall see, such circumstances are rare in spontaneous speech. There is one last point about Table 2.1. Unlike the phonemic transcription, the soundfile has intonation – there is a falling tone (as we have noted) which starts on the prominent syllable in column 2 and continues over the non-prominent syllable in column 1. In presenting speech units in tables like this, tones always start on the syllable in column 2 and continue over the syllable, or syllables, in column 1 – if there are any.

The world of the soundfile is different from the world of phonemic symbols. It is a world of sound substance, pitch movements, speed, and social information such as the gender and age of the speaker. It is unlike the phonemic transcription because it is not a coded instruction on how to pronounce segments. It is not so much 'a pronunciation' as 'a listening' – a version of the word for hearing and imitating.

2.2   The citation form and prominence

Generally, words do not occur in isolation. They are grouped with other words and they have sound-shapes which are different from the citation form. It is the job of the window on speech to help us capture the speaker-created rhythmic patterns of spontaneous speech and thereby to help us identify the different soundshapes that words can have. We will now see what happens when the word *association* occurs with other words, as in Table 2.2. One of the most important things which happens is the emergence of squeeze zones.

Table 2.2 is a representation of a double-prominence speech unit, with the syllables in columns 4 and 2 being prominent. Row 1 shows *association* with the five syllables of the citation form (as in Table 2.1), but in row 2 it shares the cells with four other words which precede it.

Table 2.2: Extract 2.3 *Association* at the end of a speech unit

	5	4	3	2	1
1	as	SO	ci	A	tion
2	you should	JOIN	the associ	A	tion

In the citation form (row 1) the syllables with word stress occur with prominences in columns 4 and 2, but in row 2 the single syllable of *join* is prominent in column 4. Consequently the second syllable of *association* becomes non-prominent and is therefore squeezed into column 3, which now contains four non-prominent syllables *the.as.so.ci*. The one-to-one relationship between prominence and word stress that we hear in the citation form in row 1 is broken. The speaker's choice is to highlight the word *join* and, because the secondary stress in *association* is not the focus of the speaker's attention, this syllable becomes downplayed and non-prominent.

You can perhaps still hear that the second syllable of *association* stands out more than its three unstressed syllables. However, in the window on speech we assign word stresses which are not highlighted by the speaker to the same level as unstressed syllables – non-highlighted word stresses are transcribed as non-prominent.

Applying the window on speech requires us to pay attention to speakers' choices – the words they highlight, and the syllables they make prominent, and we ignore the properties which the words would have had in the citation form. In our framework speakers are regarded as the creators of speech units and the soundshapes they contain, we therefore give the speakers' choices priority over the careful speech model's predictions about what will happen to the citation forms.

In Table 2.3 we see another soundshape for *association*, where it occurs early in a speech unit and is followed by four words *with the green party* in which the word *green* is prominent.

Table 2.3: Extract 2.4 *Association* early in a speech unit

	5	4	3	2	1
1	as	SO	ci	A	tion
2	in a	SO	ciation with the	GREEN	party

In row 2 *association* occurs early in the speech unit and is spread over columns 5, 4, and 3. The second syllable is prominent, and is therefore placed in column 4. But the fourth syllable, which has primary stress in the citation form, is non-prominent along with its neighbouring syllables *-ci-a-tion* and the words *with the*. This gives us five non-prominent syllables *-ci-a-tion-with-the* in column 3. In this case, the fourth syllable of *association* which receives primary stress in the citation form, is squeezed so that it becomes weaker than the secondary stress on the second syllable, giving *aSSOciation* rather than *aSSOciAtion*. This is an example of **stress shift**, a feature which we will deal with in Chapter 9.

In the examples in Tables 2.2 and 2.3 *association* has three different soundshapes: the citation form with two prominences, and then two single-prominence versions with either the second or the fourth syllable being prominent. Below we will see cases in which it receives no prominences at all.

2.3   Non-prominent syllables in squeeze zones

Table 2.4 shows a further example of *association* in a double-prominence speech unit, but now all syllables are non-prominent in the squeeze zone in column 3.

Table 2.4: Extract 2.5 Non-prominent *association* in a squeeze zone

5	4	3	2	1
it was	DONE	in association with the	SPORTS	council

There are two prominent syllables: on *done* and *sports*. The other syllables are non-prominent. However, the eight syllables in column 3, including the five of *association*, are spoken in a fast blur in which its soundshape is very different from the citation form. We get something like *so-say-shun* or *show-shay-shun*. Table 2.5 shows us that something similar happens when *association* occurs in column 5.

Table 2.5: Extract 2.6 Non-prominent *association* in column 5

5	4	3	2	1
the association is	LOOK	ing for another	CAN	didate

Here the speech unit is dominated by the prominences on *look* and *can*. The five syllables of *association* share column 5 with two other syllables, *the* and *is*, to make a very fast blur of seven syllables which precede the first prominence. Just as with column 3, column 5 is a squeeze zone where words are transformed into an acoustic blur.

Where a word occurs before a pause, in column 1, it is less likely to be squeezed into new shapes, as we can see in Table 2.6. This phenomenon is known as **pre-pausal lengthening**.

Table 2.6: Extract 2.7 Non-prominent *association* in column 1

5	4	3	2	1
but it was op	POSED	by the british	MED	ical association

In Table 2.6 *association* occurs in column 1 as part of a seven syllable group *i-cal-a-sso-ci-a-tion* which is preceded by the prominent syllable on the first syllable of *medical*. As with all syllables in column 2, a tone starts and continues over the syllables in column 1. In this case, it is a falling tone. It is likely that you will be able to hear the word stress of *association* in the tail of the falling tone. Non-prominent syllables in column 1 undergo pre-pausal lengthening and a consequent slowing down, which results in the word stresses remaining audible even though they are not highlighted by the speaker.

The point to grasp from these tables is that *the window on speech records the occurrence of speaker choices of prominence*. It does not record the occurrence of primary and secondary word stress unless they happen to coincide with prominences. A transcription made using the window on speech is therefore a transcription of speaker choices, not of word or sentence stress.

Remember that Ying (Chapter 1) wondered whether words 'change somewhere ... in a sentence'. We have now seen, using the word *association*, how words can have a variety of soundshapes according to the position they have in speech units. In particular we have seen that the non-prominent columns 5 and 3 are squeeze zones – places where syllables and words are squeezed together into fast bursts of sound substance. In Chapter 3 we will deal with other sizes of speech unit, which have similar squeeze zones.

2.4   Non-prominent syllables and speaker choice

Non-prominent syllables or **non-prominences** are syllables which are not highlighted by speakers – they are quieter, less clear, shorter and faster and they follow pitch movements, rather than being the starting points for them. As with the placement of prominences, the occurrence of non-prominent syllables is a matter of speaker choice at the moment of speaking. The choices are related to the speakers' ideas of what they need to do in the context to make their meaning clear to their listeners. We will cover this point in more detail in future chapters, when we consider the evidence of spontaneous speech provided by a variety of speakers.

So, as we learn to use the window on speech, we attend to the occurrence of prominent syllables in relation to non-prominent syllables in speech units. In effect we ignore word-level stress, primary stress and secondary stress. Usually, however, where a word has a prominence assigned by the speaker, that prominence will be placed on a primary or secondary stress. However, in spontaneous speech, unlike with the careful speech model, *any* syllable in *any* word – including primary-stressed and secondary-stressed syllables – may be downplayed by the speaker, with the result that we will transcribe them as non-prominent.

2.5   Spontaneous speech

The recordings used so far in this chapter were scripted and recorded deliberately to demonstrate the relationship between prominence and word stress, and to demonstrate the existence of the squeeze zones that cause Ying's dilemma. It is now time to see how our framework works on an example of spontaneous speech. We will hear Corony, a university lecturer, who had a number of interesting short-term jobs after she finished university. For a brief time she was a batik artist, and when she was asked 'Were you successful as a textile artist?' she answered:

> i i didn't make an awful lot of money in the first couple of years erm but i sold a lot of
> things it was obviously very popular

Corony speaks this using five speech units as given in Table 2.7.

Table 2.7: Extract 2.8 Corony *i didn't ... very popular*

	5	4	3	2	1
01	i i didn't	MAKE	an awful lot of	MON	ey
02	in the	FIRST	couple of	YEARS	
03				ERM	
04			but i	SOLD	a lot of things
05	it was	OB	viously very	POP	ular

The prominent syllables are shown in columns 4 and 2, and non-prominent syllables are shown in columns 5 and 3 (the squeeze zones) and in column 1. Note that the two-syllable words *didn't*, *awful* (row 01), *couple* (row 02), and *very* (row 05) all occur in squeeze zones. Although you may be able to detect word stress in these words, they are not highlighted by Corony herself. Therefore they are transcribed as non-prominent.

Three of the units – in rows 01, 02 and 05 – are double-prominence speech units of the type we were looking at with *association* earlier. In row 01 the squeeze zone in column 3 looks, in transcription, as though it should have five syllables *an.aw.ful.lot.of*, but these reduce to four syllables, giving us something close to *an.aw.flot.a*. Similarly, in row 02, the squeeze zone in column 3 looks as though it should have three syllables *coup.le.of* but this reduces to two syllables *coup.luv*. In row 05 the squeeze zone in column 3 has four syllables (counting *-vious-* as one) going at 9 syllables per second (very fast, cf. Chapter 7) and with the final syllable of *obviously* sounding close to *klee*.

The number of non-prominent syllables that can occur in any single squeeze zone is not fixed, but the maximum we will see and hear in this publication is twelve (cf. Chapter 8.11).

The speech units in rows 03 and 04 are single-prominence units. In row 03 *erm* is the only syllable, whereas in row 04 the single prominence is preceded and followed by non-prominent syllables, with the falling tone which starts on *sold* continuing over the syllables of the phrase *a lot of things*. These four words have phrasal stress with a perceptible rhythmic beat on *lot* and *things* but because Corony does not highlight them, they are transcribed as non-prominent.

2.6   Displaying speech units

Normally we will not use a table to present our transcriptions of recordings in speech units. Though visually helpful and useful for making concepts clear, tables are somewhat cumbersome. It is often more convenient, therefore, to present them in lines of transcription as shown in Extract 2.9.

Extract 2.9 Corony *i didn't ... very popular*

```
01 || i i didn't MAKE an awful lot of MOney ||
02 || in the FIRST couple of YEARS ||
03 || ERM ||
04 || but i SOLD a lot of things ||
05 || it was OBviously very POpular ||
```

The numbers to the left are reference numbers for each line. The prominences are shown in upper case letters and the non-prominences are shown in lower-case letters.

2.7   Clauses and speech units

The examples of speech units that we have seen so far (with the exception of *erm* in Extract 2.9) have all been complete clauses. However, it would be a mistake to believe that the relationship between clause and speech unit is always as regular as in the examples we have seen. Although such regularity is predicted and encouraged by the careful speech model, in spontaneous speech the relationship is often very irregular. To illustrate, let us take Corony's last clause as an example. It was contained in a double-prominence speech unit, as in Extract 2.10.

Extract 2.10 Corony *it was ... popular*

```
|| it was OBviously very POpular ||
```

But it need not have been this way. The pressures of creating speech in real time might have resulted in the version in Extract 2.11, with two single-prominence speech units followed by one double-prominence unit.

Extract 2.11 Corony *it was ... popular* in three speech units

```
01 || IT ||
02 || WAS ||
03 || OBviously very POPular ||
```

In speech units 01 and 02 the single syllables have level tones (cf. Chapter 4) on them, as the speaker is buying time in order to decide what to say next and in 03 the words *obviously very popular* are spoken very fast as the speaker has decided what to say, and delivers it very quickly. In Chapter 6 we will see that the words in speech units 01 and 02 are examples of **stepping stones**, and in Chapter 07 we will see that this sequence of a number of slow speech units, followed by a quick one, is a fairly common occurrence in spontaneous speech.

2.8   Summary and what's next

This chapter and the preceding one have presented a sufficient number of the components of the window on speech for you to embark on reading any chapter in this book, namely the concept of prominence and non-prominence, the notion that there are speech units of different sizes and the fact that prominence and non-prominence have no fixed relationship to word stress. Most important however, are these two points: it is the blurring of syllables in the squeeze zones which is most likely to cause Ying's dilemma; and (contrary to what the careful speech model would have us believe) in spontaneous speech it is the speaker, not 'the language' who is the creator of the soundshapes that learner listeners have to cope with.

In this and the first chapter we have focused mainly on the double-prominence speech unit, but we have also seen that there are other sizes of speech unit. How, you might naturally ask, does one divide up the stream of speech into speech units of different sizes? The remaining three chapters of Part 1 provide more information and examples which will answer this question for you. They provide the tools for you to be able to begin transcribing speech on your own. In Chapter 3 we will look in more detail at speech units of different sizes. In Chapter 4 we will look at the tones and contours of the speech unit and in Chapter 5 we will examine the scientific status of the transcriptions made using the window on speech and compare it to other transcription systems. If you would like to skip these chapters, or return to them later, you may do so. After reading thus far, you are sufficiently well equipped (provided you have been reading reasonably carefully!) to embark on any other part of the book. So if you are interested in the concept of a variety of soundshapes, and in understanding Ying's dilemma, you should go to Part 2 *Describing spontaneous speech*. If you would rather explore the more sociolinguistic and affective dimensions of speech, you should go to Part 3 *Accents, identity and emotion in speech*. Or if your interest is primarily in teaching, you can go directly to Part 4 *Teaching listening*.

2.9   Further reading

The approach to speech units and prominence outlined in this chapter is based on the theoretical framework known as *Discourse Intonation* (Brazil, 1997), which has also been shown to have practical value in both teaching (Bradford 1988, Cauldwell 2002, Hewings, 2007) and research (Hewings, 1993; Pickering, 2001).

Syllables are an important component of our descriptive framework. For decisions on how to divide up words into syllables, see the introductions to Roach et al. (2011) and Wells (2008), or for more technical discussions Roach (2009: Chapters 8–9) or Wells (1990). Word stress is dealt with in Roach (2009: Chapters 10–11), and the classic treatment of prominence can be found in Brazil, (1997: Chapter 2) and pedagogic treatments can be found in Bradford (1988), Hewings (2007) and Cauldwell (2012). The notion of non-prominence is related to the notion of downgrading (Wells, 2006: 228).

2.10   Language awareness activities

Activity 1: Prepare and perform

Look at Table 2.8 below, and prepare a 'read-aloud' performance of the speech units it contains. Make the syllables in the even columns – the prominent syllables – loud and clear, and make the syllables in the odd-numbered columns – the non-prominent syllables – quieter and less clear.

- Unit 01 is the citation form of *acceleration* with two prominent syllables.
- Unit 02 has three prominences, but *acceleration* has only one, on the fourth syllable.
- Unit 03 has two prominences, but *acceleration* has only one, on the second syllable.
- Unit 04 has two prominences, but neither of them are on *acceleration*.

For Unit 04 you need to squeeze *accleration* so that it becomes much less like the citation form – say it with just three syllables *sell ray shun* – but remember the only prominent syllables are on *fast* and *all*. Read aloud these speech units to a friend, a colleague or a fellow teacher.

Table 2.8 Squeezing *acceleration*

	7	6	5	4	3	2	1
01			ac	CEL	e	RA	tion
02	it had the	FAST	est accele	RA	tion of	ALL	the cars
03			its ac	CEL	eration is fan	TAS	tic
04			it had the	FAST	est acceleration of	ALL	the cars

Make notes about how easy or difficult you found this to do.

Activity 2: Record and observe

Find a section of an unscripted recording in which several content words of at least two syllables are repeated several times. Copy each occurrence of each word out of the recording, and paste them next to each other in the same sound file. What do you notice about the soundshapes? Are they the same? If not, how do they differ? What is the relationship between each soundshape and the citation form? Make notes about your findings, and discuss them with a friend, colleague, or fellow-teacher.

3   Transcription I: Speech units

This chapter, together with Chapters 4 and 5, provides preliminary training in how to listen to and transcribe recordings in a way which throws light on the sound substance of spontaneous speech. These chapters are accessible, and repay close attention, but you may want to delay reading them until you get more of an idea of how useful the window on speech can be. You can do this by reading Parts 2-4. If you decide to do this, then you can refer back to these chapters as needed – they can act as reference chapters for you.

This chapter explains how recordings of spontaneous speech can be transcribed into speech units of five different sizes. These sizes are determined by the number of prominences they contain: single, double, triple, quadruple and incomplete – speech units with no tone. The five sizes of speech unit form the basis of the *Phonology for Listening* framework – they are the window on speech, a way of capturing the speaker choices which exert a major influence on the soundshapes of words. The written transcription then becomes an observational tool which you and your students can use to explore and learn about the realities of the sound substance of the stream of speech.

These chapters will give you practical training in the process by which the transcriptions of extracts in *Phonology for Listen*ing have been produced. You do not have to be an expert in transcribing in this particular way in order to get full value from looking at and hearing these extracts. However, if you want to understand the principles and practice that underlie these transcriptions, and you are keen to use this method of transcription for yourself, then working on these chapters, together with the supplementary materials available on the website will be of enormous benefit. There are other transcription frameworks (some of which are mentioned in Chapter 5) which you might prefer to use. Nevertheless, whichever framework you use, I hope you will apply the techniques of zooming in to short extracts of recordings, and then dividing them up into short bursts of between 0.5-2.0 seconds in length to investigate the soundshapes of individual words, and groups of words, and to discover how the speaker's choices have influenced these soundshapes.

3.1   Single-prominence speech units

At the end of the previous chapter we looked at an extract from a recording by Corony and noted that it had two single-prominence units which are shown in separate rows in Table 3.1. You will notice that the table has a three-part pattern.

Table 3.1: Extract 3.1 Corony *erm ... a lot of things*

	3	2	1
01		ERM	
02	but i	SOLD	a lot of things

The units have different rhythmic patterns: row 01 has the smallest rhythmic shape possible for a single-prominence speech unit, a single syllable in column 2 – *erm*. Row 02 has a larger rhythmic shape, with the prominence in column 2 being preceded and followed by a number of non-prominent syllables. As with speech units of all sizes, the tone starts in column 2. In the case of row 01 it is a level tone and in the case of unit 02 it is a falling tone which continues over the syllables in column 1. The filled pause *erm* (also spelled *um*) is very common in single-prominence units (cf. Chapter 6), but any monosyllable may occur in such units – whether they are short responses (*yes, no*) function words (*and, but, so, where*) or content words (*found, books*).

As we saw in Chapter 2.5, the phrasal stress of *a lot of things* can be heard, but it is not shown in our transcription. Instead Corony has chosen to place a prominence on *sold*, with a falling tone continuing over the remaining syllables. These are not highlighted by Corony and are therefore non-prominent.

Speakers have a choice of how to package what they say into speech units. As Extract 3.2 shows, Corony could have said this clause with two or three prominences, thereby producing speech units of different sizes.

Extract 3.2 Corony *sold...things* three different ways

```
single      || but i SOLD a lot of things ||
double      || but i SOLD a lot of THINGS ||
triple      || but i SOLD a LOT of THINGS ||
```

Single-prominence speech units account for about 40% of the speech units in spontaneous speech (count based on Cauldwell, 2002).

3.2   Double-prominence speech units

We saw in Chapter 2 that the double-prominence speech unit has a five-part structure. It must contain two prominent syllables – without them it would not be a double-prominence speech unit. However, the three other parts are optional. The rhythmically smallest size is therefore a unit with two syllables, and the rhythmically most complete size is where all five parts contain syllables. A range of versions of this size of speech unit are shown in Table 3.2 (one unit per row), taken from a recording by Bob.

Table 3.2: Extract 3.3 Bob *dreadful ... leaves*

	5	4	3	2	1
01	is a	DREAD	ful time of	YEAR	
02	all those	WET		LEAVES	
03		VE	ry	HEA	vy
04		WET		LEAVES	

Bob explains why working as a road-sweeper in south-east London is a difficult job in Autumn, when it rains a lot.

All four of these units are double-prominence speech units, because they have prominent syllables in columns 4 and 2. The units vary in length from two syllables (row 04) to seven (row 01). Row 01 has two syllables in column 5 and three in column 3. These are the squeeze zones (cf. Chapter 2.3). All of these rows have at least one empty cell, but row 04 has three empty cells, leaving only the prominent syllables *wet* and *leaves*.

Prominence is a matter of speaker choice, so although Bob produced the words *is a dreadful time of year* as a double-prominence speech unit, he could have said them as either a single or a triple-prominence speech unit, as in Extract 3.4.

Extract 3.4 Bob *dreadful ... leaves* three different ways

```
single      || is a DREADful time of year ||
double      || is a DREADful time of YEAR ||
triple      || is a DREADful TIME of YEAR ||
```

Double-prominence speech units account for over 40% of speech units (count based on Cauldwell 2002). Thus single and double-prominence units together make up over 80% of speech units in spontaneous speech.

3.3 Triple-prominence speech units

The triple-prominence speech unit has seven parts, as shown in Table 3.3. There are three compulsory parts - the prominences in columns 6, 4 and 2, without which they would not be triple-prominence units. The other parts are optional, and may consist of any number of syllables, although the likely maximum is illustrated in row 02, where five syllables appear in column 5.

Table 3.3 Triple-prominence speech units Extracts 3.5

	7	6	5	4	3	2	1
01	the	FIRST	ob	SESS	ion is with vo	CAB	ulary
02	for	TELL	ing people how to	STRING	the words	GETH	er
03		PRAPS*		FIVE		DAYS	
04	he can	TURN	his	HAND	to	AN	ything

Rows 01-02 come from Geoff's seminar on the history of English grammar. Row 03 is from Maggie and row 04 from Gail. Maggie's *perhaps* is spoken as a single syllable.

Rows 01 and 02 have rhythmically complete versions of the triple-prominence speech unit, in that all seven parts have one or more syllables. Row 03 appears to have a nonsense word in column 6, but this is *perhaps* spoken as a single syllable, as it often is at the beginning of a speech unit (Roach et al, 2011; Wells, 2008). Unit 03 has two other prominent monosyllables: *five* and *days*. This is the rhythmically smallest form of the triple-prominence speech unit, with no non-prominent syllables. With the additional column for non-prominence (column 7) our framework has an additional squeeze zone in which words can be squeezed into difficult-to-catch soundshapes.

Maggie could have said the words *perhaps five days* as either a single or a double-prominence speech unit, as illustrated in Extract 3.6.

Extract 3.6 Maggie *perhaps five days* three different ways

```
single      || praps five DAYS ||
double      || praps FIVE DAYS ||
triple      || PRAPS FIVE DAYS||
```

Triple-prominence speech units are relatively rare, and account for fewer than 10% of speech units (count based on Cauldwell, 2002).

3.4   Quadruple-prominence speech units

Even rarer than triple-prominence units are quadruple-prominence units, which have a maximum of nine parts. We have reached the limits of what a table can usefully show us, so we will view three quadruple-prominence speech units in normal transcription, shown in the three lines of Extract 3.7.

Extract 3.7 Quadruple-prominence speech units

```
01 || he's CURRently THINKing of MOVing aGAIN ||
02 || who is the AUTHor of the GREAT FRENCH DICtionary ||
03 || apPLY for a JOB at the UNiversity of WARwick ||
```

The examples are spoken by three different people: unit 01 from Gail, unit 02 from Geoff and unit 03 from Rachel.

All speech units have four prominences – without any one of them, they would not be quadruple-prominence speech units. Gail's clause in unit 01 need not have been spoken as a quadruple-prominence speech unit, it could have been a single, double, or triple-prominence speech unit, as you can hear in Extract 3.8.

Extract 3.8 *He's currently ... again* four different ways

```
single || he's currently THINKing of moving again ||
double || he's currently THINKing of moving aGAIN ||
triple || he's currently THINKing of MOVing aGAIN ||
quadruple || he's CURRently THINKing of MOVing aGAIN ||
```

As you listen to triple and quadruple-prominence speech units, you will perhaps get a sense of the rhythm of English speech, which is often referred to as **stress timing**. You probably sense that the prominent syllables are occurring at equal intervals of time, and that you could tap a pencil to the regular beat of the prominent syllables. We will return to the topic of stress timing in Chapter 10.

Quadruple-prominence speech units are rare in spontaneous speech, accounting for about 1% of speech units (count based on Cauldwell, 2002).

3.5   Larger speech units

Speech units with more than four prominences are extremely rare, but they do exist. A six-prominence speech unit occurs in a recording by the twentieth century British poet, Philip Larkin, (Larkin, 1965) reading the title of his poem MCMXIV (Roman numerals for 1914). The speech unit contained six syllables, all prominent, and with a falling tone on the last syllable.

Extract 3.9 MCMXIV

```
|| EM CEE EM EX ONE VEE ||
```

Such speech units are most likely to occur where scripted language is being read aloud.

3.6   Incomplete speech units

It is common in spontaneous speech for speakers to start to say something, and change their minds, stop and re-start. These moments are part of the **drafting phenomena** that are described in detail in Chapter 6. They typically consist of a number of non-prominent syllables, but they may contain a prominent syllable. Their defining feature is that they do not contain a tonic syllable - if they did, they would become a single-prominence speech unit. In Extract 3.10, units 02 and 03 have incomplete speech units.

Extract 3.10 Corony *there's a space ...artwork*

```
01 || there's a SPACE aVAILable over their WINdow ||
02 || ... that ... ||
03 || ... they wouldn't other be ... ||
04 || WISE be USing for ||
05 || a piece of ARTwork ||
```

Unit 02 has a single non-prominent syllable which is rhythmically distinct from both the speech unit that precedes it, and the speech unit that follows it. Similarly, the incomplete unit 03 is also rhythmically distinct from what follows. Corony makes a slip – having started on the word *otherwise* she mistakenly omits the last syllable and starts on the verb phrase with *be*. She then corrects herself by supplying the final syllable of *otherwise* as the first prominence in unit 04.

Incomplete speech units account for about 5% of speech units (count taken from Cauldwell, 2002).

This completes our survey of the five different sizes of speech unit. We will now look at three issues which arise when you first embark on transcribing:

- how to decide whether syllables are prominent or not
- how to decide where speech unit boundaries occur
- the relationship between speech units and clauses.

3.7   Prominent or non-prominent?

When you start transcribing, the first stage consists of listening to short sections of the recording and deciding which syllables are prominent and which are non-prominent.

Extract 3.11 comes from Geoff and it contains fourteen prominences over seven speech units. There are three triple-prominence units (01, 03 and 07), two double-prominence units (05, 06) and two single-prominence units (02, 04).

Extract 3.11 Geoff *the first ... words together*

```
01 || the FIRST obSESSion is with voCABulary ||
02 || and THEN ||
03 || ONCE THAT'S been eSTABlished ||
04 || once the MARKet for that has been established ||
05 || PEOPle begin to REALise ||
06 || that there is ALso a MARKet ||
07 || for TELLing people how to STRING the words toGETHer ||
```

In order to decide whether a prominence occurs, you need to ask yourself the question 'At this moment, in this context, is this speaker highlighting this word relative to the other words?' If the answer to this question is 'Yes' then that word has (at least) one prominent syllable. If the answer is 'No' then that word has no prominent syllables. Speech units 03 and 04 demonstrate this quite nicely for us. In 03 Geoff clearly highlights the words *once*, *that's* and *established* and we therefore have prominent syllables (shown in upper case) in these three words. However, in 04 the only word that is highlighted is *market*, so it is transcribed as having its first syllable prominent.

If we had encountered 04 as a speech unit isolated from its neighbouring speech units, we would probably have transcribed it as a triple-prominence speech unit, as in Extract 3.12.

Extract 3.12 Geoff *once...established* with three prominences

```
04 || once the MARKet for THAT has been eSTABlished ||
```

However when you listen to it in the context of its neighbouring units, it is clear that all the important words except *market* have already been mentioned in unit 03, and crucially the benchmark for what counts as prominent is set by the level of highlighting of the prominences in unit 03: *once*, *that's* and *-stab-*. Therefore, if you listen to Extract 3.11 as a whole, you will hear that none of the syllables in *for that has been established* are highlighted in unit 04. They may have audible word stress, but they are not highlighted in the way that the prominent syllables of 03 are highlighted.

So after hearing units 01-03, and we come to 04, it becomes clear that the first syllable of *market* is the only prominence – the only syllable to be highlighted – and that the remaining eight syllables are non-prominent.

Geoff however need not have done it this way. He could have produced a double or a triple-prominence unit instead, as illustrated in Extract 3.13.

Extract 3.13 Geoff *once...established* three different ways

```
04a || once the MARKet for that has been established ||
04b || once the MARKet for that has been eSTABlished ||
04c || once the MARKet for THAT has been eSTABlished ||
```

The versions in units 04b and 04c may have sounded odd and over-explicit in this context, but nevertheless these choices are available to the speaker.

As you listen to extracts, and view their transcriptions, you may find yourself disagreeing with the transcriptions. This is entirely normal, for a variety of reasons, and you may be right – the transcription may be wrong. We will return to this issue in Chapter 5.

3.8   Boundaries

Most approaches to the transcription of speech attach great importance to the placement of boundaries. The generally accepted view is that a speech-unit boundary will normally co-occur with a syntactic boundary of some kind. In particular it is often asserted, in books associated with the careful speech model, that speech unit boundaries will normally co-occur with clause boundaries.

However, when we transcribe a recording using the window on speech our criteria for transcribing a boundary do not lie with the underlying grammar: the criteria we use are features of the sound substance itself. These include the rhythms of the sound substance, the occurrence of pauses (wherever the speaker puts them), and the location of tones (wherever the speaker puts them). When we adopt this point of view, we find that the boundaries of speech units can occur anywhere. However, it is a convention of the window on speech that boundaries must be placed wherever there is a pause, and they must occur to prevent more than one tone occurring in a speech unit. These conventions have the great advantage of helping us divide up spontaneous speech into rhythmic units where we can identify sources of Ying's dilemma.

Therefore, when transcribing a stretch of speech the important things to bear in mind are:

- the location of prominences
- the location of pauses
- the location of tones (described in Chapter 4)
- changes in rhythm

There is no expectation that speech units should necessary coincide with grammatical and syntactic categories, because grammar and syntax are not the cause of Ying's dilemma – the cause lies in the choices made by speakers. The rhythmic events are not those of the clause, or the phrase, or the sentence. It is the alternation of prominent and non-prominent syllables in rhythmic groups, together with the squeezing together of words into rhythmic bursts of sound substance that cause her dilemma.

3.9   Speech units, clauses, noun groups, verb groups

To illustrate the kind of relationship that does occur between speech units and syntactic categories, we will look at another extract from Corony:

> While I was at university I was very involved with the students Arts Society which was called the Arts Umbrella.

If we were to view these words as a script, we might suggest (according to the expectations of the careful speech model) that it should be spoken in three speech units which respect the clause structure. This would result in a sequence of a double, quadruple, and a triple-prominence speech units, as in Extract 3.14. Remember this extract is here being treated as a script, being read aloud in a particular way – one which complies with the careful speech model.

Extract 3.14 Corony *while...umbrella* **in three units**

```
01 || WHILE i was at uniVERsity ||
02 || i was VEry inVOLVED with the STUdents' ARTS society ||
03 || which was CALLED the ARTS umBRELla ||
```

This is an acted version, treating Corony's original spontaneous speech as a script.

But the rhythmic characteristics of Corony's original spontaneous speech are best captured over six units, with unit 02 of Extract 3.14 becoming four units in Extract 3.15.

Extract 3.15 Corony *while...umbrella* **in six units**

```
01 || WHILE i was at uniVERsity ||
02 || i was VEry inVOLVED ||
03 || with THE ||
04 || STUdents' ||
05 || ARTS society ||
06 || which was CALLED the ARTS umBRELla ||
```

This is Corony's original version, spontaneous speech.

The sound substance of the second clause ('I was very involved with the students Arts Society') contains gentle changes of rhythm and slight pauses which results in it being transcribed as four units. The occurrence of level tones on *involved*, *the* and *students* were an important factor in the decision-making for this transcription, because it is a rule of this approach to transcription (cf. Brazil, 1997) and therefore a rule of the window on speech, that there can only be one tone in a speech unit. It is now time to address the issue of tones, and that is the topic of the next chapter.

3.10   Summary and what's next

This chapter has described the five sizes of speech unit, and their rhythmic variants, which can be used to describe and analyse the stream of speech. We have also taken some first steps in demonstrating how to listen to recordings of spontaneous speech in the way that is demonstrated throughout *Phonology for Listening*. You do not have to become an expert in using this framework to benefit from applying these ideas and principles to the teaching of listening. You can, indeed, develop your own system of transcription which will work for you and your students. But the important thing is for you and your students to zoom in to short stretches of recordings on a regular basis to look at the details of the sound substance and the different soundshapes that words have. In Chapter 4 we will look at the tones, tunes, and contours of speech units.

3.11   Further reading

The account of speech unit sizes given in this chapter derives from the work of Brazil (1997), whose approach – known as Discourse Intonation – had its origins in applying the approach of Halliday (1970; 1994) to spontaenous speech. Halliday's approach is itself exemplified with recordings in Halliday & Greaves (2008). Crystal (1969) has also outlined an approach and exemplified it in Crystal & Davy (1975). Meanwhile Tench (2011) offers both scripts and recordings and a step-by-step approach to learning to transcribe speech units.

3.12   Language awareness activities

Activity 3.1: Soft focus listening

Soft focus is a term which is borrowed from the cinema: actors and actresses are sometimes portrayed with a soft focus lens – resulting in the details and edges of their faces becoming blurred and giving them a dream-like quality, usually at falling-in-love moments. It is the blur of speech that is the object of our attention.

Next time you are out with a group of friends, and you can take a rest from the conversation without appearing rude, stop listening for meaning and direct your attention instead to the sound substance of speech. If you do not want to risk appearing rude, do this with an appropriate YouTube video. Listen for pauses, changes of rhythm and fragments of speech (incomplete speech units). Listen also for sequences of prominent syllables, where the speaker is highlighting a number of syllables in quick succession (triple-prominence speech units). Listen for single-prominence speech units on sounds like *um* and words like *and*. Make notes about what you hear.

Activity 3.2: Listen and decide   Answer key page 73

Listen to Extract 3.16, and look at the two transcriptions below. Which transcription best represents the sound substance of the extract? As you consider the transcriptions, make notes about what you hear.

Extract 3.16 Maggie *i'm going ... long weekend*

Version 1

```
01 || i'm GOing to be GOing aWAY ||
02 || for aNOther LONG weekEND ||
```

Version 2

```
01 || i'm GOing to BE ||
02 || GOing ||
03 || aWAY FOR ||
04 || aNOther ||
05 || LONG weekEND ||
```

4   Transcription II: Tones, contours and key

This chapter continues the presentation of the window on speech. We examine the five tones, the three choices of key and the contours associated with them.

People do not speak in a monotone – their voices fall, rise, glide, step up and down, giving shape to the sound substance of speech. The movements that occur within and over a number of speech units gives speech **contours** – the sound substance's equivalent of mountain peaks and valleys that one might see in a landscape. Contours are important for keeping speech interesting for the listener – without them, speech would be boring, monotonous and difficult to listen to.

The window on speech framework has two mechanisms by which to transcribe the contours of speech: **tone** and **key**. In this chapter we begin by describing the five tones: a system of falling, rising and level pitch movements which start on the last prominence of a speech unit. Then we describe key: a system of three pitch levels, which can occur on any prominence.

We will deal with meaning in Chapter 5 (grammatical meaning) and Chapter 15 (attitudinal meaning).

4.1   Principles and terminology

Tones are the major pitch movements in a speech unit that start on the final prominence. They are important for two reasons. First they are a major contributor to the soundshape of the stream of speech. Second, their occurrence is used to determine where speech units end. There are five tones: fall (or falling), rise-fall, level, rise (or rising), fall-rise.

Key is the name of the system of steps up and down that speakers choose when making a syllable prominent. There are three of these steps: high, mid, and low.

Choices of tone and key may be made in clearly contoured ways, such as when someone is speaking to a child, or over-acting, or speaking to a large group of people without the aid of a microphone and sound system: the falls, rises, and steps up and down are given explicit and clear realisation. They are like the contours of a landscape with high peaks, steep slopes and deep valleys. But most commonly the contours of spontaneous speech are not steep. Instead they have low levels of realisation, which are more like the gently rolling hills and shallow slopes of the English countryside. The low levels of realisation often make it difficult to determine with certainty which tone or key choice has occurred, so we have to accept that any transcription is accompanied by a level of uncertainty. This is a topic we will return to in Chapter 5.

4.2   Five tones on a monosyllable

There are five tones: the fall (or falling tone), the rise-fall, the level, the rise (or rising tone), and the fall-rise. These tones can occur either on a single syllable, or over a number of syllables. Table 4.1 shows the five tones on the single-syllable word *then*, with both steep and shallow contours.

Table 4.1: Extract 4.1 Tones on a monosyllable,

name	symbol	steep	shallow
fall	↘	THEN	THEN
rise-fall	↗↘	THEN	THEN
level	→	THEN	THEN
rise	↗	THEN	THEN
fall-rise	↘↗	THEN	THEN

Each row gives the name of the tone, the symbol, the sample word and two typical shapes of the tone: one with a steep/long contour; the other with a shallow/short contour. For the level tone, the adjective 'steep' is not appropriate: 'long' and 'short' are better adjectives for the level tone.

The tones are defined by their final movement, which starts in the middle of the syllable. Notice, however, that the shape of the falling tone includes a slight jump up before the final falling movement starts. Similarly the rise is preceded by a slight jump down before its final rising movement. These initial movements are sometimes heard as the tone by people who have not had ear training, so a fall might be heard as a rise, a rise as a fall, etc. But the consensus among scholars of intonation is that the final movement of the tone is the one by which we define it.

4.3   Five tones over two syllables

It is a convention of the window on speech that if a tone occurs, then the prominence on which it occurs is the last prominence in a speech unit. Therefore (logically) tones always start on the last prominent syllable of a speech unit, the **tonic prominence**. However, tones may continue over any non-prominent syllables which follow it. In Table 4.2 the two-syllable word *Bradford* (a city in Yorkshire) has prominence on the first syllable and the contour of the tone continues over the second syllable.

Table 4.2: Extract 4.2 Tones over two syllables

name	symbol	steep	shallow
fall	↘	BRADford	BRADford
rise-fall	↗↘	BRADford	BRADford
level	→	BRADford	BRADford
rise	↗	BRADford	BRADford
fall-rise	↘↗	BRADford	BRADford

As with Table 4.1, each row shows the name of the tone, its symbol, and the sample word with both a steep and shallow contour, or long and short for the level tone. The tone starts on this prominent syllable, and continues over the second non-prominent syllable.

It is worth repeating the important convention: if a tone occurs, then **the prominence on which the tone starts is the last prominence in a speech unit**. This convention consequently means that **there is only one tone per speech unit.** It is also a convention of the notation that the symbol for the tone is given at the start of the speech unit, even though the tone does not start until the last prominence.

In the speech unit in Extract 4.3 , from Bob, the symbol for the fall-rise is given before the words of the speech unit, but does not start until the final prominence, the tonic syllable (or tonic prominence), on the word *then.*

The Window on Speech

Extract 4.3 Bob *it was...then*

```
01 ||  ↘↗it was aROUND THEN ||
```

This speech unit is the first one in Extract 4.4, in which Bob explains how he went from working as a roadsweeper in London to becoming a teacher in Sudan. Read Extract 4.4 to yourself slowly, speech unit by speech unit, taking note of the tone symbol at the beginning of each speech unit and performing the tone on the last prominent syllable of each speech unit, which is underlined. Then listen to the original, and to a slow over-acted version, and imitate what you hear.

Extract 4.4 Bob *it was... el-oBeid* – original

```
01 ||  ↘↗ it was aROUND THEN ||
02 ||  → THAT ||
03 ||  → of a MATE ||
04 ||  ↘ of MINE FROM BRADford ||
05 ||  → ERM ||
06 ||  ↘ a GUY called JAY ||
07 ||  → ER ||
08 ||  ↘ SENT me a POSTcard ||
09 ||  ↘ i got a POSTcard from a PLACE called el-oBEID ||
```

El- Obeid (also spelled Al-Ubayyid) is a city in Southern Sudan.

Bob's original, in Extract 4.4, is unscripted spontaneous speech and it contains some interesting features that are very common in spontaneous speech, namely filled pauses in 05 and 07 and a slip in 03 where he inserts the word *of*. The undulations of his tones are reasonably clear, but it may take you a little while, and a few re-listenings, for you to be satisfied that you can hear what the transcription indicates.

Extract 4.5 is a re-recorded version of Bob's original, in which his original version was treated as a script. It is somewhat slower, and the peaks and valleys (the contours) are exaggerated in a way that someone who is over-acting might perform it.

Extract 4.5 Bob *it was... el-oBeid* – over-acted version

```
01 ||  ↘↗ it was aROUND THEN ||
02 ||  → THAT ||
03 ||  → of a MATE ||
```

```
04  ||  ↘ of MINE FROM BRADford ||
05  ||  → ERM ||
06  ||  ↘ a GUY called JAY ||
07  ||  → ER ||
08  ||  ↘ SENT me a POSTcard ||
09  ||  ↘ i got a POSTcard from a PLACE called el-oBEID ||
```

In Extract 4.5, the tones are far more clearly delineated than in Extract 4.4, but the ones in the earlier extract are more typical of spontaneous speech. Listen to both extracts to compare the steep contours of the over-acted extract with the normal, shallow contours of the original extract.

Most of Bob's tones occur on monosyllables, apart from units 04 and 08 where the tones extend over the non-prominent second syllables in the words *Bradford* and *postcard*. Incidentally, it is possible that you (or even a well-trained expert) will disagree about which tones occur in each speech unit. This is entirely natural, and it is an issue we will return to in Chapter 5.

4.4   Five tones over many syllables

The five tones can extend, not just over the remaining syllable(s) in a word, as we saw with *Bradford*, but also over a number of words which form the non-prominent tail of the tone. Table 4.3 shows the five tones spread over six syllables. They start on the tonic prominence *had* and continue over *human* (two syllables) and *scientists* (three syllables) after the tonic syllable.

Table 4.3: Extracts 4.6 Tones over three words

fall	↘ that HAD human scientists
rise-fall	↗↘ that HAD human scientists
level	→ that HAD human scientists →
rise	↗ that HAD human scientists
fall-rise	↘↗ that HAD human scientists

The Window on Speech

You will notice that although the words *human scientists* are non-prominent, you can still hear the word stress of each of these words. Remember that the focus of the window on speech is on capturing speaker choices of highlighting (through prominences), and non-highlighting (non-prominences), and does not analyse below the level of non-prominence (cf. Chapter 2).

The speech unit used in Table 4.3 originally occurred in a recording by Rachel, who is talking about her degree course at Oxford University where she studied Human Sciences. Extract 4.7 shows three speech units in a row which have a fall-rise tone.

Extract 4.7 Rachel *and each ... after us* original

```
01 ||  →  AND ||
02 ||  ↘↗ EACH COLLege ||
03 ||  ↘↗ that HAD human scientists ||
04 ||  ↘↗ had ONE TUTor ||
05 ||  ...who... ||
06 ||  ↘ who looked AFTer us ||
```

This extract has an incomplete speech unit (05) containing the rhythmically isolated *who* which has no tone. There is one monosyllabic speech unit (01) which has a level tone on *and*, which is an example of a stepping stone (cf. Chapter 6). There are also four speech units in which the tone starts on the last prominent syllable and continues over the remaining syllables: the second syllables of the words *college* (02) and *tutor* (04), the five syllables of *human scientists* (03), and the second syllable of *after*, plus *us* in 06.

Extract 4.8 is an acted version of Rachel's speech units in which the tones are more steeply contoured than they are in the original.

Extract 4.8 Rachel *and each ... after us* acted version

```
01 ||  →  AND ||
02 ||  ↘↗ EACH COLLege ||
03 ||  ↘↗ that HAD human scientists ||
04 ||  ↘↗ had ONE TUTor ||
05 ||  ...who... ||
06 ||  ↘ who looked AFTer us ||
```

The careful speech model (Chapter 1) would tell us that the level and fall-rise tones signal non-completion, whereas the falling tone signals completion. Rachel's sequence of tones (level, three fall-rises and a fall) is an example of this pattern in action. However, as we shall see in Part 2, spontaneous speech is not always as tidy as this.

4.5   Key: high, mid, low

Up to this point, we have concerned ourselves with those parts of the contours of speech units – the tones – which start on the last prominence. But all prominences, not just the last one, can feature a choice of key, and it is to this aspect of the contours of speech that we now turn.

On any prominence, speakers can choose between three pitch levels of **key**, meaning that any prominence can be high, mid, or low in the speaker's individual and current **vocal range**. Extract 4.9 illustrates the different choices available.

Extract 4.9 Rachel *it's no ... course* – original

```
01 || → IT'S ||
02 || → ↑NO more DISparate ||
03 || ↘ than ANy other MOdular ↓COURSE ||
```

In 02, there is a vertical arrow pointing upwards before the prominence on *no* and in 03 there is a vertical arrow pointing down before *course* - these vertical arrows signal high key and low key respectively. All the other prominences have no vertical arrows in front of them, and the absence of an arrow signifies that the prominence has mid key. Extract 4.10 gives an acted version, in which the choices of key are more clearly contoured than they are in the original.

Extract 4.10 Rachel *it's no ... course* – acted version

```
01 || → IT'S ||
02 || → ↑NO more DISparate ||
03 || ↘ than ANy other MOdular ↓COURSE ||
```

Mid-key choices are by far the most common. The careful speech model predicts that high key occurs at beginnings (however defined) and low key occurs at endings (however defined), but this neat arrangement is not borne out by the evidence of spontaneous speech. High key is a choice that can occur anywhere, and the same is true of low key.

4.6   Frequency of tones

In the Received Pronunciation (RP) accent of the UK (as exemplified in Cauldwell, 2002), the most frequent tone is the fall, and the least frequent tone is the rise-fall. Table 4.5 lists the tones and their frequency, including a percentage for uncertain tones.

Table 4.5 Frequency of tones in British English

fall	level	rise	fall-rise	rise-fall	uncertain
35%	34%	12%	12%	1%	6%

The most common tones were the fall and the level tone, with the least common tone being the rise-fall. The rise-fall is much more frequent in non-standard accents of English (such as Welsh English or Irish English) where its occurrence is heard as normal. However, in RP the rise-fall is an unusual event, and therefore tends to be interpreted as cuing an attitudinal meaning (cf. Chapter 15). Extract 4.11 shows an example from Rachel.

Extract 4.11 Rachel *erm ... a long story*

```
01  ||  →  ERM ||
02  ||  ↗↘ WELL ||
03  ||  ↘↗ it's a LONG STOry ||
```

Rachel begins an answer to a question about how she ended up being employed at the University of Birmingham.

The rise-fall occurs in unit 02, on *well*, a **discourse marker** – a word that helps with the organisation and planning of speech. To a speaker of RP, the effect of the unusual rise-fall tone on *well* seems to convey an attitudinal meaning which we could explain as 'You will be intrigued by this'. But *well* as a discourse marker can convey this meaning without this tone (cf. Carter & McCarthy, 2006: 152) and for those for whom this tone occurs more frequently (for example people with Welsh accents) it will not sound unusual. It will not therefore cue the presence of an attitudinal meaning (cf. Chapter 15 for more on attitudinal meanings).

4.7   Vocal range

When people speak, their vocal range drifts up and down over periods of time, so that one minute they are making choices in a vocal range which is relatively high and the next minute they are making choices in a vocal range which is relatively low. Thus there are no absolute landmarks, even in the speech of a single speaker, for what constitutes high, mid, and low key. Instead of landmarks, there are constantly (often gently, sometimes dramatic) shifting reference points which establish a for-the-time-being reference norm for that speaker at that moment. Changes in vocal range are not represented in the window on speech.

4.8   Capturing the whole contour

With the three choices of key and the five choices of tone, the window on speech is able to capture the broad outline of the contour of a speech unit. But there may be a variety of small movements up and down which the transcription does not capture. Our framework transcribes the choices made by the speaker, not the fine phonetic detail of these choices. A transcription is a window through which the fine detail can be observed, but it is not in itself a representation of the fine detail. Thus in the two speech units of Extract 4.8, the transcription does not give any information about the contour of the non-prominent syllables which precede the first prominence.

Extract 4.12 Geoff *towards...to avoid*

```
01 || ↘ towards the END of the book ||
02 || ↘ so that you'ld KNOW exactly what to a VOID ||
```

These units are from Geoff's university seminar on the history of English grammar.

In unit 01, there is no information about the contour before the word *end*. We can see only that the words *towards the* have not been highlighted (because they are in lower case and therefore non-prominent), but there is no information about whether they approach the prominence on *end* from above or below. Similarly with the three syllables at the beginning of 02, there may be small slopes in the contour but there is no attempt to capture them in the transcription. But of course these contours can be heard in the recording.

Other frameworks use more symbols to capture finer details of the contours of speech. Whereas our framework has a total of eight choices associated with the contour of a speech unit (five of tone, three of key) Crystal has at least four times as many (1969: 142, 177). This was appropriate for his research, but it made the representation of lines of speech problematic (1969: 299-300). Our descriptive framework aims to be economical so that it is possible to display a reasonable number of lines of transcription for the purposes of analysis, presentation, and teaching.

4.9 Summary and what's next

This chapter has completed the presentation of formal components of the window on speech framework, a descriptive apparatus which aims to capture in transcription the choices that speakers make at the moment of speaking. These choices are:

- whether or not to highlight a word by making a syllable prominent
- which of the five sizes of speech unit to use
- which of the five tones to use
- which of the three choices of key to use

Transcriptions which use the window on speech framework arise from careful listening to the rhythmic properties of the sound substance of speech. They are thus particularly useful in identifying the squeeze zones which are likely to cause Ying's dilemma. In Chapter 5 we will look at further issues which arise when transcribing a recording using this framework, and in particular we will examine the relationship that a transcription has to meanings.

4.10 Further reading

There are many accounts of the tones of English. The approach adopted in *Phonology for Listening* is very close to that of Brazil (1997). Other influential approaches to tone can be found in Crystal (1969: 141ff), Halliday & Greaves (2008: 40ff), Roach (2009: 119ff), and Tench (2011: 158ff). Wells (2006: 15-25) provides practice in hearing tones of different types.

4.11 Language awareness activities

Activity 4.1: Soft focus listening

Next time you are out with a group of friends, and you can take a rest from the conversation without appearing rude, stop listening for meaning and direct your attention to the sound substance of speech.

If you do not want to risk appearing rude, do this with an appropriate YouTube video. Listen to the sound substance of speech for its contours. Notice the difference between moments when speech has steep clear contours, and when it has very shallow contours, and think why these occur. Make notes about what you notice (again, if you can do so without appearing rude). Do not worry if you cannot determine what type of tone has occurred – this takes some time to learn. Discuss what you have noticed with a friend, colleague or fellow teacher.

Activity 4.2: Listen and decide   Answer key page 74

Listen to extract 4.13. There are five speech units, each with a different tone starting on the tonic prominence (underlined). All five tones – fall, rise-fall, level, fall-rise, and rise – occur once. Where do they occur?

Extract 4.13 *i'm going ... of autumn*

```
01 || i'm GOing to be GOing aWAY ||
02 || for aNOther LONG weekEND ||
03 || perHAPS FIVE DAYS ||
04 || into SHROPshire ||
05 || AT the beGINning of AUTumn ||
```

5   Transcription III: Reliability and meaning

In this chapter we first examine the relationship between the careful speech model and the spontaneous speech model. We then review the scientific status of the transcriptions which emerge using our framework – the window on speech. We consider levels of reliability, we compare it with other transcription methods and we look at its relationship to meaning. In this chapter we will occasionally need to use a single term to refer generally to the complete set of the components of the framework (prominence, speech units, tone, key), plus the equivalent concepts in other frameworks. We will use the terms **prosody** and **prosodic** to do so. These terms will be used to refer to the complete range, across all frameworks, of the concepts and tools used to capture those aspects of the sound substance of speech that the particular framework deems important.

The usefulness of a model of speech needs to be judged by the goals it sets for itself. To act as a reminder, here are the goals that we have set ourselves:

- Ying's dilemma – we need to identify those moments in the stream of speech in which words are squeezed out of shape into unfamiliar forms which learners cannot recognise
- the plight of the learner listener – we focus on helping the learner who has to cope with a sound substance that arrives at their ears at speeds and levels of clarity over which they have no control.

5.1   An additional model of speech

As mentioned in Chapter 2, the window on speech is a framework for the analysis, description and transcription of spontaneous speech. This framework, in combination with the findings of the analyses which emerge from it constitute the spontaneous speech model – a model of speech for the teaching of listening. It is designed to represent the realities of the sound substance of speech which learner listeners have to cope with. As we have seen in the previous chapters, it captures the choices that speakers make of prominence, speech units, tone, and key. It places no prior restriction, nor expectation, on what can happen. In fact any given prosodic feature can occur anywhere, within the limits of physical possibility.

The spontaneous speech model is a counterbalance to the careful speech model. It is not something to copy, or emulate. It is something to get used to – something to become familiar and comfortable with. It is a descriptive model, not an emulation model. As we shall see in Part 2 (Chapters 6-10) the spontaneous speech model can help learners and teachers get to grips with the realities of spontaneous speech, which is much less tidy, much less rule governed, much wilder than the careful speech model would have us believe.

5.2   What does a transcription represent?

A transcription represents an interpretation of a recording, not objective fact. It is a visible record of the transcriber's interpretation of the choices which the speaker made in the prosodic systems of the window on speech.

A transcription is a graphic (written) metaphor which represents, but stands in the place of the recordings of the stream of speech. Whereas the recording retains the properties of invisibility and transience, the transcription makes the words of the recording visible and permanent. Its convenience is that it has made the transient readable, and treatable as if it were a written text, but it does this at the cost of misrepresenting the essential nature of the stream of speech.

5.3   Reliability of a transcription

Every transcription includes an element of uncertainty. Transcriptions of the same recording by the same person at different times can differ by 15%; and transcriptions by different people, using the same framework, can differ by 35%, giving only a 65% level of agreement. This can be improved to 90% by a process of comparison and discussion, but getting to that level of agreement may require two sets of independent analyses and discussions to attempt to resolve differences (cf. Cauldwell, 1997). It is an expensive and time-consuming process, and therefore is not practical for large amounts of recorded material.

Transcribers face a number of difficulties when dealing with spontaneous speech. The clear categories of the prosodic systems (prominence versus non-prominence and falling tone versus rising tone) have to be applied to a sound substance that is infinitely variable and mostly shallow-contoured (cf. Chapter 4). Sometimes transcribers are uncertain whether a tone is a fall or a fall-rise, or whether a syllable is prominent or non-prominent. When such problems are encountered, the transcriber can have recourse to repeated listenings and to the help of computer analyses. But even with these tools, levels of uncertainty remain. In such cases, two principles are applied: the **principle of best fit**, and the **principle of the listener's plight**.

5.4   The principle of best fit

The principle of best fit works in the following way: when faced with a case of uncertainty, the transcriber writes down the two competing ways of representing the prosodic feature in question, then performs both ways to him or herself before choosing the version that is the closest match to the original.

For example in Extract 5.1, Corony says the words *in the first couple of years*. It is pretty certain that there are prominences on *first* and *years*. But is there one on the first syllable of *couple*?

Extract 5.1 Corony *in the ... years*

```
|| in the FIRST couple of YEARS ||
```

The procedure is to write down two competing versions, one with two and the other with three prominences, and for the transcriber to perform them matching the speed, volume and level of clarity of the words as closely as possible to the recording, but making the single difference between them as distinct as possible, as in Extract 5.2.

Extracts 5.2.1-2 Corony *in the ... years* – two performances

```
A || in the FIRST COUPle of YEARS || (performance 1)
B || in the FIRST couple of YEARS || (performance 2)
```

The transcriber then compares these versions to the original. In this case, the preference was the two-prominence version because the prominences on *first* and *years* are clearer, at a higher level of realisation than the first syllable of *couple*. This higher level of realisation sets the reference point for what is prominent in this speech unit. So the final transcription is a double-prominence speech unit, as in Extract 5.3.

Extract 5.3 Corony *in the ... years* - original

```
|| in the FIRST couple of YEARS ||
```

5.5   The principle of the plight of the learner

The second principle to apply in cases of difficulty relates to the purpose of providing the transcription. The purpose of our transcriptions is to aid the teaching of listening. We want to help identify moments in the stream of speech which are likely to create instances of Ying's dilemma, where familiar words are rendered unrecognisable because they have a soundshape which is very different to the citation form. So the guideline is as follows: in cases of uncertainty as to whether a syllable is prominent or not, transcribe it as non-prominent, as this is indicative of a possible decoding difficulty for learner listeners.

5.6   Levels of transcription

Often contours of speech will be shallow and fast. This makes it difficult for the transcriber to be certain about what prosodic features have occurred. This is particularly the case with private speech within close social groups. Although the speech is not tune-less, the level of uncertainty about which prosodic feature has occurred is likely to be extremely high, particularly with tones.

In the remaining chapters of *Phonology for Listening* we will vary the degree of precision of the transcription according to that required by the topic being addressed. Most of the time we will use transcriptions which show speech units with prominence and non-prominence, but we will omit the symbols for tone and key. Where it is important to represent tone and key (for example in Chapter 15) then we will use the full transcription system.

5.7   Relationship to Discourse Intonation

The window on speech is derived from *Discourse Intonation* (Brazil, 1997) and is endebted to it for:

- the focus on spontaneous speech
- the concepts of prominent and non-prominent syllables
- distinguishing prominence from word stress
- the five tones, and three types of key
- the concept of speech units of different sizes
- the absence of a relationship to grammatical categories
- the absence of a relationship to attitudinal meanings

However, the window on speech differs from Discourse Intonation (DI) in three ways. First, DI used the term *tone units*, where we use the term *speech units*. Second, for DI **key** only applies to the first prominence in a speech unit. DI recognises a separate system of **termination**, which is similar to key because it consists of high, mid and low steps in pitch, but it applies only on the tonic prominence of a speech unit. Third, DI holds that speakers' choices of tone represented discoursal meanings. Thus, for DI, a falling tone has a *proclaiming* meaning – which indicated that the speaker was presenting the contents of the tone unit as *something the hearer needed to be told* and a rising tone has a *referring* meaning – which indicated that the speaker was presenting what he/she meant as *something that was part of shared understanding*. However, the window on speech regards tone as having no systematic relationship to meaning, whether grammatical, discoursal, or attitudinal. We return to the issue of meaning in 5.9 below.

5.8   Comparison with other frameworks

Transcriptions using the window on speech will usually have higher counts of prosodic phenomena than transcriptions from other frameworks. For example, Halliday (1970) has the utterance in Extract 5.4 as a single tone group (his term for a speech unit):

Extract 5.4 Halliday *with ice ... soda please*

```
//...1 ^ with / ice / ^ a / slice of / lemon / ^ and a / tiny / splash of / soda / please //
```

The soundfile is not the original one. It has been re-recorded for our purposes.

There is a falling tone which starts on the first syllable of *soda*. This is shown by the number 1 at the start of the tone group. In addition, and internal to the tone group, there are rises on the words *ice* and *lemon*, which are signalled by the three dots prior to the number 1. (For Halliday, these rises are secondary tones in the pre-tonic segment of the tone group; they are not tones – cf. Halliday, 1970.)

The transcription of the tone group in the window on speech results in three speech units as in Extract 5.5.

Extract 5.5 Halliday *with ice ... soda please*

```
01 || ↗ with ICE ||
02 || ↗ a SLICE of LEMon ||
03 || ↘ and a TINy SPLASH of SODa please ||
```

Because our framework allows only one tone per speech unit (cf. Chapter 4.3), the rising tones have to occur in separate units, thus creating three speech units out of Halliday's original single tone group.

Halliday's framework is designed specifically to show the relationship between prosodic features and grammatical systems, and in particular the relationship between clauses and tone groups. This is why his transcriptions contain fewer speech units than would be the case with our framework.

A more recent comparison with Tench (2011: 183) shows three of his intonation units becoming seven when transcribed using the window on speech framework. The three intonation units of Tench's transcription feature one incomplete unit (01) and two which end in falling tones on *road* and *scout* as shown in Extract 5.6.

Extract 5.6 Tench *and then ... scout hut*

```
01 | and then one.|
02 | one day we were in up Prospect \Road|
03 |.near the \scout hut|
```

A transcription using the window on speech model results in seven units as shown in Extract 5.7.

Extract 5.7 Tench *and then ... scout hut* in the window on speech

```
01 || ...and then... ||
02 || → ONE ||
03 || ↗ one DAY we were in ||
04 ||...up... ||
05 || ↘ PROSpect ROAD ||
06 || → NEAR the ||
07 || ↘ SCOUT hut ||
```

This transcription has four more units than the one for Extract 5.6. There is one more incomplete unit (04) and a rising tone on *day*, which therefore means it has to be in a unit (03) on its own. Meanwhile unit 06 features a level tone on *near*, which therefore requires a separate speech unit. So our framework typically has more speech units, more tones, and in particular, more level tones and rising tones than other frameworks.

5.9   Relationship to meaning

Most scholars agree that prosody is multi-functional:

- it conveys attitudinal meaning revealing the emotions and feelings of the speaker (O'Connor & Arnold 1973)
- it conveys information structure, determining which parts of the message are given or new, and where the focus of information is located (Halliday, 1994)
- it differentiates between types of relative clause, between questions and statements, types of tag question, and makes sentences less ambiguous (Roach, 2009: 156)
- there is a discourse function where rising tones convey referring meaning and falling tones convey a proclaiming meaning (Brazil, 1997)

Our framework, however, is optimised for the teaching of listening: it records the choices that speakers make, and it is very sensitive to changes in rhythm, and makes transcriptions on the basis of the patterns in the sound substance, rather than on the expectations of the careful speech model. It is one of the consequences of not adopting the careful speech model that we have what some people might regard as the disadvantage of not showing relationships to the clause and to information structure. Furthermore, we use the window on speech in Chapter 15 to demonstrate that in spontaneous speech there is no systematic relationship between attitudinal meanings and prosodic choices.

The view of *Phonology for Listening* is that, contrary to what many textbooks maintain, there is no systematic, generalisable relationship between prosody and meaning. Statements such as 'a high falling tone means surprise' and 'uncertainty is shown by a fall-rise tone' are simply not borne out by the evidence of spontaneous speech.

The function of prosody is to give shape to the sound substance of speech – to make it interesting, listenable to and oriented towards both the speaker's purposes and the hearer's needs. The meaning of a prosodic choice arises in the moment as a non-generalisable coming together of all the elements of speaking (words, syntax, context, situation, converging biographies of speaker and hearer). It is simply not generalisable to other contexts.

In spontaneous speech, speaker choices, performance factors and drafting phenomena (cf. Chapter 6) militate against a tidy relationship between prosody, clause elements, and meaning.

5.10   Summary and what's next

The window on speech framework is a transcription method for representing speaker choices. It gives an auditory view (an ear's 'eye-view') of the sound substance of the recording. It is a written representation of what to listen for in the recording, it is not a replacement for the recording. The transcription is a way of dividing a continuous stream of speech into bite-sized pieces to help reveal how speaker choices interact with the properties of words to create Ying's dilemma.

It provides a tool for the analysis of recordings of unscripted speech. This usefulness will become apparent in Part 2 (Chapters 6-10) where we will use it to explore the nature of spontaneous speech on its own terms. We will look at the soundshapes of frequent forms (including weak forms), the soundshapes of content words, the speed of speech and the nature of English speech rhythms. In Part 3 *Accents, identity and emotion in speech* we will use the window on speech as a presentational and analytical tool to explore accents from around the world and to analyse the relationship between attitude and prosody. And in Part 4 *Teaching Listening* we will see how the window on speech can be used in the classroom to help learners grapple with the realities of spontaneous speech.

5.11   Further reading

Cauldwell (1997) explores the issues of reliability of transcriptions and Knowles (1991) specifically discusses the issues of determining the location of tone group boundaries.

5.12   Language awareness activities

Activity 5.1: Soft focus listening

Listen to conversations between your friends, or between strangers in public places, such as a cafe or a train station. Can you hear emotions being expressed? How are they expressed? Is it the words themselves which express this meaning, or is it *how* the words are said? What is the role of facial expressions, and body language in the expression of emotional meanings? Make notes about what you observe and then discuss them with a friend, colleague or fellow teacher.

Activity 5.2: Listen and decide   Answer key page 75

Listen to Extract 5.8 and write a commentary on the transcription, paying particular attention to the relationship between speech units and clause structure. Consider how it might be different if it were to be transcribed by Tench's framework (cf. Section 5.8 above). Which transcription method do you find most useful, and why?

Extract 5.8 Geoff this is ... for reading

```
01 || → ↑THIS IS ||
02 || ↘ a MANual ||
03 || → FOR ||
04 || → BOTH ||
05 || → READing ||
06 || ↘ and WRITing ||
07 || ↘↗ ef↓FECTively ||
08 || → its a MANual ||
09 || ↘ well well its MORE of a manual for WRITing in fact ||
10 || ↘ EVen though it is for READing ||
```

References for Part 1

Audacity 2.0 (2012) *Audacity*. [Digital audio editor]. http://audacity.sourceforge.net

Bradford, B. (1988) *Intonation in Context*. Cambridge: Cambridge University Press.

Brazil, D. (1994) *Pronunciation for Advanced Learners of English*. Cambridge: Cambridge University Press.

Brazil, D. (1995) *A Grammar of Speech*. Oxford: Oxford University Press.

Brazil, D. (1997) *The Communicative Value of Intonation in English*. Cambridge: Cambridge University Press.

Brown, G. (1990) *Listening to Spoken English*, [2nd edition]. Harlow: Longman.

Cauldwell, R. (1997) The incompatibility of transcriptions: Implications for speech in computer corpora. [Departmental Paper]. EISU, The University of Birmingham.

Cauldwell, R. (2002) *Streaming Speech: Listening and Pronunciation for Advanced Learners of English*. [CD-ROM] Birmingham: Speech in Action.

Cauldwell, R. (2012) *Cool Speech: Hot Listening, Cool Pronunciation*. [iPad application]. Birmingham: Speech in Action.

Crystal, D. (1969) *Prosodic Systems and Intonation in English*. Cambridge: Cambridge University Press.

Crystal, D., and Davy, D. (1975) *Advanced Conversational English*. Harlow: Longman.

Field, J. (2008) *Listening in the Language Classroom*. Cambridge: Cambridge University Press.

Goh, C. (1997) *Metacognitive awareness and second language listeners*. ELT Journal, 51/4, 361-369.

Halliday, M. A. K. (1970) *A Course in Spoken English: Intonation*. London: Oxford University Press.

Halliday, M. A. K. (1994) *An Introduction to Functional Grammar*, [2nd edition]. London: Edward Arnold.

Halliday, M. A. K. and Greaves, W. S (2008) *Intonation in the Grammar of English*. London: Equinox.

Hewings, M. (1993) *The English intonation of non-native speakers*. [Unpublished dissertation]. Birmingham: University of Birmingham.

Hewings, M. (2007) *Pronunciation in Use: Advanced*. Cambridge: Cambridge University Press.

Knowles, G. (1991). Prosodic labelling: The problem of tone group boundaries. In Johansson, S. and Stenström, A. (eds.), *English Computer Corpora: Selected Papers and Research Guide*, 149-163. Berlin: Walter de Gruyter.

Larkin, P. (1965) *Philip Larkin reads 'The Whitsun Weddings'*. [Audio Cassette]. London: The Marvell Press.

O'Connor, J. D. and Arnold, G. (1973) *Intonation of Colloquial English*. Harlow: Longman.

Pickering, L. (2001) The role of tone choice in improving ITA communication in the classroom. *TESOL Quarterly*, 35/2, 233-255.

Roach, P. (2009) *English Phonetics and Phonology: A Practical Course*, [4th edition] Cambridge: Cambridge University Press.

Roach, P., Setter, J., and Esling, J. (eds.) (2011) *Cambridge English Pronouncing Dictionary*. Cambridge: Cambridge University Press.

Tench, P. (2011) *Transcribing the Sound of English: A Phonetic Workbook for Words and Discourse*. Cambridge: Cambridge University Press.

Wells, J. C. (1990) Syllabification and allophony. In Ramsaran, S. (ed.) *Studies in the Pronunciation of English: A Commemorative Volume in Honour of A. C. Gimson*, 76-86. London: Routledge.

Wells, J. C. (2006) *English Intonation: An Introduction*. Cambridge: Cambridge University Press.

Wells, J. C. (2008) *Longman Pronunciation Dictionary*. Harlow: Pearson Education.

Answer key for Part 1

Chapter 3

Activity 3.2: Listen and decide

Extract 3.17 Maggie *i'm going ... long weekend* **– Version 2**

```
01 || i'm GOing to BE ||
02 || GOing ||
03 || aWAY FOR ||
04 || aNOther ||
05 || LONG weekEND ||
```

Version 2 represents Maggie's rhythms and pacing better than Version 1, for the following reasons:

- in units 02-05, she dwells slightly on the words *be* and *going* and *for* with level tones
- she dwells on them for a sufficient time to ensure that there is no continuity of rhythm
- in units 04-05 *another long weekend* is in two rhythmic chunks: *another* is rhythmically distinct from her final two words *long weekend*
- there is a falling tone on *another*, which as we will see in Chapter 4 is the reason for having it in a speech unit of its own

In Chapter 6 will refer to level tones on words such as *be, going to,* and *for* as **stepping stones**, words on which speakers dwell briefly as they decides what to say next.

Version 1 of the transcript – shown in Extract 3.18 – represents Maggie's words as being contained in two triple-prominence speech units, resulting in a total of six prominences.

Extract 3.18 Maggie *i'm going ... long weekend* **– Version 1**

```
01 || i'm GOing to be GOing aWAY ||
02 || for aNOther LONG weekEND ||
```

The Window on Speech

This is the kind of speech, with its resultant transcription, which we might get if both Maggie and ourselves knew in advance what she was going to say, and used the rules of the careful speech model to predict how she would say it. We might reasonably expect that the two units would be spoken in a continuous rhythm. But in the spontaneous speech of Extract 3.17, this is not what Maggie does.

Chapter 4

Activity 4.2: Listen and decide

The tones occurred as shown below.

Extract 4.13 *i'm going ... of autumn*

```
01 || ↗ i'm GOing to be GOing aWAY ||
02 || ↘↗ for aNOther LONG weekEND ||
03 || → perHAPS FIVE DAYS ||
04 || ↗↘ into SHROPshire ||
05 || ↘ AT the beGINning of AUTumn ||
```

The symbols for the tones are shown at the beginning of each speech unit, but the tone itself starts on the centre of the last prominence in the speech unit. These prominences, known as tonic prominences, are underlined for the purpose of this exercise.

In 01 the rising tone occurs on a single syllable, *-way*. The rise is preceded by a slight jump downwards from *a-* to *–way*. Hearing tones on single syllables is sometimes difficult, so do not worry if you cannot hear it at first.

In 02 the fall-rise tone is preceded by a slight jump upwards from *week* to *end*.

In 03 the level tone occurs on a single syllable *days*.

In 04 there is a slight jump down from the second syllable of *into* to the beginning of *Shropshire* and then the rise-fall tone starts on *Shrop-* and continues over *-shire*.

In 05 the falling tone starts on the first syllable of *autumn* and continues over the second syllable.

Chapter 5

Activity 5.2: Listen and decide

There are a number of comments to be made about the relationship between clause structure and speech units. In these units, Geoff is slowly piecing together what he wants to say. He is audibly considering his choice of words in 01-06 but, once he has decided what to say, he then speaks very fast in units 09-10. This occurrence of slow speech units followed by very fast ones is very common in spontaneous speech. We will address this issue in Chapter 7.

Below are a few more specific points which are likely to arise in any discussion.

- Units 01-06: The clause *this is a manual for both reading and writing effectively* is divided into six units because it contains so many level tones, or **stepping stones** (cf. Chapter 6).
- Unit 07: The status of *effectively* is indeterminate – it could either be an adverb which means 'for reading and writing in an effective way' or a sentence adverbial meaning 'in fact' or 'more or less'. This kind of indeterminacy is common in spontaneous speech.
- Unit 8: This unit consists of a complete clause – it has a subject,verb and complement – but it seems incomplete, as it is simply a restatement of what Geoff has said in units 01 and 02. Geoff rephrases it in 09.
- Units 09 and 10: each contain a full clause.

A transcription following the guidelines of Tench (2011) looks like this, but remember it's not the only possible one.

```
01 | this is. a \manual|
02 | .for both reading and \writing|
03 | efVfectively|
04 | its a manual.|
05 | well well its more of manual for \writing in fact|
06 | even though it is for \reading|
```

The Window on Speech

Points to notice are that the Tench-style transcription:

- has fewer units
- includes notation for pauses (the full-stops in units 02 and 04)
- is better at preserving the relationship between clause structure and speech units (Tench refers to them as intonation units)
- does not recognise level tones

PART 2

Describing spontaneous speech

Part 2   Describing spontaneous speech

In Part 2 we use **the window on speech framework** to help us describe the sound substance of spontaneous speech. Our aim is to create a model of spontaneous speech to use in teaching listening. To achieve this, we need to pay attention to the moment-by-moment details of the sound substance of speech. These details are best treated not as a sequence of individual sounds, but as short bursts of continuous sounds. Therefore the unit of analysis will be the speech unit (cf. Chapter 1.1). We keep the plight of the learner listener in mind by focusing on those aspects of spontaneous speech which are most different from the careful speech model. Throughout Part 2, but especially in Chapters 8 and 9, we will be focusing on those aspects of speech that are most likely to cause **Ying's dilemma** (Chapter 1.2). We will be searching for **Ying moments** – moments when words are squeezed into unfamiliar and unrecognisable shapes by the forces of spontaneous speech. Each chapter ends with two language awareness activities. Most ask you to listen to an extract (or make your own recording) and analyse it using the concepts presented in the chapter concerned. There is an answer key for these activities after Chapter 10.

Chapter 6 *Drafting phenomena* looks at pauses, filled pauses, repetitions, markers of vagueness and softeners. These contribute to the sound substance of the stream of speech by interrupting it, taking it forward very slowly, adding references to speaker roles (*you know, I mean*) and adding vague language (*kind of, sort of*).

Chapter 7 *Speed of Speech* looks at benchmarks of slow and fast speech. We will see that the speed of speech changes moment-by-moment. Neighbouring speech units have speeds at the extremes of fast and slow speech.

Chapter 8 *Soundshapes I: Function words* looks at what happens to the soundshapes of function words, weak forms and frequent forms when they are squeezed together in the non-prominent parts of speech units.

Chapter 9 *Soundshapes II: Content words* looks at what happens to content words when they encounter the squeezing forces of the speaker's choices in speech units.

Chapter 10 *Rhythms of speech* looks at the nature of the rhythms of English. Spontaneous speech is not stress-timed. Despite this, classroom activities which are labelled 'stress timing' are useful. In spontaneous speech, rhythms change so frequently that no single rhythm has the chance to establish itself.

Remember you need the recordings. Download them from www.speechinaction.com

6   Drafting phenomena

Many types of language are carefully prepared and planned. In writing we have poems, novels, Acts of Parliament, whereas in speaking we have political speeches, news reading, and sermons. Before publication or performance, these forms undergo extensive preparation. They are subjected to the processes of drafting, reviewing, changes of mind and editing, all of which are invisible in the final product. However, our interest is in language which is spontaneously created. Of course in the written language there are spontaneous forms such as emails, tweets and instant messages, but our focus will be on spontaneous speech, in which the processes of drafting, reviewing and changes of mind leave audible traces in the invisible, transient sound substance. These traces, which include filled pauses, restarts, repetitions and reformulations, are sometimes treated as if they are symptoms of something wrong in speech. For this reason some teachers feel strongly that it is inappropriate to teach them. They are often labelled **disfluencies**, and discussed using words with negative connotations such as 'hesitation' and 'indecision'. Indeed the early history of such research seems to have been influenced by research into stuttering in children (cf. Eklund, 2004). However, they are in fact the natural result of the processes of constructing meaning in real time. They are absolutely normal and contribute significantly to the sound substance of spontaneous speech. As we are concerned with the plight of learner listeners as they encounter spontaneous speech, we need to include them in our description.

We will use the term **drafting phenomena** as a collective term for the audible output of these processes. We will look at pauses (both silent and filled), repetitions, restarts, interjections and vague language such as *sort of* and we will use the window on speech to present the examples. It is best to have read the Introduction and Chapters 1 and 2 before embarking on this chapter.

Many of the examples in this chapter come from Dan, a doctor, who talks about his singing experiences at primary and secondary school, and later as an adult. His experiences include being the soloist (aged ten) in a school choir which reached the final of a competition at London's Royal Festival Hall. Dan's musical ability was so impressive that he was made leader of the school orchestra which is unheard of for someone who couldn't play the violin. Dan also had an audition for the television programme Pop Idol (a predecessor of the more famous X-Factor) in front of the much-feared producer, Simon Cowell. There will also be examples from Toby, a thirty-year-old teacher from the UK whose hobby is climbing;

from Terry a university lecturer from Dublin; from Mohamed, a university academic from Sudan; from Ellen a student from the USA, and Jess a teacher who is also from the USA.

6.1 Silent pauses

Silent pauses are gaps in the sound substance of speech. Researchers have different criteria for what counts as a pause. Following Laver (1994: 536), we will treat any silence of 0.2 seconds or greater as a pause, (written [pause 0.2]).

Silent pauses happen for a variety of reasons, for example they occur because the speaker needs to breathe, because the speaker needs time to decide what to say next or because the speaker has decided to insert a **pause for effect**. They also occur at points where there is a change of speaker, between a question and an answer, or between turns in a conversation. Silent pauses go mostly unnoticed, but they may cause awkwardness for the participants if they are long or frequent. In a speaking test, for example, they may result in students getting a low mark. According to the careful speech model, pauses occur at the end of each turn and at sentence, clause or phrase boundaries.

However, in spontaneous speech the relationship between pauses and syntactic boundaries is not so neat. Pauses can occur anywhere, even in the middle of noun groups and verb groups . In Extract 6.1, Dan describes his role as a solo singer at primary school. Two other children provided the harmony and he sang the main tune.

Extract 6.1 Dan *and then ... stuff*

```
01 ||...and then I'D sing the... ||
02 || the MAIN ||
[pause 0.8]
03 || STUFF ||
```

Unit 01 is an incomplete speech unit (cf. Chapter 3). Ying moment: *and then* sounds like *annen* (cf. Chapter 8.4).

Notice how Dan interrupts a noun group – *the main stuff* – by inserting a pause of 0.8 seconds in between the adjective *main* in 02 and the noun *stuff* in 03. *Stuff* is an example of vague language which we will explore further in 6.5.

Pauses can also occur in the middle of verb groups. In Extract 6.2 Dan gives an example of how his music teacher treated him as a favourite pupil.

Extract 6.2 Dan *he made me ... the violin*

```
01 || he made me LEADer of the ORchestra ||
  [pause 0.3]
02 || Even though i COULDn't ||
  [pause 0.6]
03 || PLAY the vioLIN ||
```
Ying moment: in 01 *made* sounds like *may,* resulting in something close to *he may me.*

Between 01 and 02 there is a short pause (0.3 seconds), but there is a pause which is twice as long in the middle of the verb group *couldn't play.* Such pauses, which break up noun and verb groups, are normal and usually go without notice.

Silent pauses, and indeed any drafting phenomenon, can be used strategically by speakers *for effect* – to add emphasis to a particularly important point. Dan makes strategic use of the pause in Extract 6.3, when he talks about one of the highlights of his singing career as a young adult.

Extract 6.3 Dan *and I sang ... Simon Cowell*

```
01 || and i SANG in FRONT of ||
  [pause 0.4]
02 || SIMon COwell ||
```

Simon Cowell, at the time of the recording, was one of the most influential, and most feared people in show business. Ying moment: in 01 *front of* – the final |t| of *front* is realised as a glottal stop.

Dan pauses for effect after the prepositional phrase *in front of* in order to add more impact to his saying the name of a very famous person.

Pauses can happen anywhere in spontaneous speech that speakers choose to place them. In the *careful speech model*, pauses are only acceptable when they occur at syntactic boundaries, and they are regarded as disfluencies when they occur mid-structure. When competent speakers speak together, pauses generally go unnoticed, and are unproblematic unless they are so long, or occur so often, that they go beyond the threshold of acceptability. And that threshold will be dependent on the participants' familiarity with each other's speech habits and the extent of their willingness to cooperate in social interactions which focus on meaning, and not on the forms of speech.

Silent pauses are not the only type of pause. In the next section we look at two other types of pause: the vocalised filled pause and the lexical filled pause, or stepping stone.

6.2   Filled pauses: vocalised pauses and stepping stones

Filled pauses are extremely common and they come in a variety of soundshapes. In writing they are spelled in different ways: *erm, er, um, uh, ah,* etc. Their use is often deplored. In fact, they are often edited out of recorded interviews by broadcasters in a process known as 'de-umming'. People can train themselves to avoid them in their own speech by attending sessions of an organisation called Toastmaster. In these sessions someone acts as an 'ah-counter' whose role is to record any word or sound 'used as a crutch'. These include interjections such as *you know* and *I mean*, filled pauses such as *ah, um, er* and repetitions of words such as the first person *I* at the beginning of a sentence (Toastmaster, 2011).

The view is that educated people, speaking carefully, should have sufficient skill to hide their drafting phenomena. However, for most people this can only be achieved if their speech is in some way prepared.

Filled pauses are a normal feature of spontaneous speech. In Extract 6.4 you can hear Dan explaining which song his choir sang in the final.

Extract 6.4 Dan *um ... something about you*

```
01 || UM ||
02 || and we SANG ||
[pause 0.3]
03 || LEVel forty-TWO ||
[pause 0.8]
04 || UM ||
[pause 0.5]
05 || SOMEthing aBOUT you ||
```

Level 42 is an English pop-rock band which had a number of hits during the 1980s and 1990s. *Something about you* is one of their hit songs. Unit 05 contains a Ying moment: *something* sounds like *sumpning* (cf. Chapter 9.2).

In 01 and 04, we see typical *ums* appearing as the only syllables in their respective speech units, with the one in 04 preceded and followed by a pause, which is a common occurrence. Filled pauses almost always occur with a level tone, as they do here. Filled pauses can also occur in speech units which contain other words, as in Extract 6.5.

Extract 6.5 Dan *the um*

```
|| THE UM ||
```

In this unit *the* occurs before *um* and has the full vowel |ðiː| and the transition to *um* involves a yod, giving |ðiːjʌm| – *thee yum*.

Filled pauses act as points in the stream of speech where speakers dwell (in the sense of *wait*) for a short time while making a non-word, i.e. non-lexical, noise. This enables speakers to buy themselves time while they decide what to say next. However, such dwelling points can occur on lexical items as well, in which case they are traditionally termed **lexical filled pauses.** We, however, will refer to them as **stepping stones,** for reasons which are explained below. Most commonly, speakers dwell on function words such as *and*, *but*, *the*, and *which* by extending the vowel and using a level tone. Dan gives us an example of this on *the* in Extract 6.6.

Extract 6.6 Dan *and then ... kind of thing*

```
01 || and THEN THE ||
02 || the ROYal festival hall and the queen eLIZabeth hall ||
03 || was more of like a GOSpel kind of THING ||
```

Dan describes the song that his choir planned to sing in the final of the singing competition. Ying moments: in 01 *and then the* sounds close to *an.nen.ee*; in 03 *was more of like a* sounds close to *wuz morve lakka*.

In 01 there is a double-prominence speech unit (cf. Chapter 3.2), with a level tone on *the* on which Dan dwells before embarking on the two speech units which follow.

Speakers also use content words as stepping stones. Extract 6.7 shows Dan explaining how he got into singing at the age of eight.

Extract 6.7 Dan *um it started ... in Oliver*

```
01 || UM ||
```

```
02 || it STARTed ||
03 || when i was the ROSE seller ||
04 || in OLiver ||
```

Oliver! is a famous musical with words and music by Lionel Bart. It is based on Charles Dickens's *Oliver Twist*.

In unit 02 the word *started* is elongated, and it has a level tone. The occurrence of the word itself pro-gresses Dan's explanation, but the elongation of the word slows the explanation. Meanwhile the fact that it is stretched out with a level tone buys him planning time for what to say next. It is not so much a pause as a stepping stone, where the rhythm is interrupted, the speed slows and the speaker dwells on a word which is advancing the discourse.

6.3   Repetitions

When we learn to write, we are told to avoid repetitions of words, to use a variety of words, to avoid saying the same things over and over again, and to vary our sentence patterns. To follow this advice you need the time to plan and edit – a characteristic feature of prepared language. In spontaneous speech it is quite normal for there to be repetitions of words, meanings and structures which would be edited in writing and severely censured by the 'ah counter' of the Toastmaster organisation. In this section we look at the range of repetitions which are normal in spontaneous speech.

6.3.1 Exact repetitions *again and again and again*

Toby loves climbing rocks and mountains. In Extract 6.8 he describes how he practises climbing indoors where, if he falls, he falls safely onto a mat.

Extract 6.8 Toby *because while ... again and again*

```
01 || because WHILE you're only a METre ||
02 || off the GROUND ||
03 || and you've GOT the CRASHmat there ||
04 || ...you just CLIMB it... ||
 [pause 0.4]
05 || DO the move aGAIN and again and GAIN ||
```

In 05 the word *again* occurs three times. Toby is a very enthusiastic and lively speaker and he enjoys acting out meanings. Rather than *You repeat the move* which he might have chosen to say in prepared speech, he uses *again* three times in a very colloquial, commonly occurring pattern.

Often it is the personal pronoun at the start of a clause which is repeated. In Extract 6.9 Dan talks about a tour he made of Africa as a newly qualified medic.

Extract 6.9 Dan *and we ... in Kenya*

```
01 || and WE ||
02 || we STARTed off in KENya ||
```

Ying moment: the second |t| of *started* is a glottal stop, and the final syllable sounds close to *udd* (rhymes with *bud*).

Dan says *we* twice: in 01 it occurs as a stepping stone (cf. 6.2). It is elongated, it has level tone and has its full vowel quality. In 02 it occurs in its weak form as the subject of the clause.

Although such repetitions normally occur as part of the drafting processes of spontaneous speech, they can also be used for strategic effect. In Extract 6.10 Mohamed explains his desire to live in France. He wanted to:

Extract 6.10 Mohamed *as it were ... and the culture*

```
01 || AS it were imMERSE myself ||
02 || in in in in the LANGuage and the CULture ||
```

In 02 the word *in* occurs four times in succession, and conveys the sense of someone completely in control of what he is saying, and very comfortable making this kind of repetition. He sounds very professorial.

6.3.2 Meanings re-worded

Meanings are often repeated by being immediately re-worded. Extract 6.11 shows Dan talking about an eagle owl which he saw on his trip to Africa.

Extract 6.11 Dan *absolutely massive*

```
01 || ...this... ||
02 || BIRD ||
```

```
03 || is ABsolutely MASSive ||
04 || HUGE ||
```

Ying moment: *absolutely* undergoes stress-shift (cf. Chapter 9.1).

In 03 and 04 Dan describes the size of the eagle owl in words which make it very clear that it is very big. He has no need to add *huge* but he does so. This type of repetition, of re-worded meanings, is very characteristic of spontaneous speech.

6.3.3 Repeated clauses

Clause structures can also be repeated. In Extract 6.12 Ellen describes the area around her house.

Extract 6.12 Ellen *there were...there was*

```
01 || there were a LOT of WHEAT fields ||
02 || around my HOUSE ||
03 || and there were VEry few HILLS ||
04 || and there was a VEry small town i lived in ||
05 || and there was a UniVERsity there ||
```

Ellen is a student and she was born and brought up in Washington State in the USA.
Ying moment: in both 04 and 05 *and there* sounds like *an air*.

In these five speech units there are four clauses beginning with *there*. This demonstrates two very common features of spontaneous speech. First, repetitions of words and phrases and second, the additive nature (*this-plus-this-plus-this* rather than *although-this, nevertheless-this*) of syntactic structures.

In Extract 6.12 there is a neat co-occurrence between clause and speech unit, but sometimes the relationship between clause and speech unit is not so neat, as we can see from Extract 6.13 (a continuation of Extract 6.8). Toby explains the advantages of practising climbing indoors when you are only a metre off the ground.

Extract 6.13 Toby *do the move ... and falling*

```
01 || DO the move aGAIN and again and GAIN ||
02 || and keep MISSing it and keep MISSing it and FALLing ||
03 || and keep MISSing and FALLing and MISSing and FALLing ||
```

Units 02 and 03 contain three and four non-finite clauses respectively. Such repetitions act out the meaning of repeated activity. It is symptomatic of the here-and-now nature of spontaneous speech that situations are described in this acted-out way, in which the clauses are repeated in imitation of the repeated action, rather than in an after-the-event edited wording such as 'you repeat the move'.

6.4   Restarts

Speakers very often begin speaking and then change their mind about what they are going to say, or how they are going to say it. In Extract 6.14, Dan begins a reply to a question about his feelings when his Pop Idol experience ended.

Extract 6.14 Dan *well i didn't ... pop idol*

```
01 ||...well i DIDn't... ||
02 || at the TIME ||
03 || it was POP idol ||
```

In passing it is worth noticing that there is a clear fall-rise tone on *time* in 02, and a falling tone starting on *pop* in 03. Ying moment: there is a vocalised |l| at the end of *idol* (cf. Chapter 11.4.4).

In unit 01 Dan begins his response *Well I didn't…* and quickly changes his mind. He then begins again in 02 with the construction of a longer reply which only later on (in speech units which are not shown) answers the question. This stopping and restarting, or 'recasting' (Carter & McCarthy, 2006: 89b) is very common. Here, as is often the case, the discarded words are in an incomplete speech unit (cf. Chapter 3.6).

6.5   Markers of imprecision *like ... kind of*

Markers of imprecision and vagueness are also characteristics of spontaneous speech which are avoided in prepared language. In Extract 6.15 Dan talks about both the style of singing, and the clothes that he wore.

Extract 6.15 Dan *was more of like ... you know*

```
01 || was more of like a GOSpel kind of THING ||
02 || where i had to WEAR like a BLACK SUIT ||
03 || with GLITTery ||
 [pause 1.0]
```

```
04 || THINGies ||
05 || YEAH ||
06 || laPELS ||
07 || you KNOW ||
```

Unit 05 is a response token from Richard. Ying moment: in 02 *more of like a* sounds like *morve lakka*.

In 01 there are two markers of imprecision: *like* and *kind of thing*. The word *like* has an indeterminate meaning, roughly equivalent to *similar to* or *so to speak* or *as it were* or even *you know*. The words *kind of thing* signal that the term *Gospel* is not a completely accurate description of what the choir was going to sing. In 02 Dan uses non-prominent *like* once more, which – as in 01 – has a *not-quite-exactly* meaning. After all the vagueness and imprecision of 01 and 02, Dan in 03 dwells on a stepping stone of great precision – the adjective *glittery* – after which he pauses for one whole second before saying the noun *thingies*, which is as vague as it is possible to be. Dan then explains what he means by *thingies* when he re-words it as *lapels* in 06 and then finishes with a brief appeal to the listener's perspective – *you know*.

In writing, *etcetera* or its abbreviation *etc.* shows that a list of indeterminate length is being suggested. In speech this function is often performed by *and that kind/sort/type of thing* or *and stuff like that*. Extract 6.16 shows four examples.

Extract 6.16 *And that kind of thing, and things like that, and stuff*

```
01 || DRAma and THAT kind of THING ||
02 || and STUFF like THAT ||
03 || and things like THAT ||
04 || and STUFF ||
```

These units come from Corony, who is British (01), and Ellen (02) and Travis (03-04), who are from the USA.

In 01 Corony's *that kind of thing* ends her list of evening classes that she was organising; in 02 Ellen ends a list of games that she would play in the street with her childhood friends; and in 03-04 Travis ends a list of subjects that he studied at university – his *and stuff* is equivalent in meaning to *and things like that*.

6.6   Softeners

Softeners are another type of imprecision marker, examples of which include *sort of, kind of* and *just*. In Extract 6.17 Toby talks about special shoes which he uses while climbing.

Extract 6.17 Toby *so your feet ... sort of thing*

```
01 || so your FEET stick to the ROCK ||
02 || sort of THING ||
```

In 01 he makes a statement which, if interpreted literally, means that he would not be able to move, but in fact this is equivalent in meaning to *so your feet get a good grip on the rock*. In 02 Toby's *sort of thing* is an overt indicator of imprecision, which makes any possible dispute ('You don't literally mean stick, do you?') less likely.

Our example of *kind of* is from Jess from the USA, who – in Extract 6.18 – talks about the time when she moved house and wanted to make new friends.

Extract 6.18 Jess *kind of hard*

```
01 || UM ||
02 || ... and SO it was ...||
03 || kind of HARD to find FRIENDS ||
```

Note that in 03, the words *kind of* are in the squeeze zone, part 5 of the five-part pattern of a double-prominence speech unit (cf. Chapter 3).

In 03 *kind of* softens the strong meaning of *hard*, but, as you will hear, it has become virtually monosyllabic. Instead of |kaɪnd əv|, it sounds something close to *ka*. This is because the consonant cluster at the end of *kind* is elided, along with the word *of*. Meanwhile the vowel is not the diphthong |ai|, as we might expect, but is closer to the short vowel |æ|.

There is a clearer version of *kind of* from Dan in Extract 6.19, but our focus here is on the two occurrences of *just*. Dan describes his feelings when he had finished his audition in front of Simon Cowell.

Extract 6.19 Dan *just kind of ... just glad*

```
01 || ...and i JUST kind of... ||
02 || i was just GLAD to be OUT of there ||
```

In 01 *kind of* appears to be heading for an indeterminate, softened meaning to which the preceding prominent *just* is contributing. But in 02 there is a change of stance, where *just* is used to emphasise the precision of the following adjective. For more on the varied meanings of *just* cf. Carter & McCarthy (2006, section 47).

Describing Spontaneous Speech

6.7   References to speaker roles *you know, I mean*

Two frequent phrases in the sound substance of speech make reference to the discourse roles of speaker and hearer: *you know* and *I mean*.

The two words *you know* seem to have special status. They occur very frequently, mostly in a speech unit on their own and have a short sharp rising tone on *know*. Of the twenty-three occurrences of *you know* in Cauldwell (2002 & 2004), fourteen occur on their own. Extract 6.20 shows an example from Dan, in which he explains the advice he got from people when he had problems with his voice.

Extract 6.20 Dan *you know*

```
01 || and they were like DON'T SPEAK ||
02 || you KNOW ||
03 || just REST it ||
```

Ying moment: in 01 *and they were like* goes at 11.5 syllables per second (very fast, cf. Chapter 7) and sound close to *nairwuhlike*.

In 02 Dan gives a typical *you know* in a speech unit on its own which is at the very fast speed of 480 words per minute, or 8 syllables per second.

Unlike *you know*, the phrase *I mean* is most often used with a following clause within the same speech unit. In this way it is similar to *like*. In Extract 6.21, Jess from New Mexico praises her home town – Santa Fe.

Extract 6.21 Jess's *I mean*

```
01 || it's the SOUTH west ART capital of the u S ||
02 || i mean it's VERy arTISTic ||
03 || we have a WORLD class OPera ||
```

In 02 *I mean* occurs in the first squeeze zone of a double-prominence speech unit (cf. Chapter 2.3). The speed of *I mean* is 600 words per minute, or 10 syllables per second – very fast indeed. It is equivalent in meaning to *as it were* or *in other words*. Of course, *I mean* can occur in other relationships to the clause to which it relates. Here is Terry explaining his age at the time of an incident in his early life.

Extract 6.22 Terry's *I mean*

```
01 || and THERE i am in my PRIME i mean ||
02 || in my TWENties early TWENties ||
```

In 01 Terry's *I mean* occurs at the end of a speech unit. For more on *I mean* see Carter & McCarthy (2006: 52b).

6.8   Summary and what's next

Spontaneous speech involves juggling with past, present and future time. At the moment of speaking, speakers utter in the present what they have just planned to say in the past, while simultaneously planning what to say in the immediate future. It is no surprise, therefore, that spontaneous speech is characterised by the audibility of its drafting phenomena. And even some of those scholars who adopt the vocabulary of disfluency think that it is a symptom of something good:

> And just personally I am glad that there is actually some disfluency in what most people say because it means that we haven't gone around and we are not saying things that are practised and rehearsed. (Michael Erard, BBC 2008)

We have seen that drafting phenomena contribute to the sound substance of spontaneous speech and that they are a significant part of the difference between the careful speech model and the spontaneous speech model. We have seen that drafting phenomena can occur at very slow speeds, where they are very clear – what we referred to as filled pauses and stepping stones. More problematically, however, they can also appear at a very fast speed and in ways which produce Ying moments – moments when words are squeezed into new soundshapes. It is now time that we examine the topic of the speed of speech, which we will do in Chapter 7.

6.9   Further reading

Carter & McCarthy (2006: 82–122) is a good source for information on the patterns of spontaneous speech. Brazil (1995: 71–73) provides a readable description of indeterminacy in spontaneous speech. For vague language, Channell (2004) is the classic text. Erard (2007) investigates the meanings of *um* and other drafting phenomena. Research into silent pauses can be traced through the work of Goldman-Eisler (1972) and Hawkins (1971).

6.10 Language awareness activities

Activity 6.1: Prepare and perform   Answer key page 149

Add drafting phenomena to the following text from a conversation about the films that people have seen recently. Make it resemble spontaneous speech as much as possible. Then perform your version to a friend, colleague, or fellow teachers.

```
01 || i've MADE some bad CHOIces seeing FILMS ||
02 || i get VEry enGROSSED in films ||
03 || they REAlly TAKE me IN ||
04 || and IF it's VIolent ||
07 || i get VEry upSET ||
```

Activity 6.2: Listen and comment   Answer key page 149

Listen to Extract 6.23 and comment on the drafting phenomena. Make notes on the differences between this extract and what the careful speech model would recommend. Then compare notes with a friend, colleague, or fellow teacher.

Extract 6.23 Philip *well i was ... literature*

```
01 || WELL i was i was DOing ||
02 || ERM ||
03 || a MOdern languages degree in OXford ||
04 || IS ||
05 || ERM ||
06 || a STUdy of ||
07 || MOdern LANGuages ||
08 || AND ||
09 || of the LANguage ||
10 || AND ||
11 || LIterature ||
```

7 Speed of speech

It is often easy to notice when the speech of other people is particularly fast or slow, but usually we are unaware of the speed at which we ourselves speak. So although we might notice that broadcast commentaries of solemn events are slow, or that horse racing commentaries (particularly at the end of a race) are really fast, we are generally unaware of the extremes of speed in everyday spontaneous speech. This lack of awareness can extend to the language classroom and for language learners this is a problem because speed of speech is one of the major reasons for their difficulties with listening. Because of our plight-of-the-listener stance, speed is also an important issue for us to address because speed increases the problems associated with the transience and plasticity of speech (cf. Chapter 1.6-7). Speed is a major contributory factor to the defamiliarising effects of the squeeze zones of speech units (cf. Chapter 2.3), where words acquire new soundshapes – an area which we will address specifically in Chapters 8 and 9.

We therefore need to develop an accurate sense of speed of speech, firstly to understand how speed affects the soundshapes of words, secondly to be able to judge which parts of a recording are likely to cause learners most difficulties (cf. Chapter 19) and thirdly to be able to demonstrate – in class – speech of different speeds (cf. Chapter 18). In what follows, we will use the window on speech framework (Part 1) and in particular the notion of speech units (cf. Chapter 3) to explore issues relating to the speech of speech.

We will look at what research suggests about the benchmarks for fast, average and slow speech and how the speed of speech varies moment-by-moment. However, we begin with the man who holds the world record for speed of speech in English.

7.1 Unreliable judgements

At the time of writing, the world record for fast speech in English is held by Steve Woodmore, who can speak at a staggering 637 words per minute. Steve claims that his record speed is nearly six times the speed of his normal speech – which he claims is about two words per second, or a hundred and twenty words per minute. However, in saying this he is underestimating the speed at which he is speaking. A quick analysis of the nearly thirty seconds of speech which include this quotation shows that he is speaking at over 180 words per minute, which is 50% faster than he thinks (BBC Wales, 2006).

Describing Spontaneous Speech

It is also frequently the case that teachers of English – even experienced ones – are not good judges of their own speed of speech. Here is Beth describing what happened when she wanted to demonstrate to an Arabic speaker that he was speaking too fast:

> I decided to demonstrate to him how much faster his speech was compared to mine and recorded myself saying the same utterances as we had recorded him saying earlier. I then counted the syllables per minute for his version and my version ... Mine was faster! (Personal communication)

Beth is not alone. Teachers who participated in a study reported in Derwing and Munro (2001: 325) all claimed to have reduced their speed of speech when talking to a group of students, but subsequent analysis showed that one third of them had not moderated their speed at all.

7.2 Benchmarking the speed of speech

It would be convenient if there were universal benchmarks for what constitutes fast, average (that is normal) and slow speech, but there is no objective way of providing such absolute measures. This is because what counts as fast, normal or slow depends on the speech style (audio book, news bulletin, commentary on a state funeral) each individual's style of speech, and on the norms that specific social groups have for speaking in different contexts (Laver, 1994: 542). Nevertheless, researchers have provided us with useful benchmarks, or rules of thumb, for speed. They have used both words (Pimsleur et al, 1977) and syllables (Tauroza & Allison, 1990) as the units of counting, and have analysed different speech styles: French and American newsreading in the case of Pimsleur et al, and a variety of speech styles (lectures, conversations, interviews) in the case of Tauroza & Allison. Although their figures do not match precisely, the suggestions that emerge from both publications (and those from Laver, 1994) are broadly compatible. It is therefore possible to derive some broad rules of thumb as to what constitutes slow, average and fast speech. These are shown in Table 7.1.

Table 7.1 Benchmarks for speed of speech (speaking rate) in wpm, sps

SLOW	AVERAGE	FAST
90 wpm	180 wpm	240 wpm
2.0 sps	4.0 sps	5.3 sps

The speed of speech is shown in both words per minute (wpm), and syllables per second (sps), for reasons we will come to in the next section. The figures are approximate and are intended as a rough guide. You should regard them as approximate mid-points of a range of speeds: thus the 90 wpm of the 'slow' category is the centre point of the range 60-120, and the 180 wpm of the 'average' category is the centre point (or close to) of the range 120-220. There is therefore the possibility of overlapping between the categories: speech of speeds of 140 wpm might be classed as 'slow' or 'average', depending on the speech style and other contextual factors.

These benchmarks are intended to be interpreted as content and context neutral, which means that they can apply to speech of any type in any context. However, they are approximate and subject to disagreement. This is because ultimately judgements on whether somebody's speech is *slow* or *fast* will come down to personal or social judgements about whether a speed complies with, or falls outside, the norms for a particular speech style in a particular social context. For example if, as Wikipedia (2011) claims, the norm for recording an audiobook is 150–160 words per minute, then anything recorded substantially faster will be thought of as *too fast* even though it would be within the *average* category given in Table 7.1. Thus the contextual dimension is unavoidable, as we will see as we examine syllable-to-word ratios.

7.3   Words and syllables

Measuring the speed of speech requires decisions both about what to include in the calculation and what units of measurement to use. The **speaking rate** is a measure of the speed of speech which includes the time taken by silent pauses and other drafting phenomena in the calculation. The **articulation rate** is a measure of the speed at which a speaker produces a continuous series of sounds and typically excludes silent pauses. It may also exclude other drafting phenomena (Jacewicz et al., 2009). In this chapter we will use both measures. We will use speaking rate including pauses when we discuss average speeds of stretches of speech of ten seconds or more. However, when we focus on individual speech units, we will use articulation rates excluding pauses.

But what should we count? The options include words, syllables with word stress, syllables, prominences and vowels/consonants. In this chapter we will count both words and syllables, for reasons which will become clear. Extract 7.1 shows two speech units which demonstrate why this issue is important. They come from Rachel, who describes her degree course at Oxford.

Describing Spontaneous Speech

Extract 7.1 Rachel *and that* and *multidisciplinary degree*

```
01 || and THAT was the WAY to do WELL on the course ||440/7.3
02 || it's a MULTidisciplinary deGREE || 110/5.3
```
These two speech units come from different parts of Rachel's recording.

The pairs of numbers after each of these speech units (440/7.3 and 110/5.3) give separate measures of speed for each unit: words per minute (wpm) – 440 and 110, and syllables per second (sps) – 7.3 and 5.3 respectively.

Units 01 and 02 have the same number of syllables – eleven – but they have different numbers of words: eleven and four respectively (counting *it's* as one). Unit 01 consists of monosyllabic words and therefore has an equal number of words and syllables, resulting in a syllable-to-word ratio of 1. In contrast, unit 02 has different numbers of words and syllables because two words are polysyllabic, with seven and two syllables: *mult-i-dis-ci-plin-ar-y* and *de-gree*, resulting in a syllable-to-word ratio of 2.75. If we compare the speeds of the two units in words per minute, we can see that unit 01 is four times faster than unit 02 – 440 wpm compared to 110 wpm. However, if we measure the two units in syllables per second, the difference between the two is greatly reduced: unit 01 is less than 40% faster – 7.3 sps compared to 5.3 sps. The danger, therefore, is that if we use words as the unit of measurement of speed, then we are not comparing like with like.

Whilst most people would agree that it is easier to count words than syllables, it is clear that the number of syllables better represents the sound substance of speech as a rhythmic sequence of prominent and non-prominent syllables. On the other hand the number of words better represents the number of units of meaning that need to be understood. Both measures have their uses. In this chapter we will give two speeds for each speech unit: words per minute (wpm), and syllables per second (sps), but in other chapters we will prefer the sps count.

There are two additional points to make about counting syllables and words. Filled pauses (*um, er*, etc.) and contractions (*it's, she's*, etc.) are counted as one word and one syllable. Where words do not have a fixed number of syllables (for example *actually* which can have four, three or two syllables |æk.tʃu.əl.i|, |æk.tʃəl.i|, |æk.ʃi| the basis for counting will be explained for each example.

7.4   Syllable-to-word ratio

We saw in the previous section that Rachel's *it's a multidisciplinary degree* had a syllable-to-word ratio of 2.75, meaning that each word had, on average, close to three syllables. This is an extremely high ratio. Longer extracts of spontaneous speech generally have a ratio of between 1.2 and 1.5 syllables per word.

The reason for this variation in ratio can be found in the topics that are spoken about – there is a correspondence between word size and topic. Conversations about being a student at university are likely to contain the names of academic subjects and departments – polysyllabic words such as *developmental psychology* and *humanities*. Similarly, an academic seminar on the history of grammar is likely to contain polysyllabic words such as *seventeenth century* and *grammar*. But if someone is telling a personal anecdote the proportions of monosyllabic words (e.g. *and what we do*) is likely to be much greater. The syllable-to-word ratio can vary substantially depending on the topic of the conversation.

As another rule of thumb therefore, we can state that – for recordings of minutes or more in length – the average ratio between syllables and words can vary between 1.2 to 1.5 depending on the topic. This may not seem a large range, but it is a 25%, difference, and – as we have seen with Rachel's units in Extract 7.1 – individual speech units can have much larger ratios.

7.5   Accelerations

Of course, speakers do not speak at their average speed all of the time – they vary their speed moment-by-moment, as Corony demonstrates in Extract 7.2.

Extract 7.2 Corony *I was ... very popular*

```
01 ||... i WAS ... || 170/2.8
[pause0.14]
02 || quite sucCESSful || 130/4.5
03 || i i didn't MAKE an awful lot of MOney || 330/7.3
04 || in the FIRST couple of YEARS || 270/5.2
[pause 0.46]
05 || ERM || 070/1.2
06 || but i SOLD a lot of things || 370/6.2
07 || it was OBviously very POpular || 260/9.3
```

Corony is answering the question *Were you successful as a textile artist?* The speeds at the end of each speech unit are articulation rates (cf. 7.3 above).

Extract 7.2 has a speaking rate of 5.8 sps and 250 wpm – which puts it into the fast category of Table 7.1. However, the individual units (articulation rate) vary greatly in speed: between a low of 1.2 sps (05) and a high of 9.3 sps (07). Corony's two slowest units, 01 and 05, are both associated with drafting phenomena (cf. Chapter 6). We will return to this point in the next section.

There are two noticeable accelerations in this extract: the first over units 01-04, where there is an acceleration from 2.8 to 5.2 sps, and the second over 05–07, where there is an acceleration from 1.2 to 9.3 sps. These short bursts result in the juxtaposition of very fast and very slow units. This is a phenomenon which creates difficulties for learners even in recordings where average speeds are low.

7.6   Content, speed and length of speech units

There seems to be a correlation between the speed of speech units, and their content. In the recordings of Cauldwell (2002), the majority of slow speech units (around 2.0 sps and below) consist principally of single monosyllabic words (*yes*, *no*) filled pauses (*erm*, *er*), function words, together with content words which are used as stepping stones – the drafting phenomena described in Chapter 6.

This seems to be part of a general picture: there is a correlation between the speed of speech units, and the number of words and syllables they contain – the fewer words a speech unit has, the more likely it is to have a slow speed and the more words a speech unit contains, the more likely it is to have a fast speed. This is illustrated in Extract 7.3 in which Rachel describes how she decided to apply for a job at the University of Warwick.

Extract 7.3 Rachel *that was ... of Warwick*

```
01 || THAT WAS || 120/2.0
02 || CLOSE enough || 130/3.3
03 || to acaDEmic adminisTRAtion || 110/6.6
04 || TO || 080/1.3
05 || ERM || 090/1.5
06 || ...for ME to... || 250/4.2
07 || aPPLY for a JOB at the University of WARwick || 240/6.8
```

This extract illustrates the correlation between speed and the amount of content in a speech unit. The slowest speech units are 04 and 05 which contain monosyllabic drafting phenomena: unit 04 has a stepping stone level tone on *to*, followed in 05 by a level tone filled pause. Then as the number of syllables increases, the speed goes up and the content moves away from drafting phenomena onto topic related lexis. It must be emphasised that this correlation is more of a tendency than a fixed rule because (of course) the pacing of speech and the division into speech units is under the control of the speaker.

7.7   Speed in L2 English speech

Up to this point we have been examining the speed of L1 speech – so how does this compare with L2 speaker performance in English? Roach (1998) gives some idea of the difficulties of conducting such a comparison, but Hincks (2010) gets around these difficulties by comparing the speed of presentations given by master's degree students of engineering in both their native language (Swedish) and in English. Hincks found that their performances in English were on average 23% slower than in Swedish but there was a correlation between individuals. Hincks states that 'speakers who speak relatively slowly in their L1 also tend to do so in the L2'.

Derwing and Munro (2001) reported that when the speed of speech of L2 speakers was altered electronically – with a slight speeding up – they were judged to be as 'less accented and more comprehensible' than when they were heard speaking at normal speed. They also found, contrary to what we might expect, that 'slowing down the speech of L2 learners by about 10 per cent rarely leads to better rate evaluations from listeners' (2001: 325). But Hincks disagrees: 'Studies have shown that comprehension for both L1 and L2 users improves as rates slow' (2010: 6).

7.8   Summary and what's next

In this chapter we have seen and heard that people – including teachers – are often unreliable judges of the speed of their own and other people's speech. We have also learned that the speed of speech varies from moment to moment and that there are patterns of acceleration in speech which mean that extremes of slow and fast speeds frequently occur in neighbouring speech units. We have also noticed that there is a correlation between size, speed and content of speech units. We found that the slower the speech unit, the more likely it was to consist of single words and drafting phenomena such as stepping stones and filled pauses. In Part 4 *Teaching listening* (Chapters 16-20) we will examine in more detail the implications of these findings for the teaching of listening. This is because we need to help learners acclimatise to speech which is continually changing in speed. Even if they are comfortable with the average speed of speech found in the typical ELT coursebook, in the real world they have to be prepared for bursts of speech that come much faster.

In the next two chapters we will look at the variety of soundshapes which are created when words are spoken at high speed in the squeeze zones of speech units. In Chapter 8 we will see that function words, weak forms and other frequent forms occur in clusters which are squeezed into soundshapes, thus creating Ying moments. In Chapter 9 we will see that content words can also have a wide variety of soundshapes.

7.9   Further Reading

The key works in research into speed of speech are by Pimsleur et al. (1977) and Tauroza and Allison (1990). Griffiths (1991) gives a critical survey of research in speed of speech up to 1990. Altenberg (1987) reports research that shows a correlation between genre of speech and speed of speech. Cauldwell (2007) demonstrates that the distribution of speeds of speech units in oral examinations helps differentiate between passing and failing performances.

7.10   Language awareness activities

Activity 7.1: Listen and decide   Answer key page 151
Look at and listen to Extract 7.4 below (it lasts 9.8 seconds) and do the following:

1. Look at the speed of each speech unit, which is given in syllables per second at the end of each line. Using the benchmarks given in 7.2, write 'slow', 'average', or 'fast' after each unit. Make notes on any issues that arise as you do this.
2. What do you notice about the relationship between speed, the number of syllables and the contents of these speech units?

Extract 7.4 Geoff *this is ... in fact*

```
01 || THIS IS || 1.5
[pause 1.1]
02 || a MANual || 5.7
[pause 0.5]
03 || FOR || 1.5
```

```
04 || BOTH || 2.5
05 || READing || 3.3
06 || and WRITing || 3.5
07 || efFECtively || 7.3
08 || it's a MANual || 8.8
09 || well well it's MORE of a manual for WRITing in fact || 8.3
10 || Even though it is for READing || 8.3
```

Activity 7.2 Record and analyse

Record yourself speaking to a class or to a friend. Choose a twenty-second extract where you are speaking continuously and then, using Appendix 2 *Calculating the speed of speech* to help you, do the following tasks.

1. Calculate your speaking rate for the whole extract.
2. Identify pauses of 0.2 seconds or more.
3. Divide your extract into speech units (do not worry too much about getting them exactly right – just do a quick rough-and-ready analysis).
4. Calculate the articulation rate of each speech unit in syllables per second.
5. As you do these tasks, keep a log of any problems you have.
6. Finally, what did you learn about your own speed of speech?

Report your findings to a friend, colleague, or fellow teacher.

8   Soundshapes I: function words

In this chapter we will look at the ways in which the soundshapes of words are squeezed into shapes which are dramatically different from their citation forms. Our focus will be on the most frequent words in English – function words – in common combinations such as *and the*, *in the*, and *we were*. We will focus on content words in Chapter 9.

The main causes of the variations in soundshape of a word are the choices made by the speaker in context: choices of which syllables should be made prominent, which non-prominent, and choices of speed and the level of clarity required by the context. We will observe these choices, and their effects on the sound substance of spontaneous speech, using the window on speech framework.

Function words are far more frequent than content words, and they are typically taught and learned early in language teaching. It might therefore be expected that they are easily decoded when encountered in spontaneous speech. However, Field (2008) reports that – surprisingly – learners perceive known function words less accurately than known content words. The disparity was close to 20% and his research suggests that this disparity does not improve as learners move to higher levels of competence.

We begin with some definitions and remind ourselves of Ying's dilemma, which we first encountered in Chapter 1.

8.1   Definitions and a reminder of Ying's dilemma

Studies of English vocabulary distinguish between **function words** (*and*, *the*, *we*) and **content words** (*farmed*, *departments*, *tutors*). Function words express grammatical relationships and they are often monosyllabic. They include auxiliary verbs, conjunctions and prepositions. Content words are those words which enable us to tell what speech is about – who and what is involved (nouns), what they look like (adjectives), what is happening (verbs) and how things are being done (adverbs).

Two processes that very commonly happen when words come into contact are **assimilation,** where a segment such as a consonant changes in some way because of the sound which immediately precedes it, or follows it (*ten people* becomes *tem people*), and **elision**, where the sound disappears (*last night* becomes *las night*).

Ying's dilemma (Chapter 1) refers to the situation when someone believes they know a word, but cannot recognise it when they hear it spoken. We will use the five-part pattern of the double-prominence speech unit (first seen in Chapter 2) to show those parts of speech unit structure – the squeeze zones – where Ying's dilemma is most likely to be caused. Table 8.1 shows five speech units which demonstrate Ying's dilemma.

Table 8.1: Extract 8.1 Ying's dilemma – Prominent and non-prominent *where*

	5	4	3	2	1
01	but i	WAS	n't sure	WHERE	
02		WHERE		MAR	ket street was
03			where she'd	SAID	
04	where there were	STREET		LIGHTS	
	WHERE ... WHERE ... where ... where				

The last line gives the four different soundshapes of *where* side-by-side, so that you can clearly hear the differences.

Columns 5 and 3 are **squeeze zones** – stretches of non-prominent syllables where words are squeezed and reshaped into bursts of the stream of speech. Simply put, the squeeze zones are the cause of Ying's dilemma although, as we will soon discover in 8.6 below, this is an over-simplification. We will also use a seven-column version of this table whenever we need to deal with a triple-prominence speech unit.

8.2   Function words and weak forms

Function words dominate the list of the top 100 most common words and forty-eight, or nearly half of these function words, are known as 'weak forms'. Cruttenden (2001: 252-253) gives both an accented soundshape and between two and four unaccented soundshapes for each of these weak forms. For example, *has* is shown in accented form as |hæz| and four unaccented forms |həz| |əz| |z| |s|. The list of weak forms was first published by Gimson in 1962 and he made it clear that it was not intended to be a complete list. However since its original publication many teachers and textbook writers seem to have been under the impression that this is a complete list, failing to appreciate that all words (and not just function words) have a wide variety of soundshapes.

8.3   Word clusters and phonetic indeterminacy

When extracted from a recording, individual function words often sound like bleats, clicks and burps. But function words frequently occur in clusters – pairs, trios or even longer combinations – and their soundshapes are influenced by the very fact that they are clustered. It is necessary therefore, to deal with these function words as clusters of words (Carter & McCarthy 2006: 828-837) which are squeezed into bursts of the stream of speech which are indivisible into their component words.

In these squeezed bursts it is not always possible to be absolutely certain which words were intended. Sometimes the soundshapes which emerge seem to be between alternatives – not quite one thing or the other. Such phonetic indeterminacy – where it is impossible determine whether it is *x* or *y* in the sound substance – is common and unproblematic for expert speakers of the language, for whom it either does not matter, or is resolved by contextual considerations. However, for language learners such as Ying this is the very crux of the matter. Such moments – 'Ying moments' – in the stream of speech, where familiar words are de-familiarised, have to be given pedagogic treatment through explicit instruction if learners are to achieve an adequate level of mastery of the sound substance of the spoken language.

8.4   Phonetic symbols and informal representation

In this chapter and the next we will use two kinds of written help to draw attention to the features of the sound substance: phonetic symbols and (where the spelling of English allows) informal representations in ordinary writing of the features of the recording (e.g. *un.en.at.wuzz.at* for *and then that was that*). Neither the phonetic symbols nor the informal representations should be thought of as indicating precisely what has happened. Instead they should be interpreted as guides to alert your ears to the results of the squeezing processes that occur in the sound substance of the recording. We need to bear in mind the warning of Brown (1990: 7) 'the stretches of obscure acoustic blur often no longer permit any representation on a segment-by-segment basis' and accept that there will always be difficulties in bridging the gap between sound substance and the written form.

8.5   The many soundshapes of *and*

Carter and McCarthy list *and* as the third most frequent word in their spoken corpus (2006: 12). It has a large number of soundshapes. In Extract 8.3, Dan illustrates some of these different soundshapes in British English. There are six occurrences of *and*, all of which are non-prominent.

Describing Spontaneous Speech

Extract 8.2 Dan *and i ... didn't get through*

```
01 || and I just STARTed ||
02 || and my VOICE just went [creak] ||
03 || and NOTHing came OUT ||
04 || and Everyone just WENT ||
05 || [SIGH] ||
06 || oh POOR YOU ||
07 || and then THAT was THAT ||
08 || and WE ||
08 || didn't get THROUGH ||
       and ... and ... and ... and ... and ... and
```

Dan, who is a very good singer, is talking about the time when his voice failed at a public concert. Unit 06 *Oh poor you* is a sympathetic interjection from Richard. The last line gives the different soundshapes of *and* side-by-side, so that you can clearly hear the differences.

The six *and's* are all non-prominent. They occur before the first prominence in their respective speech units and sound close to *an, em, n, on, an* and *um*. The first *and* has a vowel close to |æ|, as does the fifth, but the others approach |e| |ɒ| and |ʌ|.

Dan's extract gave us six very different soundshapes for *and* in a very short space of time. If you survey a large number of people, you may well find many more soundshapes. In the USA, research by Greenberg (1999) found eighty different soundshapes for *and* of which the most frequent included |æn|, |en|, |in|, |ən|, |n|, with the full form |ænd| coming only seventh on the list (Greenberg & Fosler-Lussier, 2000). Although Greenberg's findings were for American English, it is likely that there is similar variability for Englishes of all kinds.

It is worth noting two Ying moments in Extract 8.2 which involve content words. In 02 *and everyone* sounds close to *an error one*, whilst the four syllables *and my voice just* |ænd maɪ vɔɪs dʒəst| sound close to |əmævɔɪʒəs| where the final consonant of *voice* and the first consonant of *just* squeeze together to form a sound close to |ʒ| – the sound of the consonant in the middle of *azure*.

We will now return to function words and examine *and* in combination with other words.

8.6   *And then, and that*

Carter and McCarthy list *and then* as among the most common two-word clusters in speech (2006: 829). Other very common two-word clusters with *and* are *and that*, *and there* and *and the* – all of which feature the consonant |ð|.

In Extract 8.3 Rachel talks about her studies at Oxford.

Extract 8.3 Rachel *and that ... on the course*

```
|| and THAT was the WAY to do WELL on the course ||
```

The words *and that* have the citation forms |ænd ðæt|, but Rachel gives us |ənnæʔ| – *annat* – where the |d| of *and* along with the |ð| of *that* are elided (omitted) and the final |t| of *that* is realised as a glottal stop.

In Extract 8.4 we can hear a similar example from Dan who says *and then that was that* (meaning 'that was the end of the matter') as a somewhat sad conclusion to his description of his voice failing in a public concert.

Extract 8.4 Dan *and then that was that*

```
|| and then THAT was THAT ||
```

In this unit, |ænd ðen| becomes |ənen| – *un.en* – where the |d| of *and* along with the |ð| of *then* are elided. This shows us that when *and* is the first word in a cluster, and it precedes |ð| both the final consonant of *and* along with the initial |ð| of *then* are likely to disappear.

There are three other Ying moments to notice in Dan's example. The initial consonant |ð| in the first *that* is also elided, and when the remainder is added to |ən.nen| we get |ən.nen.æʔ| – *un.en.at*. In the second *that* the initial consonant again disappears and there is a lengthening of the |z| of *was* to take its place, giving |wəzː.æʔ| – *wuz.zat*. Lastly the |t| at the end of both occurrences of *that* are realised as glottal stops |ənnenæʔwəzːæʔ| – *un.en.a'.wuzz.a'*.

We can see and hear with these examples that it is not just in the squeeze zones that words have non-citation form soundshapes: the three instances of *that* in 8.5 and 8.6 are all prominent in their respective speech units.

8.7   *In the*

The word cluster *in the* is listed by Carter and McCarthy (2006: 829) as the fourth most common cluster in their spoken corpus. We will use Dan's recording to illustrate this, but in Extract 8.5 and the others from Dan which follow in this chapter, we change topic. He now speaks about his adult life when, as a trained medic, he made a trip to Africa, where he helped a colleague in a small hospital.

In Extract 8.5 Dan says *in the* twice: at the end of 01 and at the beginning of 02.

Extract 8.5 Dan *in the*

```
01 || and then i would TREAT in the ||
02 || in the room NEXT door to the main consulTATion room ||
```
Ying moment: *treat* sounds half-way between *chreat* and *dreet*.

In 01 Dan pronounces *in the* somewhere between |ɪn ðə| and |ɪn nə| and in 02, he gives us |ɪn ə| which sounds indistinguishable from *in a* – which, of course, the grammar would allow. However, in Extract 8.6, the grammar of units 03-4 indicates he is more likely to be saying *in the* rather than *in a*.

Extract 8.6 Dan *she was like ... in the garden*

```
01 || she was like WHY don't you GO out to AFrica ||
02 || and STAY with ANNa ||
03 || she says she LIVES in the MIDDle of a WILD life conSERvancy ||
04 || and there's HIPPos in the GARden ||
```
The soundshape of the word cluster *in the* that precedes *middle* in 03 and *garden* in 04 are not |ɪn ðə| but something closer to |ɪn nə|.

Again, in Extract 8.7 we can be certain that the intended target is *the* not *a*, but the soundshape is definitely closer to *a*.

Extract 8.7 Dan *and then the ... come through*

```
|| and then the NEXT patient would come THROUGH ||
```
The comes as part of a very fast (12.5 sps) group of three non-prominent syllables *and then the* |ənenə| which occur before the first prominence on *next*.

We have seen and heard several examples of *the* sounding like a reduced form of *a*. This illustrates an extremely important point about the sound substance of spontaneous speech and its relationship to the careful speech model. This is that the grammatical distinctions which we insist upon when teaching pronunciation are often absent or inaudible in the sound substance of spontaneous speech. In spontaneous speech, definite articles sound like indefinite articles and past tenses sound like present tenses. These are facts about the sound substance of spontaneous speech that we have to take into account when we teach. We will examine the consequences of these facts in Part 4 *Teaching listening*.

8.8   *We were*

In Extract 8.8, Toby talks about a friend he played badminton with when he was at primary school. He uses *we were* twice in a triple prominence speech unit which goes at 7.7 sps.

Extract 8.8 Toby *and we were ... like ten*

```
|| and we were in a BADminton CLUB together when we were like TEN ||
```
This speech unit has three prominences *bad-*, *club* and *ten*. Preceding and between them there are three groups of non-prominent syllables with five, two, and seven syllables respectively. The five syllables *and we were in a* go at over 12.3 sps and are squeezed together in a way which we can represent informally as *nwiwerinna*.

However, it is in the third group of seven syllables that the squeezing effects are most strongly at work. Following the rules of connected speech (e.g. Roach, 2009: 107ff) we might expect *when we* to become *whem we*, with the final consonant of *when* changing to |m| in preparation for the consonant |w| which begins *we*. However, the squeezing forces are so strong that the resulting stream of sounds becomes almost impossible to transcribe with symbols. The reason for this extreme squeeze is that the cluster *when we* is preceded and followed by other non-prominent syllables – *together ... were like* – and these neighbouring words exert forces which result in the extreme squeezing of *we were*. One possible transcription of these syllables is |təgerənwiːwəlaɪʔ| – *tegedderunwewuhlike* – in which *when we* has become |ənwiː| informally *un we*.

8.9   Negatives

You may have noticed that in Dan's account of his voice failing at a concert (Extract 8.2) his *didn't* sounds closer to *ding*. This speech unit is repeated in Extract 8.9.

Describing Spontaneous Speech

Extract 8.9 Dan *didn't*

```
01 || and WE ||
02 || didn't get THROUGH ||
```

In 02, *didn't* becomes |dĩ| – the symbol above |ɪ| is known as a 'tilde', which indicates that the symbol below it is a nasalised segment.

The situation is similar for *could/couldn't* in the examples in Extract 10.10, from different parts of Dan's recording.

Extract 8.10 Dan *couldn't*

```
01 || well i COULDn't SING it ||
02 || i LITerally couldn't SING it ||
03 || but i just COULDn't SING ||
       couldn't ... couldn't ... couldn't
```

The final line gives the different soundshapes of *couldn't* side-by-side, so that you can clearly hear the differences .

In both 01 and 02, *couldn't* sounds monosyllabic. In 03 *couldn't* sounds as if it has two syllables with |ṇ| as the second syllable.

There is potential for a decoding problem here in the very fast, fleeting and distorted appearance of the *n't* at the end of both *didn't* and *couldn't*. Although such occurrences are a common, and completely normal, feature of the sound substance of spontaneous speech, we must emphasise once again that grammatical distinctions which are clearly heard in the careful speech model may be absent in the sound substance of spontaneous speech.

8.10   Function words with content words

Clusters of frequent forms do not occur in isolation. Instead they blend with the content words around them to make the sound substance of spontaneous speech. In Extract 8.11 Toby talks about his favourite hobby, climbing. There are two triple-prominence speech units in this extract. We begin by focusing on *where* in unit 02.

Extract 8.11 Toby *there's just ... at all*

```
01 || there's just LOTS of different TYPES of CLIMBing ||
```

```
02 || BOULDering is where you DON'T use a ROPE ||
03 || at ALL ||
```

In between the first two prominences of 02 are five non-prominent syllables: the last two syllables of *bould.er.ing* plus the three syllables *is where you*. On listening to these speech units we can observe the following points:

- the two syllables *where you* are squeezed into one |wei| – *way*
- the vowels of *where you* |weə juː| have become a diphthong |wei|
- the three syllables *er.ing.is* sound close to |ɪrɪŋz| – *irringz*
- |zwei| *zway* is a squeezed version of *is where you*
- thus five syllables have become three, |ɪ.rɪŋz.wei| – *ir.ringz.way*

There are two other Ying moments in this extract. The first involves another very frequent combination of frequent forms: *there's* and *just* in 01. This becomes *ez juss* |ezʤəs| with no audible |ð| at the beginning of *there's* and with the final |t| of *just* being elided (for more on *just* see Chapter 9.7.2). The second Ying moment concerns the content word *different* in 01. Pronunciation dictionaries give citation forms with either two or three syllables |dɪf.rənt| or |dɪf.ə.rənt| but in both cases the last syllable has four segments |rənt|. However, in 01 this last syllable has only one segment – the syllabic consonant |n̩| thus giving us |dɪf.n̩| – *diffun*.

8.11   An extreme squeeze

We end this chapter by looking at a speech unit which has a large number of both function words and content words in the middle squeeze zone of a double-prominence speech unit. This unit comes from a university seminar given by Geoff. It consists of sixteen words (counting *I'm* as two words) and nineteen syllables (counting *I'm* as one syllable). It lasts 2.1 seconds and was spoken at 9.3 sps, which is extremely fast.

Extract 8.12 Geoff *this is one … detail in fact*

5	4	3	2	1
this is	ONE	i'm going to be looking at in slightly more	DE	tail in fact
		i'm going to be looking at in slightly more		

Geoff is from the British West Midlands and his pronunciation of one |wɒn| is typical of someone from that region.
The second line gives the contents of the middle squeeze zone on its own.

There are two prominent syllables: *one* and the first syllable of *detail*. The rest of the syllables are non-prominent. What follows is a description of some of the features of the soundshapes in column 3:

- *I'm* has a final consonant |ŋ|, thus |aɪŋ|
- *going* loses its final syllable, thus |ɡəʊ|
- *to* and *be* are inaudible in the recording
- *looking* loses |k| and is monosyllabic
- the two vowels of *looking* merge into |ʊ|, thus |lʊŋ|
- *at* acquires |j| thus |jæt|
- the vowel of *more* is close to |u| thus |mu| – *moo*

These soundshapes demonstrate the extreme results that are possible when words are squeezed between two prominences at speeds of 9.3 sps (430 wpm).

8.12 Summary and what's next

Frequent forms are likely to undergo extreme squeezing when they are clustered with other frequent forms and when they occur in the squeeze zones of speech units.

The argument is frequently made that it is not necessary for students to recognize fast, non-prominent function words because they are relatively unimportant and do not therefore contribute much to meaning. There are two points to make against this view. First, essential meanings are often communicated in fast non-prominent syllables – as we have seen with *didn't* and *couldn't*. Second, non-prominent syllables constitute a very important part of the rhythmic flow of the sound substance of speech. Therefore if learners want to become effective listeners then they need to become familiar and comfortable with such stretches of spontaneous speech. This will become an essential part of our goal for listening in Part 4 *Teaching listening*.

We have seen in this chapter that distinctions which are very important in the careful speech model are either absent or inaudible in the sound substance of spontaneous speech. For example, definite and indefinite articles can sound the same and negative morphemes may not be audible. These are the realities of spontaneous speech, and we need to take them into account when teaching learners about the sound substance of spontaneous speech. To help with the plight of the learner listener, we need to be honest about what is present and (just as importantly) what is absent from the sound substance at any given moment in the recordings we use. We therefore need to change the current situation in which many teachers and textbook writers seem either to be reluctant to tackle these realities or to pretend that they do not exist. We will turn to teaching issues in Part 4 *Teaching listening*.

In Chapter 9 we continue to look at the soundshapes of words, but our focus will turn to content words.

8.13 Further reading

Brown (1990: 57-88), Shockey (2003: 14-48) and Greenberg (1999) provide detailed analysis of the variety of soundshapes which words have. For the relationship between prominent and non-prominent syllables and soundshapes, see Greenberg et al (2003). Tench (2011: 119-120) has more on *not* and *there*.

8.14 Language awareness activities

Activity 8.1: Listen and decide   Answer key page 152

Listen to Extract 8.13 and describe what happens to *him that* (01), *and that* (02), *recorded that* (03) and *and that was* (04).

Extract 8.13 Dan *it was...a lad called*

```
01 || it was HIM that WROTE it ||
02 || and THAT was at ABBey ROAD ||
03 || we reCORDed THAT ||
04 || and that was called CRUEL TIMES ||
05 || with a lad CALLED ||
06 || [name removed] ||
```

Unit 06 is not present in the recording. The name has been removed to preserve anonymity.

Compare notes with a friend, colleague, or fellow teacher.

Activity 8.2: Record and analyse

Go back to the recording you made for Exercise 7.2 and look for clusters of frequent forms such as *and that*, *and the*, and *in the* etc. Listen to them carefully – if necessary use a digital audio editor such as Audacity to copy these words out of the recording and paste them into a separate sound file. What do you notice about these word clusters in your own speech? Report your findings to a friend, colleague or fellow teacher.

9 Soundshapes II: Content words

In this chapter we will look at the variety of soundshapes that content words can have in speech units. Content words (e.g. *farmed*, *department*, and *tutor*) are those words which enable us to find out what speech is about – nouns, verbs, adjectives and adverbs. Content words are less frequent than function words, and are more likely to have syllables which speakers make prominent. However, content words are subjected to the same squeezing pressures as function words, and this results in their having a wide variety of soundshapes.

Most L1 speakers of English are not aware of the wide variety of soundshapes that content words have in the speech they produce and the speech they hear. Even experienced teachers of English seem unaware – and this results in Ying's dilemma (cf. Chapter 1), and Anna's anger (cf. Chapter 16).

We will start with long words which feature both primary and secondary stress in their citation forms, and which undergo changes in soundshape due to stress shift, contrastive stress and repeated mentions. We will then go on to look at smaller content words (e.g. *produced*) and examine what can happen to them when they are squeezed by the forces of spontaneous speech. We will pay particular attention to content words which refer to the truth value of what is being said (*actually*, *literally* and *certainly*) and vague language (*something* and *perhaps*). As always, our ultimate aim is help the plight of the listener by examining the realities of the sound substance of spontaneous speech.

9.1   Stress shift

The words *guaranteed* |ˌgærənˈtiːd|, *absolutely* |ˌæbsəˈluːtli| and *observation* |ˌɒbzəˈveɪʃən| have secondary stress on the first syllable and primary stress on the third syllable. The citation forms translate into double-prominence speech units as in Extract 9.1.

Extract 9.1 *Guarantee, absolutely* **and** *observation*

```
|| GUAR an TEE ||
|| AB so LUTE ly ||
|| OB ser VA tion ||
```

Describing Spontaneous Speech

In all three words the secondary stress occurs as the first prominence, and the primary stress occurs as the tonic prominence, that is on the last prominence in the speech unit. We will now see what happens to the soundshapes of these words when they occur in spontaneous speech.

In Extract 9.2 Dan is talking about the time he visited Africa. He says the word *guaranteed* twice. Listen to what happens to the soundshape of *guaranteed* in both units 02 and 03.

Extract 9.2 Dan *guaranteed*

```
01 || it's LIKE a ||
02 || GUARanteed WILD life exPERience ||
03 || you're GUARanteed to SEE ||
04 || LIon ||
     GUARanTEED ... GUARanteed ... GUARanteed
```

The last line gives three soundshapes of *guaranteed*: the citation form and then the versions from 02 and 03.

In both 02 and 03 Dan makes the first syllable of *guaranteed* prominent, and he makes the syllable with primary stress in the citation form (*-tee-* the third syllable) non-prominent. On both occasions *guaranteed* occurs early in a speech unit, with the tonic prominences occurring on the words *experience* (02) and *see* (03) respectively. In both units, the pressure of Dan's choices of prominence squeezes the syllable that receives primary stress in the citation form (*-teed*) into non-prominence.

Something similar happens with *absolutely* in Extract 9.3 in which Dan describes an eagle owl.

Extract 9.3 Dan *absolutely*

```
01 || this ||
02 || BIRD ||
03 || is ABsolutely MASSive ||
04 || HUGE ||
     ABsoLUTEly ... ABsolutely
```

The last line gives two soundshapes of *absolutely*: the citation form, and then the version from 03.

In unit 03 *absolutely* precedes the adjective *massive* and this adjective is the location for the tonic prominence in a double-prominence speech unit. This results in the syllable with primary stress in *absolutely* (*-lute-*) becoming squeezed into non-prominence.

The third of our examples is *observation* in Extract 9.4, which features Geoff reading out the final four words of the title of a book, an early grammar of English, in unit 03.

Extract 9.4 Geoff *observations*

```
01 || the RUDiments of english GRAMmar ||
02 || aDAPTed to the use of SCHOOLS ||
03 || with OBservations on STYLE ||
      OBserVAtions ... OBservations
```

The last line gives two soundshapes of *observations*: the citation form and then the version from 03.

In 03 *observations* shares a double-prominence speech unit with *style* which receives the tonic prominence. This results in the third syllable of *observations*, which receives primary stress in the citation form, being squeezed into non-prominence.

Pronunciation dictionaries generally indicate which words are subject to stress shift. Although neither Wells (2008) nor Roach et al (2011) indicate the possibility of stress shift in their dictionary entries for *observation*, they nevertheless state that stress shift can occur 'on a syllable ... that is capable of receiving stress' (Roach et al. 2011: xvi,) and 'to any word that has a secondary stress before its primary stress' (Wells, 2008: 784). For Brazil, (1997: 17-20) primary and secondary stress are best viewed as potential prominences – syllables where prominences may, but need not, occur. We will encounter another instance in section 9.3 below.

Table 9.1 shows the word *absolutely* followed by its stress-shifted version from Extract 9.3.

Table 9.1: Extract 9.5 Stress-shift *absolutely*

	5	4	3	2	1
01		AB	so	LUTE	ly
02	is	AB	solutely	MASS	ive

Why are the columns numbered in reverse order? See Chapters 2 and 3.

Using the five-part structure of a double-prominence speech unit, we can explain stress shift as follows. We start with unit 01 in the table featuring *absolutely* which has both primary and secondary stress in the citation form. In unit 02 *absolutely* has to share a double-prominence speech unit with the words *is*

... massive. Because column 2 is occupied by a syllable from another word (in this case the first syllable of *massive*) then the primary stress (in this case *-lute-* of *absolutely*) becomes non-prominent in column 3. We can therefore think of stress shift as a movement to the left in this structure, from column 2 to column 3, bringing with it the unstressed syllables which follow it. Of course, as we saw in Chapter 2 with the example of *association*, the word *absolutely* can appear in any of the slots in this structure – becoming entirely non-prominent if all of its syllables occur in columns 5, 3 or 1.

9.2   Stress shift to the right

Occasionally stress shift works in the opposite direction - to the right. For example the citation form of *administrator* has primary stress on its second syllable *-min-*, and there is no secondary stress |əd'mɪnɪstreɪtə|. But listen to Rachel in Extract 9.6, talking about one of her jobs.

Extract 9.6 Rachel

```
|| where i was a reSEARCH adminiSTRATor ||
      adMINistrator ... adminiSTRATor ...
```
The last line gives two soundshapes of *administrator*: the citation form, and then Rachel's version.

Rachel has made the syllable with primary stress *-min-* non-prominent, and has placed the prominence on the penultimate syllable *-strat-*, which is unstressed in the citation form. This type of stress shift to the right is rarer than the one to the left which we saw in Section 9.1. However, both types of stress shift contribute to the range of different soundshapes that content words can have in spontaneous speech and thereby creating Ying moments.

9.3   Contrastive stress

In Extract 9.7 we will hear two different processes at work: stress shift and contrastive stress. The adverb *fundamentally* |ˌfʌndə'mentəli| has primary stress on its third syllable *-men-*, which Geoff makes non-prominent on two occasions. In unit 02 it is non-prominent because it shares the same double-prominence speech unit as the adjective it is modifying – *prescriptive* – and in 04 it shares a double-prominence speech unit with the verb *intended*. This is absolutely consistent with what we saw happening to *guaranteed* in extract 9.2, but observe what happens to the word *descriptive*.

Extract 9.7 Geoff *fundamentally, descriptive*

```
01 || it IS ||
02 || FUNdamentally preSCRIPTive ||
03 || RAther than DEscriptive ||
04 || and it is FUNdamentally inTENDed ||
05 || to be PRACtical ||
      deSCRIPTive ... DEscriptive ...
```

The last line gives two soundshapes of *descriptive*: the citation form and then the version from 03.

The citation form of *descriptive* has stress on the second syllable |dɪˈskrɪpt.ɪv|, but in unit 03 Geoff makes the first syllable prominent, changes the vowel quality in that syllable |ˈdiː.skrɪpt.ɪv| and demotes the primary stress to non-prominence. Why does Geoff do this? He does so because, in this context, he needs to distinguish clearly between two words (*descriptive* and *prescriptive*) which are differentiated solely by their weak, unstressed first syllables |prɪ| and |dɪ|. They have otherwise identical middle and final syllables |ˈskrɪptɪv|, with primary stress on |ˈskrɪpt|. This means that if he had simply left the words in their citation form, it would have been difficult for his listeners to catch the difference in sound-shape, and therefore the difference in meaning. In order to make his argument easier for his listeners to follow, he made the differentiating syllable *de* – normally unstressed in the citation form – prominent. Contrastive stress such as this is yet another way in which the forces of spontaneous speech can change the soundshape of words.

9.4   Climbing

We now focus on shorter content words starting with *climbing*. Toby is passionate about this hobby. On its first mention, in Extract 9.8, *climbing* is clear and full.

Extract 9.8 Toby *climbing*

```
01 || CLIMBing's ||
02 || one of my MAIN HOBBies really ||
```

In 01 *climbing* is very close to the citation form |ˈklaɪm.ɪŋ|. However, in Extract 9.9 – taken from slightly later in his recording – both *climbing* and *twelve* are prominent on their first mention, but non-prominent on their second mention.

Describing Spontaneous Speech

Extract 9.9 Toby *climbing, twelve*

```
01 || but CLIMBing itSELF i ||
02 || i got INto it aBOUT ||
03 || i've BEEN climbing TWELVE ||
04 || twelve YEARS i think ||
      CLIMBing's ... CLIMBing ... climbing
```

The last line gives three soundshapes of *climbing*: one from Extract 9.8, followed by the two from Extract 9.9.

In Unit 01 of Extract 9.9 *climbing*, although still prominent |ˈklamın| has two differences from its soundshape in 9.8 – the vowel in the first syllable has changed, becoming less of a diphthong, and the final segment is |n| rather than |ŋ|. There is a dramatic change in 03 where *climbing* loses its final syllable and the vowel is reduced |klæm| – *clam* – as it is squeezed between the prominences on *been* and *twelve*.

One might think that a learner has a good chance of understanding the intended meaning of *climbing* here, despite the squeezed soundshape, because of the context: the word has been frequently mentioned and, even if it is not perceived, there are no other candidates in the immediate context for a hobby with twelve years duration. However, as we will see in Part 4 *Teaching listening*, we should not assume this to be the case – we need to check that our students have recognized the word. It is entirely possible that the obscure acoustic blur of which *clam* is now a part may be so squeezed as to make it difficult for learners to decode it, even though they have heard a clearer form of the word just seconds previously.

It is extremely important that this characteristic of the sound substance of speech (words being squeezed into different soundshapes) is taught, demonstrated, and learned from. We will see in Part 4 *Teaching listening* that a short extract like this, where two words appear both prominently and non-prominently, provides an ideal opportunity for teaching and learning about how the soundshapes of words are changed in the squeeze zones of speech units.

9.5   *Produced*

We now focus on three instances of the word *produced* |prəˈdjuːst| spoken at different moments by Geoff in a seminar on the history of English grammar.

Extract 9.10 Geoff *produced*

```
01 || proDUCED by a NON-native SPEAKer ||
02 || produced by GUY miEGE ||
03 || this is ONE produced by PRIEStley ||
      proDUCED ... produced ... produced
```

In 02, *Guy Miege* (1644-1718) is the name of a Frenchman who wrote a grammar of English; in 03 *Priestley* is *Joseph Priestley* (1733-1804), an Englishman who, besides discovering oxygen, also wrote a grammar of English.

In the last line the three soundshapes of *produced* side-by-side.

The word *produced* appears in three different positions in these speech units. In unit 01 it is close to the citation form, but without the final past tense marker |d|. The other two units provide us with Ying moments: *produced* occurs in squeeze zones in units 02 and 03 and becomes almost, but not quite, monosyllabic, with the consonant |d| in the middle being almost non-existent, thus giving us something close to *prius*.

This weakening-to-the-point-of-disappearance of a consonant in the middle of a word is something we will see again in Chapter 11, where we get *lil* for *little* and in Chapter 13 where we get *twenny* for *twenty*. We will also take advantage of this phenomenon of consonant disappearance in the classroom exercises presented in Chapter 18.

9.6   Truth value *actually, literally, certainly*

In this section we will look at a number of common content words which indicate how confident speakers are of the truth of what they are saying – *actually, literally, certainly*. These words occur frequently in spontaneous speech and they have a great variety of soundshapes.

9.6.1   *Actually*

The citation form for *actually* has either three or four syllables, with primary stress on the first syllable: |ˈæk.tʃu̯əl.i| or |ˈæk.tʃul.i|. Pronunciation dictionaries tell us that two syllable forms are also possible |ˈæk.ʃli| and |ˈæk.ʃi|. Extract 9.11 gives us an example from Toby who talks about the school friend who introduced him to climbing.

Extract 9.11 Toby *actually*

```
01 || it was ONE of my BEST mates RObin ||
02 || who i used to play BADminton with actually ||
```

Toby gives us a two-syllable version |æk.ʃi| in a non-prominent section after the tonic prominence on *badminton*. We should note in passing the Ying moment in 02: the words *who I used to play* are squeezed together at a speed of 11 sps – extremely fast – and the first four words are reduced to an obscure acoustic blur which is close to two syllables *how.is*. Extract 9.12 gives us another example of *actually* from Dan, who talks about the time when his voice went really deep.

Extract 9.12 Dan *actually*

```
01 || well i reMEMber ||
02 || something FUNNy happened ||
03 || actualLY ||
```
Ying moment: the past tense *ed* of *happened* is inaudible.

In 03 Dan's *actually* occurs in a speech unit of its own. It has three syllables and a tonic prominence with a rising tone on the final syllable, even though this is unstressed in the citation form. This is not unusual when *actually* appears at the end of a clause.

9.6.2 *Literally* and *certainly*

At the end of certain adverbs such as *literally* and *certainly*, the consonant |l| is often elided. The citation form for *literally* has primary stress on the first syllable and either three or four syllables: |ˈlɪt.rəl.i| or |ˈlɪt.ə.rəl.i|. However, the non-prominent syllables can be reduced to a single syllable, as Dan and Toby demonstrate in Extract 9.13.

Extract 9.13 Dan, Toby *literally*

```
01 || i LITerally couldn't SING it ||     [Dan]
02 || it's NOT LITerally CATCH you ||      [Toby]
       LITerally...LITerally... LITerally
```
Dan is talking about the time his voice failed and Toby is talking about about the safety of his climbing.
The last line gives (in order) the citation form, Dan's, and Toby's soundshapes for *literally*.

Both Dan and Toby have two syllables |lɪtʃ.ri|, making a four- (or three-) syllable word into a two-syllable one. However, Gail and Rachel keep the three syllables of the citation form of *certainly* |sɜːt.ən.li| in Extract 9.14, in which Gail talks about her uncle in New Zealand and Rachel talks about her degree course at Oxford.

124

Extract 9.14 Gail, Rachel *certainly*

```
01 || so he YES he CERTainly || [Gail]
02 || but CERTainly THAT was a || [Rachel]
        CERTainly...CERTainly...CERTainly
```

The last line gives (in order) the citation form of *certainly*, then Gail's, and Rachel's soundshapes for *certainly*.

However, in both cases |t| becomes a glottal stop and |l| is elided to give us |sɜːʔ.n̩.i|.

9.7   Vagueness *something, just, perhaps*

In this section we will look at a number of common content words which show that speakers are being vague – *something*, *sort of*, *like*, *perhaps*, *just,* etc. Like the words we examined in the previous section, these words occur frequently and they have a great variety of soundshapes.

9.7.1   *Something*

Extract 9.15 has five speech units containing *something* from three different speakers, Geoff, Toby, and Dan. The latter gives us three examples.

Extract 9.15 *Something*

```
01 || or SOMEthing like that || [Geoff]
02 || i'd DO something ELSE || [Toby]
03 || SOMEthing aBOUT you || [Dan]
04 || something FUNNy happened || [Dan]
05 || or SOMEthing || [Dan]
      SOMEthing...something...SOMEthing...something...SOMEthing
```

The last line gives the soundshapes of *something* in the same order that they occur in the units of the extract.

In 01 Geoff gives us a very common form |sʌmnɪŋ|; in 02 Toby gives a suggestion of an epenthetic, or inserted |p| |sʌmpni|, (cf. Wells, 2009); in 03 Dan gives |sʌmnɪn|, in 04 |sʌmʔɪŋ| and in 05 |sʌmpʔnɪŋ|. That gives us five different soundshapes.

9.7.2   *Just*

The word *just* often appears in circumstances where it is likely to lose its final consonant, as we can hear in Extract 9.16. These units are from unrelated parts of Dan's recording: 01 is when he talks about working in Africa; 02 is taken from his account of his singing audition in front of Simon Cowell.

Extract 9.16 Dan *just*

```
01 || but it JUST went REALLy DEEP ||
02 || I was just GLAD to be OUT of there ||
     JUST ...JUST ... just
```

The last line gives (in order) the citation form of *just* followed by the two versions from Dan in the extract.

The citation form of *just* is |ʤʌst|, but although *just* is prominent in 01 and non-prominent in 02, they are similar in duration and soundshape. They both last 0.25 seconds, they both lose their final consonant and they both have a reduced vowel quality – close to |ʤes| in 01 and with a vowel close to a schwa |ʤəs| in 02.

9.7.3   *Perhaps*

The word *perhaps* is |pəˈhæps| in its citation form, with two syllables and the primary stress on the second syllable. However, in spontaneous speech it is often reduced to a single syllable |præps| as we can hear in Extract 9.17, in which Maggie talks about holiday plans, and Corony talks about her business as a textile artist.

Extract 9.17 Maggie, Corony *perhaps*

```
01 || perHAPS FIVE DAYS || [Maggie]
02 || and perhaps AREN'T prepared to PAY for them || [Corony]
       perHAPS... perHAPS...perhaps
```

The last line gives (in order) the citation form of *perhaps*, Maggie's, and Corony's soundshapes for *perhaps*.

In 01, Maggie produces three successive prominent syllables. The first of them is a monosyllabic *perhaps* with both the schwa in the first syllable and the initial |h| of the second syllable being elided, resulting in |præps| – *praps*. We can hear the same elisions in Corony's non-prominent *perhaps*. Thus we have a reduced soundshape for *perhaps* which can be both prominent and non-prominent – a phenomenon that we will see again with *going*.

9.8   *Going*

The word *going* is often used to introduce reported speech, as we can hear from Dan in Extract 9.18 when he talks about his schoolmates' reactions to his voice suddenly becoming very deep.

Extract 9.18 Dan *going*

```
01 || were COMing up to me GOing ||
02 || and ALL the GIRLS are going ||
03 || WOO ||
        GOing ... GOing... going
```
The last line gives (in order) the citation form, then the two soundshapes of *going* as they occur in the extract.

In 01, *going* is close to the citation form |gəʊ.ɪŋ|, but in 02 it is quite different. It is non-prominent, shorter and quicker and becomes close to monosyllabic |gɜːŋ| – *gerng*.

Of course *going to* is also very commonly used to mark future time, as we can hear in Extract 9.19. Gail talks about her uncle, Maggie about her holidays and Bob about deciding on his career. For an explanation of why *going* is non-prominent in 01 see Chapter 5.4.

Extract 9.19 Gail, Maggie, Bob *going to*

```
01 || for the MONey he's going to MAKE || [Gail]
02 || i'm GOing to BE || [Maggie]
03 || of what i WASn't GOing to do || [Bob]
going ... GOing ... GOing
```
The last line gives (in order) the citation form, then Gail's, Maggie's and Bob's soundshapes for *going*.

Two of these instances of *going to* are monosyllabic. In 01 Gail's *going to* sounds close to |gent| and in 02 Maggie's *going to* is |gəʊnt|. However, in 03 Bob gives us what are very clearly two syllables *gunna* |gʌn.ə| for *going to*, similar to the North American *gonna*. This is normally a non-prominent form, but Bob chooses to make it prominent here, and in context it sounds perfectly natural.

9.9   Summary and what's next

Content words have a variety of soundshapes which differ from the citation form in remarkable ways. The forces of spontaneous speech squeeze them into fast-flowing transient traces: syllables are dropped, vowel quality is changed, consonants become inaudible both mid-word and at the end of words. These processes happen with content words just as they do with function words. Laver (1994: 67) writes that polysyllabic words in English have on average 'about two or three ... reorganized pronunciations for use in informal speech'. This is probably an underestimate.

The reduced soundshapes are most likely to appear in the squeeze zones of the speech units, most commonly in column 3 (between two prominences), but also in column 5 (before the first prominence), as we can see with the words *climbing* and *produced* in Table 9.2.

Table 9.2: Extract 9.20 Content words in squeeze zones

	5	4	3	2	1
Toby	i've	BEEN	climbing	TWELVE	
Geoff	this is	ONE	produced by	PRIEST	ley
	CLIMBing... climbing ...proDUCED ... produced				

You will have noticed that we have been gathering different soundshapes of the same word together at the end of a number of extracts. There is great value in doing this, not only for our own purposes, but also to help our students, as we shall see in Chapters 19 and 20.

In Chapter 10 we will use the window on speech to look at the rhythms of English and we will investigate the potential usefulness of the notions of 'stress timing' and 'syllable timing' in both the description of spontaneous speech, and in teaching.

9.10   Further reading

Reading materials are the same as for Chapter 8, but with the addition of Roach et al (2006: 482) and Wells (2008: 784) on stress-shift. Tench (2011: 199-120) has more on *just*.

9.11   Language awareness activities

Activity 9.1: Prepare and perform   Answer key page 152

Look at the speech units below. They all feature the word *absolutely*. Insert them into Table 9.3, making sure that the prominent syllables go in columns 4 and 2. The first three have been done for you.

Then, with a friend or colleague, perform them in such way to ensure that you get as many different soundshapes for *absolutely* as possible – both with and without prominences. Consult one or more pronunciation dictionaries (e.g. Wells, 2008 or Roach et al., 2011) to help you.

```
|| ABsoLUTEly ||
|| ABsolutely SOLid ||
|| he says THAT'S absoLUTEly true ||
|| his CAR'S absolutely fanTASTic ||
|| he's absolutely NOT going to aGREE to that ||
|| it's NOT absolutely CERTain ||
```

Table 9.3 Speech units with *absolutely*

	5	4	3	2	1
01		AB	so	LUTE	ly
02		AB	solutely	SOL	id
03	he says	THAT'S	abso	LUTE	ly true
04					
05					
06					

Activity 9.2 Record and analyse

Record a conversation with a friend or colleague (after getting their permission) about their schooldays and university experiences. Listen to the recording and identify moments when they repeat content words such as the names of the subjects they studied, or their feelings about these subjects and their teachers. Copy these words from the recording, and paste them side-by-side in a single sound file. Then make notes on the different soundshapes that you hear, and tell a friend, colleague or fellow teacher.

10 Rhythms of spontaneous speech

Every language has its own distinctive rhythm, and anyone who has learned another language will have noticed the rhythmic differences between the language they are learning and their first language. In this chapter we explore the rhythms of English speech. In previous chapters we have seen that words are elongated to provide planning time for the speaker (Chapter 6) and they can be squeezed together into a burst of continuous sound substance in which individual words and syllables are difficult to recognise (Chapters 8 & 9). We have seen that their soundshapes vary according to where they occur in a speech unit (their prosodic environment) and according to the speed and casualness with which they are spoken. Our description of the rhythm of English will take account of these constant variations in soundshape and of the drafting phenomena we examined in Chapter 6.

We begin with some definitions, before looking at the concept of stress timing and the reasons why, contrary to popular belief, English is not actually a stress-timed language. We then proceed to show that English speech rhythms are fleeting and ever-changing, and that the absence of a persistent rhythm aids communication.

10.1 Stress-timing: definitions

The term which dominates descriptions of English rhythm is **stress timing**. It is a term which has come to have two quite separate meanings. The first refers to a theory of the rhythms of all languages (outlined in Section 10.3 below) and the second refers to classroom pronunciation exercises which practise the alternation of prominent and non-prominent syllables. We will use **stress-timing theory** to refer to the first meaning and **stress-timing activities** to refer to the second meaning.

Stress-timing activities practise the effects of squeezing syllables and words which occur in the non-prominent sections of speech units. Such exercises are very useful in pronunciation activities, but are misleading when used as evidence concerning the rhythms of spontaneous speech. Although they may be useful in familiarizing students and making them feel comfortable with the reality of spontaneous speech, they are not demonstrations of an underlying truth about spontaneous speech for reasons we will see below.

10.2 Syllable timing: definitions

Syllable timing also has two different meanings: first as a counterpart to stress-timing in the theory of rhythms of languages and second as a shorthand term to refer to the rhythm of L2 speakers of English (e.g. French, Italian, Finnish) or of L1 speakers of non-standard accents (e.g. Caribbean and African accents). We will use **syllable-timing theory** to refer to the first and **perceived syllable-timing** for the latter. The term **rhythm** will be used to refer to alternations of prominences, non-prominences and stressed and unstressed syllables. An **isochronous** rhythm is one that is perceived to follow a series of timed events in a way which is heard to be on the beat. The term **interval** means the gap in time between two events (e.g. prominences) in speech.

10.3 Stress-timing theory

According to stress-timing theory, English rhythm is characterised by stresses which occur at equal intervals of time (they are isochronous), no matter how many unstressed syllables appear in the intervals between the stresses.

One of the consequences of the theory is that the duration of syllables has to vary in order to allow stresses to occur at equal intervals. Table 10.1 shows how.

Table 10.1: Extract 10.1 A demonstration of stress-timing

	Interval 1		Interval 2		Interval 3	
YOU	and	ME	and then	HIM	and then it's	HER

Adapted from Underhill (1994).

According to the theory, the prominent syllables in the shaded cells occur at equal intervals of time, that is in an isochronous rhythm. For this to happen, the three intervals have to be of the same duration, even though they contain different numbers of syllables. Thus the syllables in Intervals 2 and 3 have to shorten in length. The two syllables *and then* in Interval 2 have to take no more time than the single syllable of *and* in interval 1. Consequently the *and* in Interval 2 will be half the length of *and* in Interval 1. Similarly, the three syllables in Interval 3 *and then it's* have to take no more time than the first and second intervals meaning that this last *and* will be one third the length of the first *and* in Interval 1.

Stress-timing activities derived from stress-timing theory have widely-acknowledged usefulness in language teaching, particularly in the area of pronunciation (cf. Underhill, 1994: 72). However, they continue to breathe life into the theory, despite the fact that the research evidence is very much against it (cf. 10.5).

10.4   Syllable-timing theory

Syllable-timing theory is a necessary counterpart of stress-timing theory. The hypothesis is that in syllable-timed languages such as French, each syllable takes an equal amount of time to say ('syllable-isochrony'), therefore the stressed syllables do not occur at equal time intervals, because the size of the intervals are different. Table 10.2 shows how.

Table 10.2: Extract 10.2 Syllable-timing

	Interval 1		Interval 2		Interval 3	
VOUS	et	MOI	et puis	LUI	et puis c'est	ELLE

The intervals increase in duration with each additional syllable so the second interval with *et puis* is roughly twice as long as the first interval with *et*. As the number of syllables increases, the stresses are pushed further apart in time, therefore languages such as French are said to be syllable-timed.

Syllable-timing theory has been refuted by experiment (see 10.5 below), but the term lives on in the guise of perceived syllable-timing to describe the English rhythms of many L2 speakers of English and L1 rhythms of English speakers from countries like Jamaica.

Caroline, whose first language is French, provides us with a useful example in Extract 10.3 when she talks about why she enjoys walking. Listen to her pronunciation of *problems*.

Extract 10.3 Caroline *it's good ... problems*

```
01 || it's GOOD beCAUSE er ||
02 || it KEEPS your MIND ||
03 || OFF of YOUR ||
 [pause 0.5]
04 || you KNOW ||
```

05 || PROB LEMS ||

Caroline appears to give equal stress to both syllables of *problems* and the second syllable has a non-reduced vowel similar to the first syllable of British English *lemon.*

This is an example of perceived syllable-timing. The commonly-accepted view is that the syllable-timed nature of French remains audible when Caroline speaks English and this results in soundshapes of words which have fewer reduced vowels, and a different distribution of word-stress.

10.5   Experimental evidence

Stress-timing theory was clearly articulated by Abercrombie:

> every language in the world is spoken with one kind of rhythm or with the other... syllable-timed rhythm...[and]...stress-timed rhythm. (Abercrombie, 1967: 97–98)

However, Roach (1982) and Dauer (1983) found that the very factors that were supposed to *differentiate* stressed-timed languages from syllable-timed languages were *found to be the same* in both types of languages. Particularly conclusive was the finding that in both types of language the size of the intervals between stresses was proportional to the number of syllables they contained. This meant that the hypothetical differences described in 10.3-4 above were proven not to exist. Roach (adopting a position similar to Pike, 1945) concluded that:

> there is no language which is totally syllable-timed or totally stress-timed – all languages display both sorts of timing; languages will, however, differ in which type of timing predominates (Roach, 1982: 78).

Despite the weight of evidence against the stress-timing and syllable-timing theories, the concepts and terminology survive, partly because the terms live on in their other meanings – stress-timing activities and perceived syllable-timing. Another reason for the continued belief in the theory is that there is a limit to the extent humans can hear differences in timing (Laver, 1994: 524). Evidence suggests that people hear speech to be (or can persuade themselves to hear it as) more rhythmic, or isochronous, than it actually is. Lehiste (1979) found that hearers could not perceive differences in length of sounds less than 30 milliseconds but, in certain circumstances, sounds had to differ in length by one tenth of a second before they could perceive differences.

Laver sums up the research evidence thus:

> At best, the available empirical evidence could be said *sometimes* to have shown the existence of timing characteristics that *fluctuate around* a very *approximately regular* rhythm ... Laver (1994: 523) [Emphasis added]

The key words in this quotation are *sometimes, fluctuate* and *approximately.* They signal Laver's scepticism about the validity of stress-timing theory. In the following sections we will quantify how often, and within what limits, the rhythms of English are isochronous, or rhythmic. We will then give an account of the rhythms of English using the window on speech.

10.6   Isochrony in a triple-prominence speech unit

The minimum requirement for any stretch of speech to be perceived as isochronous is that there should be three events separated by two intervals which are sufficiently similar in duration for the three events to be perceived as rhythmically on-the-beat, or isochronous.

The speech unit in Extract 10.4 (from Gail) meets these criteria (cf. Cauldwell, 2000).

Extract 10.4 Gail *which she'd ... months time*

```
01 || which she'll MOVE into in FIVE months TIME ||
```

This speech-unit has three prominences – the three events required for isochrony to exist – separated by two intervals which contain the syllables *into in* and *months.* These intervals have lengths which are sufficiently similar to be heard as equal, as you can see from Table 10.3.

Table 10.3: Extract 5 An isochronous speech unit

		Interval 1		Interval 2		
which she'll	MOVE	into in	FIVE	months	TIME	
0.416	0.168	0.387	0.270	0.334	0.414	

Row 3 gives the duration in milliseconds of the words in the cells in row 2

Table 10.3 shows the speech unit divided up into prominent (shaded) and non-prominent sections, with interval 1 containing three syllables *into in*, with a duration of 387 milliseconds, and interval

2 containing one syllable *months* with a duration of 334 milliseconds. The difference in size of the intervals is 53 milliseconds, which is sufficiently small to be perceived as the same (cf. Lehiste, 1979). Therefore the intervals will be heard as having the same duration, and consequently the speech unit is heard to have an isochronous rhythm.

10.7   Isochrony in spontaneous speech is rare

In general, spontaneous speech is not isochronous. This is because spontaneous speech occurs in a series of rhythmic bursts – speech-units – most of which (close to 90%) are too short to trigger perceptions of isochrony. Triple and quadrupleprominence speech units provide the most favourable environments for isochrony, but as we saw in Chapter 3, they account for less than 10% of the total number of speech units. Most frequently – in over 90% of cases – speech units are too short to provide the three events necessary to create isochrony.

As well as rarely having the required three events for isochrony, speech units normally have different speeds and rhythms from their immediate neighbours. Additionally, their boundaries are often marked by rhythm-disrupting phenomena such as pauses, and lengthening of the tonic and post-tonic syllables. Therefore any incipient isochronous rhythm in one speech unit is disrupted by boundary phenomena as it ends, and as the next speech unit starts.

10.8   Coincidental isochrony

Much isochronous rhythm occurs by coincidence. It is a short-lived unintended side effect of speaker choices. As we have seen, it typically occurs in triple-prominence speech units (or longer), which provide optimum conditions for the perception of isochronous rhythm. These conditions occur as a result of two types of decision made by speakers: first the choice of words and second, the division of the stream of speech into speech-units. These two types of decision are illustrated in Extract 10.6.

Extract 10.6 Gail *currently ... moving again*

```
|| he's CUrrently THINking of MOving aGAIN ||
```

This unit, with four prominences, has an isochronous rhythm in that the prominent syllables occur on a regular beat. It has two non-prominent syllables between each prominence, resulting in equal numbers of syllables in the intervals, which is another favourable condition for isochrony.

There is a coincidence here: Gail has made a choice of words that happens to result in an equal number of non-prominent syllables between the four prominences. She could have chosen more common words to express the same meaning – for example, she could have chosen *now* instead of *currently* and she might have said *doing it all over again* instead of *moving again*, which would produce the different word-accent patterns shown in Table 10.4.

Table 10.4: Extract 10.7 Differing words and rhythms

			Interval 1		Interval 2		Interval 3	
01	he's	CUR	ently	THINK	ing of	MO	ving a	GAIN
02	he's	NOW		THINK	ing of	DO	ing it all over a	GAIN

The version in 02 is less likely to be perceived as isochronous because the choice of words results in an unequal number of syllables (none, two, and six) in the intervals between the prominences.

Gail has spoken these words in a quadruple-prominence speech unit possibly because she has said this about her uncle before and it is in some sense pre-packaged (cf. Section 10.9 below), but she could have spoken it in three units, as in Extract 10.8, where we have a sequence of speech units (one single-prominence, two double-prominence units) which are of the more frequent types.

Extract 10.8 Gail *he's currently* in three speech units

```
01 || he's CUrrently ||
02 || THINking of ERM ||
03 || MOving aGAIN ||
```

This version has three speech units because there are three tones – a fall rise starting on the first syllable of *currently*, a level tone on *erm*, and a falling tone on *again*. (We have seen in Chapter 4 that it is a convention of our framework that there can only be one tone per speech unit). As a result, each unit has its own rhythm. If this version had occurred, it would not be perceived as isochronous. This is because none of the units (one single-, two double-prominence units) has the required three events with equal intervals between them.

In traditional accounts of the rhythms of English the triple and quadruple-prominence speech units would be regarded as normal ways of packaging Gail's clause, in line with the careful speech model.

Describing Spontaneous Speech

From our perspective, it is a highly unusual way of doing so, because less than 10% of speech units are triple-prominence units or larger (cf. Chapter 3).

We have to recognise the force of the majority of the evidence – that 90% of speech units do not exhibit isochrony. A full description of English rhythm has to be able to account for the majority of speech which is not isochronous, such as the units in Extract 10.9.

Extract 10.9 Gail *and my ... widowed*

```
01 || AND my COUsin ||
02 || HIS DAUGHter ||
03 || ERM ||
04 || is REcently WIdowed ||
```

You will be able to hear that there is no isochrony in this extract because the conditions for it are not met. There are three double-prominence speech units and one single-prominence unit, but none of them has the required three events which create the environment for isochrony. Unit 04 has an alternation of non-prominent and prominent syllables which might result in isochrony if there were another following prominence in the same unit, as in Extract 10.10, but this did not occur.

Extract 10.10 Gail *is recently ... in a triple prominence unit*

```
04a || is REcently WIdowed aGAIN||
```

There are perceptible shifts in rhythm between the speech units of Extract 10.9 which make it rhythmically unlike the *currently thinking* speech unit of Extract 10.6. However, if these speech units were turned into a script and the careful speech model were applied, it is likely that it would be read as in unit 05 of Extract 10.11, which is rhythmically very like the earlier *currently thinking* example.

Extract 10.11 Gail *and my cousin ... orginal and in a quadruple prominence unit*

```
01 || AND my COUsin ||
02 || HIS DAUGHter ||
03 || ERM ||
04 || is REcently WIdowed ||
05 || and my COUSin his DAUGHter is REcently WIDowed ||
```

Units 01-04 are the original, unit 05 is a scripted isochronous version.

In unit 05 the four prominences occur at equal intervals of time, on a rhythmic beat, and there are equal numbers of syllables (two) between each prominence. This maximises the chances of an isochronous rhythm being heard.

Neither single-prominence speech units nor double-prominence speech units have, on their own, a sufficient number of parts to provide the three events, with two intervals, required for perceptions of isochrony. However, they they can do so in combination with other speech units, as Extract 10.12 shows.

Extract 10.12 Gail *he's currently ... eighty two*

```
01 || he's CUrrently THINking of MOving aGAIN ||
02 || he's EIGHty TWO ||
```

There is continuity between the tonic syllable on *again* in 01 and the *he's* at the beginning of 02 which leads to the two speech units being heard as part of the same isochronous rhythm. There is a short rising tone on *gain* in 01, with just the right characteristics for it to be heard as a unifying link to the next isochronous beats – the prominences in *eighty* and *two*.

10.9   Pre-packaged language

Isochronous rhythm can also occur when the language has been pre-packaged in some way, that is planned in advance of the moment of speaking. For example, pre-packaged chunks of language may have had a prior existence in writing and then later they are inserted into conversation. These moments in speech may consist of idioms, quotations from poetry, titles of books, films, etc. Extract 10.13 gives three examples of long speech units (two with five prominences) in which the language is pre-packaged.

Extract 10.13 Examples of pre-packaged language

```
01 || in SOOTH i KNOW not WHY i AM so SAD ||
02 || the seLECTed LETTers of PHILLip LARKin ||
03 || PARent TEACHer WATer aWAREness CLASSes ||
```
Unit 01 and 02 were recorded for the purposes of this demonstration. Unit 03 is from Karam, from California.

These units feature quadruple-prominence speech units or larger, all with a sufficient number of matching events to trigger perceptions of isochrony. Unit 01 is the first line from Shakespeare's

Describing Spontaneous Speech

Merchant of Venice, 02 is the title of a book and 03 is the name of a particular type of swimming class. These examples are pre-packaged in the sense that they are written down, and then said aloud. In such circumstances, the likelihood of isochronous speech units increases. Nevertheless, speakers always have the choice to say them differently, in shorter speech units. Actors, for example, are very skilled in bringing out the meaning of a script precisely by not falling into the trap of allowing an isochronous rhythm to develop unintentionally.

There is another type of pre-packaging which does not necessarily come from written language. Language which is often repeated can be spoken in long speech units which can be heard as timed in some way, as you can hear in Extract 10.14.

Extract 10.14 Gail *he can ... anything*

```
01 || he can TURN his HAND TO ANything ||
```

In 01 Gail uses an idiom which means 'he is good at everything he tries to do'. This idiom is part of the store of knowledge belonging to the community of speakers of British English who share her cultural background. It is a fixed expression which has a high probability, unlike the majority of spontaneous speech, of occurring in a triple-prominence speech unit.

Extract 10.15 shows a different kind of pre-packaging at work featuring Karam from California USA. Her favourite hobby is swimming.

Extract 10.15 Karam *our swim team ... the water*

```
01 || our SWIMteam ACTually RAN a PROgramme ||
02 || it would be HARD in the SUMMer to FIND any JOB ||
03 || i ALways LOVED the WATer ||
```
These speech units come from different parts of Karam's recording.

Karam is so fond of swimming that she often explains her enjoyment of her hobby to new people that she meets. As a result, parts of her explanation become pre-packaged through repetition. This makes it more likely that they will be spoken in large speech units with the right conditions for isochrony.

10.10 Putting stress timing in perspective

Speech is rhythmic in the sense that there is a constant alternation between prominent and non-prominent syllables. However, this alternation occurs in speech units which are almost always (90%) too short to provide the right conditions for isochrony to appear. Occasionally, either because of coincidence or because of the occurrence of pre-packaged language, isochrony may occur in one, or several, speech units in succession.

The fact that isochrony is rare is something to be thankful for. If the majority of utterances in English were isochronous, it would be difficult for hearers to attend to speech as meaningful communication. The isochronous rhythm would draw attention to itself and distract the hearer's attention from the speaker's meaningful choices. Listeners to Halliday's (1970) 'rhythmic prose narratives', or people who are used to listening to recordings of poetry, will know that the presence of a perceptible rhythm attracts attention to itself and away from the processing of the text as meaning. This is because, as Bolinger (1986: 47) argues, 'in allowing the mechanical phenomenon of even rhythm ... [to] ... assert itself … speakers will be heard to be speaking routinely and mechanically'. The rarity of isochronous rhythm is thus useful, if not essential, for effective communication. The rhythms of speech are fleeting and ever-changing and the non-occurrence of a persistent isochrony is a necessary feature of any co-operative, purpose-driven spontaneous speech.

The last words on this topic come from Classe who writes that isochronous rhythm 'only remains as an underlying tendency of which some other factor at times almost completely *obliterates* the effects' (1939: 90, emphasis added) and 'in ordinary speech and everyday prose ... the rhythmic effect is a purely automatic consequence of linguistic circumstances' (Classe, 1939: 132, cited in Dauer 1983: 60).

10.11   Summary and what's next

Stress-timing theory is (or should be) dead. The very characteristics that *supposedly differentiate* between stress-timed languages and syllable-timed languages *are the same* in both types of languages. Nevertheless, languages are, and sound, rhythmically different. To an L1 English speaker, the sound substance of French and the sound substance of English have different relationships to time, and an L1 speaker of French will feel the same about English. The rhythms of spontaneous speech in any language are created by the joint operation of speaker choices and the properties of the entire language system

– vowel and consonant inventories, syllable structure, word-order, patterns of word-stress, the extent of vowel reduction, etc. The simple hypothesis was that this difference is related to stresses, syllables, and isochrony. This hypothesis is now refuted, and other more complex explanations are required – see the further reading in Section 10.12 below. Stress-timing activities in the classroom, on the other hand, are very much alive and very useful, as we shall see in Chapter 18.

In Chapters 6-10 we have used the window on speech to go some way to producing a model of the sound substance of spontaneous speech. We have focused on those areas where spontaneous speech is most different from the careful speech model: it consists of drafting phenomena (Chapter 6); speech units go at widely differing speeds, and there seems to be a relationship between speed and size of speech unit (Chapter 7); clusters of function words occur in bursts of obscure acoustic blur created by the squeeze zones in speech units (Chapter 8); content words have a wide variety of soundshapes depending on their positions in speech units (Chapter 9); and we have seen that the rhythms of English are ever-changing, and stress-timing is extremely rare (Chapter 10). A summary of the differences between the careful speech and the spontaneous speech models can be found in Appendix 1.

In Part 3 *Accents, identity and emotion in speech* we will use the window on speech framework as an observational tool to look at a wide variety of accents (United Kingdom, Ireland, United States, Canada, Global English) and to look at the relationship between prosodic phenomena and the expression of emotion in speech.

10.12 Further reading

Crystal (1996) gives a very readable introduction to research, and makes predictions for the future (you can find it by entering the title into an internet search engine). Following Laver (1994: 528–529), Crystal suggests using the terms stress-based and syllable-based to compare the rhythms of different languages – thus removing the concept of timing from the discussion. Cauldwell (2003) argues that speech rhythms are functionally irrhythmic. Recent developments in research which retain the notion of timing can be found in Asu & Nolan (2006) and Nolan & Asu (2009), but they suggest that languages can be both syllable-timed and stress-timed – a view first articulated by Pike (1945) and subsequently, as we have seen, by Roach (1982).

10.13 Language awareness activities

Activity 10.1: Listen and decide   Answer key page 153

Listen to Extract 10.16 and identify patches of isochronous rhythm. Listen several times, tapping a pencil in time with the prominences that you hear. Explain why some speech units have an isochronous rhythm, and others do not. Report your findings to a friend, colleague or fellow teacher.

Extract 10.16 Karam *our swim-team ... give us jobs*

```
01 || our SWIM-team ACtually RAN a PROgram ||
02 || called swim aMErica ||
03 || AND ||
04 || ERM ||
05 || it's JUST ||
06 || WHERE ||
07 || our COACH is Able TO ||
08 || GIVE us JOBS ||
```

The speaker is Karam who talks about her swimming club Swim America.

Activity 10.2: Record and analyse

Take a short extract of between ten and twenty seconds in length from the recording you made for Chapter 9 (or any recording). Transcribe it, but do not worry about doing a speech unit transcription, just do a quick word-by-word transcription. Then listen to the recording repeatedly, tapping your pencil to the rhythms that you hear. Circle the syllables that you hear as being 'on the beat', and draw double vertical lines || in the transcript where you hear the rhythm change. Be strict with yourself about this – do not allow a change of rhythm to pass unmarked. It is best if you do this activity with a friend, a colleague or a fellow teacher, who will help you be strict about your marking of rhythm. Make a note of any problems you have while doing this. Then look at your rhythm transcription, and consider what it means for stress-timing/syllable-timing theories. Report your findings to a friend, colleague, or fellow teacher.

References for Part 2

Abercrombie, D. (1965) *Studies in Phonetics and Linguistics*. Oxford: Oxford University Press.

Altenberg, B. (1987) *Prosodic Patterns in Spoken English: Studies in the Correlation between Prosody and Grammar for Text-to-speech Conversions*. Lund: Lund University Press.

Asu, E .L. and Nolan, F. (2006) Estonian and English rhythm: A two-dimensional quantification based on syllables and feet. In *Proceedings of Speech Prosody* 2006, Dresden, Germany.

BBC Wales (2006) [Steve Woodmore, the world's fastest talking man]. http://www.bbc.co.uk/wales/justthejob/followyourdream/time/o_getstarted.shtml [Retrieved 13 November 2012].

Bolinger, D. (1986) The English beat: Some notes on rhythm. *Studies in Descriptive Linguistics*, 15, 36–49.

Brazil, D. (1997) *The Communicative Value of Intonation in English*. Cambridge: Cambridge University Press.

Brown, G. (1990) *Listening to Spoken English*, [2nd edition]. Harlow: Longman.

Carter, R. and McCarthy, M. (2006) *Cambridge Grammar of English*. Cambridge: Cambridge University Press.

Cauldwell, R. (2002) The functional irrhythmicality of spontaneous speech: A discourse view of speech rhythms. *Apples*, 2/1, 1-24.

Cauldwell, R. (2007) Defining fluency for air-traffic control. *Speak Out*, 37, 10-16

Channell, J. (1994) *Vague Language*. Oxford: Oxford University Press.

Classe, A. (1939) *The Rhythm of English Prose*. Oxford: Blackwell.

Cruttenden, A. (2001) *Gimson's Pronunciation of English*, [6th edition]. London: Arnold.

Crystal, D. (1996) The past, present and future of English rhythm. *Speak Out*, 18, 8–13.

Dauer, R. M. (1983) Stress-timing and syllable-timing reanalyzed. *Journal of Phonetics*, 11, 51-62.

Derwing, T. M. and Munro, M. J. (2001) What speaking rates do non-native listeners prefer? *Applied Linguistics*, 22/3, 324-327.

Eklund, R. (2004) *Disfluency in Swedish: Human–human and Human–machine Travel Booking Dialogues*. [Doctoral dissertation]. Department of Computer and Information Science Linköping Studies in Science and Technology

Erard, M. (2007) *Um: Slips Stumbles and Verbal Blunders and What they Mean*. New York: Pantheon Books.

Field, J. (2008) Bricks or mortar: Which parts of the input does a second language listener rely on? *TESOL Quarterly*, 42/3, 411–432.

Goldman-Eisler, F. (1972) Pauses, clauses, sentences. *Language and Speech*, 15/2, 103-113.

Greenberg, S. and Fosler-Lussier E. (2000) The uninvited guest: Information's role in guiding the production of spontaneous speech. *Proceedings of the CREST Workshop on Models of Speech Production: Motor Planning and Articulatory Modeling*, Kloster Seeon Germany. May 1-4, 2000.

Greenberg, S. (1999) Speaking in shorthand – A syllable-centric perspective for understanding pronunciation variation. *Speech Communication*, 29, 159–176.

Greenberg, S., Carvey, H., Hitchcock, L. and Chang, S. (2003). The phonetic patterning of spontaneous American English discourse. In *Proceedings of ISCA/IEEE Workshop on Spontaneous Speech Processing and Recognition*.

Griffiths, R. (1991) Pausological research in an L2 context: A rationale, and review of selected studies. *Applied Linguistics*, 12/4, 345-364.

Halliday, M. A. K. (1970) *A Course in Spoken English: Intonation*. London: Oxford University Press.

Hawkins, P.R., (1971) The syntactic location of hesitation pauses. *Language and Speech*, 14/3, 277-288.

Hincks, R. (2010) Speaking rate and information content in English lingua franca oral presentations. *English for Specific Purposes*, 29/1, 4-18.

Laver, J. (1994) *Principles of Phonetics*. Cambridge: Cambridge University Press.

Nolan, F. and Asu, .L. (2009) The pairwise variability index and coexisting rhythms in language. *Phonetica*, 66, 64-77.

Pike, K. L. (1945) *The Intonation of American English*. Ann Arbor: University of Michigan Press.

Pimsleur, P., Hancock, C., and Furey P. (1977) Speech rate and listening comprehension. In M. Burt, H. Dulay, and M. Finocchiaro (eds.). *Viewpoints on English as a Second Language*. New York: Regents.

Roach, P. (1982) On the distinction between 'stress-timed' and 'syllable-timed' languages. In D. Crystal (ed.) *Linguistic Controversies, Essays in Linguistic Theory and Practice*, 73-79. London: Edward Arnold.

Roach, P. (1998) Some languages are spoken more quickly than others. In Bauer, L. and Trudgill, P. *Language Myths*, 150-158. London: Penguin.

Roach, P. (2009) *English Phonetics and Phonology: A Practical Course*. Cambridge: Cambridge University Press.

Roach, P., Hartmann, J. and Setter, J. (2011) *Cambridge English Pronouncing Dictionary*. Cambridge: Cambridge University Press.

Shockey, L. (2003) *Sound Patterns of Spoken English*. Oxford: Blackwell.

Tauroza, S. and Allison, D. (1990) Speech rates in British English. *Applied Linguistics*, 11/1, 90-105.

Tench, P. (2011) *Transcribing the Sound of English: A Phonetic Workbook for Words and Discourse.* Cambridge: Cambridge University Press.

Toastmaster (2011) Website. http://www.toastmasters.org [Accessed 6 April 2011].

Wells, J. C. (2008) *Longman Pronunciation Dictionary.* Harlow: Pearson Education.

Wells, J. C. (2009) Epenthesized plosives. [Blogpost 27 January 2009].http://www.phon.ucl.ac.uk/home/wells/blog0901.htm

Wikipedia (2011) *Words per minute.* http://en.wikipedia.org/wiki/Words_per_minute (Accessed 20 January 2011)

Answer key for Part 2

Chapter 6

Activity 6.1: Prepare and perform

There are very many possibilities for this activity, and there isn't space to list all of them, so below is one example of the type of drafting phenomena that you might hear, and which actually occurred in a recording on which this task is based. You can hear it as Extract 14.1 (Chapter 14).

Part 2 Answer key Extract 1 Richard *i've ... very upset*

```
01 || ...i've...||
02 || i've MADE some bad CHOIces seeing FILMS ||
03 || ...i'm very...||
04 || i'm VEry ERM ||
05 || ... i get very ... ||
06 || i get VEry ||
07 || enGROSSED in films ||
08 || YEAH ||
09 || ...they... ||
10 || they REAlly TAKE me IN ||
11 || MMM ||
12 || AND ||
13 || IF it's VIolent ||
14 || i get VEry upSET ||
```

Units 08 and 11 are response tokens from Olivia who is listening to Richard.

Activity 6.2: Listen and comment

Part 2 Answer key Extract 2 *well i was ... literature*

```
01 || WELL i was i was DOing ||
02 || ERM ||
```

```
03 || a MOdern languages degree in OXford ||
04 || IS ||
05 || ERM ||
06 || a STUdy of ||
07 || MOdern LANGuages ||
08 || AND || 110
09 || of the LANguage ||
10 || AND ||
11 || LIterature ||
```

Your comments on Philip's extract should have included the following:

- In 01, Philip starts a sentence, but does not finish it. We have a subject and a verb group, but no complement/object which is required here and we have a repetition of *i was*.
- In 02, there is a filled pause, and Philip begins again in 03 with the subject of the sentence that he will eventually finish by the end of unit 11.
- As he proceeds, we get a further filled pause (05) and there are two stepping stones on *and* (08 & 09), and a noun group (*'modern languages* in 07) which is discarded in favour of the two noun groups in 09 and 11.

If we take the standards of the careful speech model as the norm, then Philip's extract is full of disfluencies. However, by the standards of spontaneous speech, Philip is expertly editing what he has planned to say while he is saying it, and while he is planning what to say next. If we define fluency as the skill of keeping going at your turn at speech in such a way that keeps your listener interested then Philip is demonstrating great fluency here.

If we were to apply the standards of the careful speech model to this, and de-um the recording as a BBC producer might do, we would end up with something like this:

```
03 || a MOdern languages degree in OXford ||
04 || IS ||
06 || a STUdy of ||
09 || of the LANguage ||
10 || AND ||
```

```
11 || LIterature ||
```
Note that the original speech unit numbers are given here.

Chapter 7

Activity 7.1: Listen and decide
```
01 || THIS IS || 1.5 SLOW
[pause 1.1]
02 || a MANual || 5.7 FAST
[pause 0.5]
03 || FOR || 1.5 SLOW
04 || BOTH || 2.5 SLOW/AVERAGE
05 || REAding || 3.3 SLOW/AVERAGE
06 || and WRIting || 3.5 SLOW/AVERAGE
07 || efFECtively || 7.3 FAST
08 || it's a MANual || 8.8 FAST
09 || ... MORE ... WRIting .. || 8.3 FAST
10 || Even ... REAding || 8.3 FAST
```

In Table 7.1, the benchmarks given for 'slow', 'average', and 'fast' are single numbers (2.0, 4.0, and 5.3), but none of the speeds in the units exactly match these numbers. We therefore have to decide how to describe those speeds which lie between these benchmarks:

- 2.5 (unit 04) is between 'slow' and 'average' but closer to 'slow';
- 3.5 (unit 06) is also between 'slow' and 'average' but closer to 'average'.

Because actual speeds fall between benchmarks, it is therefore extremely tempting to invent intermediate categories such as 'slow-average' and 'average-slow'. Additionally, because we reach over 8.0 sps in three units, it is also tempting to add a category above 'fast', such as 'extra-fast'.

2. What relationship do you find between speed of speech units, the number of syllables they contain and their contents?

Describing Spontaneous Speech

Below are the speech units from the extract listed in order of speed. The tendency is that the faster the speed unit, the longer it is, and the less likely it is to contain drafting phenomena. The slower the speech unit, the more likely it is to have fewer words, and these are more likely to contain stepping stones (04, 01) and words which are more grammatical in function.

```
08 || it's a MANual || 8.8
09 || well well it's MORE of a manual for WRIting in fact || 8.3
10 || Even though it is for REAding || 8.3
07 || efFECtively || 7.3
02 || a MANual || 5.7
06 || and WRIting || 3.5
05 || REAding || 3.3
04 || BOTH || 2.5
01 || THIS IS || 1.5
03 || FOR || 1.5
```

Chapter 8

Activity 8.1: Listen and decide
- In Unit 02 *that* is close to |næʔ| – *nat* – with a glottal stop for the |t|
- In Unit 03 *that* is |ðæʔ| – *that* – with a glottal stop for the |t|
- In Unit 04 *that* is |næʔ| – *nat* – with a glottal stop for the |t|
- *him that* (01) becomes close to |hɪmnəʔ| – *him.net* – with a glottal stop for the |t|
- *and that* (02) becomes |ʔənæʔ| – *un.nat* – with a glottal stop at the beginning of *and* and for the final |t|
- *recorded that* (03) becomes |ri.kɔːd.ɪ.ðæʔ| – *ri.cord.i.lhat* – with a glottal stop for the |t|
- *and that was* (04) becomes |ʔənæʔəz| – *un.nat.uzz* – with a glottal stops at the beginning of *and* and instead of |w| at the beginning of *was*

Chapter 9

Activity 9.1: Prepare and perform
The six speech units containing *absolutely* are shown in the table below

	5	4	3	2	1
01		AB	so	LUTE	ly
02		AB	solutely	SOL	id
03	he says	THAT'S	abso	LUTE	ly true
04	his	CAR'S	absolutely fan	TAST	ic
05	he's absolutely	NOT	going to a	GREE	to that
06	it's	NOT	absolutely	CERT	ain

Roach et al (2011) give the citation form |ˌæb.səˈluːt.li|, with stress-shift marked as a possibility, whereas Wells (2008) lists two stress patterns for *absolutely* |ˈæb.sə.luːt.li|, and |ˌæb.səˈluːt.li|, with stress shift marked as a possibility on the latter.

The citation form, with both primary and secondary stress, is shown in 01. The stress-shifted version is shown in 02. Wells also lists two 'casual rapid-speech forms' |ˈæbsi|, and |ˈæbsli| with the three non-prominent syllables *-so.lute.ly* reducing to single syllables *see* or *slee*.

Where the whole word is non-prominent, it is likely that the vowel in the first syllable will reduce towards schwa |əbsli| and the consonant |b| may come close to disappearing (as we saw with |d| in *produced* cf. 9.5), resulting in a pronunciation close to |əs.li| – *us.lee*

The range of soundshapes for *absolutely* therefore includes:

- four syllables: AB.so.LUTE.ly, AB.so.lute.ly, ab.so.LUTE.ly,
- three syllables: ass.lute.lee, ass.loo.lee, us.lute.lee, us.loo.lee,
- two syllables: AB.see, AB.slee, ub.slee, ub.see, us.lee.

Chapter 10

Activity 10.1: Listen and decide
These points should have emerged in your analysis of this extract:

- Unit 01 has four prominences, thus meeting the criteria for isochronous rhythm.

- Units 03-06 consist of drafting phenomena in very small speech units which are thus too small to meet the criteria for isochronous rhythm. Nor do they comprise a larger rhythmic unit of the type we saw in Extract 10.12, where two speech units – coincidentally – came together in to one rhythmic, isochronous flow.
- Unit 07 has three prominences, with single-syllable intervals, and it therefore meets the criteria for isochrony.
- On looking at the transcription of Units 07-08, it is tempting to consider that they are linked by a common isochronous rhythm of the type that we saw in Extract 10.12 (*he's currently ... he's eighty two*), but the length of the level tone on *to* in 07 is sufficient to disrupt any sense of shared rhythm between the two units.

PART 3

Accents, identity and emotion in speech

Part 3   Accents, identity and emotion in speech

In Part 3 we use the window on speech framework to shed light on two areas: accents of English (both L1 and L2) and on the relationship between prosodic phenomena and emotion and attitude. Whereas in Part 2 we focused on the different soundshapes of words, in Part 3 we examine the colours and flavours of the sound substance which come from accents and emotions. As in Part 2, we will comment on Ying moments (moments when words are squeezed into unfamiliar soundshapes) as they occur. Each chapter ends with two language awareness activities: a *Prepare and perform* activity, where you rehearse and then perform a script which focuses on an accent or issue relevant to the chapter; and a *Listen and analyse* activity, where you apply the information covered in the chapter in the analysis of a short recording. There is an answer key after Chapter 15.

Chapter 11 *British English, American English* looks at the difference in vowels, consonants, word stress and intonation between these two varieties. The comparison uses recordings from a number of young people from England and the USA.

Chapter 12 *Accents of Britain and Ireland* looks at nine accents: one from each of the countries of Britain and Ireland (Northern Ireland, Scotland, Wales, England and the Republic of Ireland) and four from cities within England (Manchester, Birmingham, Leeds and Newcastle). We will hear that many people have more than one accent. We will also tackle the issue of prejudice.

Chapter 13 *Accents of North America* looks at six accents. Five of them are from different geographical regions: Canada, New York, Virginia, Tennessee and Texas. The sixth accent is African American Vernacular English.

Chapter 14 *Accents of Global English* looks at the L2 accents of five people from Poland, Venezuela, France, Sudan and Romania. The recordings are commented on from three perspectives: the *window on speech* perspective, the accent-reduction perspective and the English as a Lingua Franca perspective.

Chapter 15 *Emotion in speech* looks at the relationship between how people say things and the emotional or attitudinal meanings that they convey. We shall see that unlike the findings for acted speech, in spontaneous speech there is no systematic relationship between attitude/emotion and prosodic phenomena.

Remember you need the recordings. Download them from www.speechinaction.com.

11   British English and American English

In this chapter we compare the accents of British English and American English. They are similar enough for their respective speakers to understand each other most of the time, but different enough to be commercial rivals in countries where English is taught to speakers of other languages. Although there are interesting lexical differences between British English and American English (*biscuit* for *cookie, trousers* for *pants,* etc.), we will focus on the differences in sound substance: vowels, consonants, word stress and intonation. We all have accents – no one is accent-free – and our accents give a flavour or a colour to the sound substance of speech which learners have to acclimatise themselves to.

There are two difficulties that face anyone comparing British English and American English. The first concerns which versions of British English and American English to use in the comparison. The second concerns what to use as the tool for comparison, that is whether to use American or British symbols.

11.1   Which British English, which American English?

Both Britain and the USA have accents which are used as reference models in English language teaching. These reference models have a variety of names: for British English this accent is known variously as 'Received Pronunciation' (RP), 'BBC English' or 'General British' and for American English it is known variously as 'General American', 'Standard American English', or 'North American English'. Defining exactly what these accents are, and whether they exist at all, is a matter of much debate, but is not appropriate for *Phonology for Listening*. We will simply accept that these reference models are defined by pronunciation dictionaries such as the Cambridge English Pronouncing Dictionary (Roach et al, 2011), the Longman Pronunciation Dictionary (Wells, 2008) and the Oxford Dictionary of Pronunciation for Current English (Upton et al, 2001).

However we must bear in mind that the accents of these reference models are notional, and it is unlikely that any single person will speak in exactly these accents. This is certainly the case with the recordings we use in this chapter. They are of people who speak in accents which are a reasonable (not exact) fit to the accents as described in these dictionaries. Features of the recordings which are different from the reference models will be commented upon as they occur. We will use the terms 'British English' (BrE) and 'American English' (AmE) during this comparison.

The majority of our examples of BrE will come from two people: Dan, a medical student from Surrey near London, and Toby, a teacher from Hertfordshire who works at a school near Oxford. Both their voices have features of Estuary English – an accent which is a mixture of an east London accent (Cockney) and RP, which was originally noted as a feature of some social groups living around the Thames Estuary (Rosewarne, 1984; Wells, 1998) but has now spread to many areas of England (Crystal, 2004: 472). We will also hear from Gail, a university administrator. The majority of our American examples will come from Jess, a teacher born in New Mexico, with further examples from Ellen from Washington state, Karam from California, Jeffrey from Tennessee and Ashley from Virginia.

11.2   Symbols

The sets of symbols used for BrE and AmE are different, in particular the symbols used for vowels. The British practice is to recognise a key differentiation between 'long' and 'short' vowels, whereas American scholars and practitioners may speak of vowels as 'tense' and 'lax', or as 'front', 'central', and 'back' (cf. Celce-Murcia et al, 2010: 117). In addition, the fact that AmE is a rhotic accent (in the word *car* the |r| is pronounced) and that BrE is a non-rhotic accent (in *car* the |r| is not pronounced) has consequences for the inventory of vowels. In AmE, the rhoticity is largely built in to the inventory of vowels, whereas in BrE |r| is always represented as a separate symbol. For the purposes of simplicity in this comparison, we will use the British symbols, with occasional uses of the American symbols where necessary.

11.3   Vowels

We will focus on four major differences in vowels, using the key words *odd, all, also, taught, authors, new* and *north*.

11.3.1 *Odd*
Dan (BrE) is a wonderful singer, and in Extract 11.1 he talks about the experience of his voice suddenly becoming very deep for a short time. It happened to his adult voice, well after puberty, so it was unexpected. We are comparing his accent with Jess's (AmE), who is commenting on the plot of a novel she is reading.

Extract 11.1 Dan and Jess *very odd*

```
BrE 01 || it was VERy ODD ||
AmE 02 || but it IS ||
AmE 03 || VEry ||
```

```
AmE 04 || very ODD ||
                    ODD ...ODD...
```

Unit 01 is from Dan (BrE) and units 02-04 are from Jess (AmE). The last line brings the two versions of *odd* side-by-side (BrE first) so that you can hear them clearly. Units 02-03 are separate speech units because Jess has three tones: level tones in 02-03 and a falling tone on *odd* in 04 (cf. Chapter 4).

In 01, Dan's BrE *odd* is |ɒd| – it has a vowel that does not occur in AmE. In 04 Jess's AmE *odd* is |ɑːd| which has the vowel used in *father*. These examples illustrate an important difference in the vowel inventory between AmE and BrE – AmE has no |ɒ| vowel. We now turn to cases where BrE and AmE have equivalent vowels, but they are used in different ways.

11.3.2 *All, north, proportion*

Jess (as well as using |ɑː| in words such as odd') also uses |ɑː| in a range of words where BrE has |ɔː|. In Extract 11.2, Jess describes what she likes to read and Dan describes his fellow tourists on a trip to Africa. Conveniently for us they both use the phrase *from all over the world*.

Extract 11.2 Jess and Dan *all over the world*

```
AmE 01 || AUTHors ||
AmE 02 || from ALL over the WORLD ||
BrE 03 || sort of THIRTy PEOPle ||
BrE 04 || from ALL over the WORLD ||
        ALL...ALL...
```

Units 01-02 are from Jess (AmE) and 03-04 from Dan (BrE). Jess's *authors* has |ɑː| thus |ɑːθəz|, where BrE would have |ɔːθəz|. In 03 *sort of* is an example of a softener (cf. Chapter 6.6). The last line brings the two versions of *all* side-by-side (AmE first) so that you can hear them clearly.

Jess's AmE *all* features |ɑː|, resulting in |ɑːl|, whereas Dan's BrE *all* features |ɔː|, resulting in |ɔːl|. It is very commonly the case that where BrE speakers use |ɔː|, AmE speakers will use |ɑː|, but not in all of cases and not with all speakers.

In fact, for many Americans the vowels |ɑː| and |ɔː| have merged (except before |r|) in what is known as the 'cot-caught merger'. However it is not a universal merger: there remain, as we will hear in Chapter 13, accents in which the merger has not happened. Nevertheless Wells (2008: xxi) tells us '...fewer and fewer Americans distinguish these two vowel sounds from one another...'.

However, even for those Americans for whom this merger is complete, |ɔː| continues to occur before |r|, as we can hear in Extract 11.3 where Jess talks about the places where she has lived.

Extract 11.3 Jess *north* and *proportion*

```
AmE 01 || but NORTH TEXas ||
AmE 02 || a CERtain proPORtion of THAT ||
       NORTH...proPORtion
```

These speech units come from different parts of Jess's recording.

Jess has |ɔː| before |r| in *north* and *proportion,* resulting in |nɔːrθ| and |prəpɔːrʃn̩|.

11.3.3 *Class, can't*

Both BrE and AmE have |ɑː| and |æ| in their inventory of vowels, but they are distributed differently. So whereas BrE has |ɑː| in words such as *class* and *pass,* AmE has |æ|. In Extract 11.4 Toby talks about an exam that he needed to take to enter university and Jess describes her home town, Santa Fe in New Mexico.

Extract 11.4 BrE – Toby, Jess *class*

```
BrE 01 || so i did my MATHS a-level ||
BrE 02 || at NIGHT-class ||
AmE 03 || i mean it's VEry arTISTic ||
AmE 04 || we have a WORLD-class OPera ||
       class ...class
```

Units 01-02 are from Toby (BrE) 03-04 from Jess (AmE). The last line brings the two versions of *class* side-by-side (BrE first) so that you can hear them clearly. Ying moment: in 01 the first four syllables *so I did my* sound close to *su.did.ma* – three syllables, going at 10 sps.

In both 02 and 04 *class* is non-prominent (cf. Chapter 2), but in both cases it is clearly audible. Toby's *class* features |ɑː| resulting in |klɑːs|, whereas Jess's *class* features |æ|, resulting in |klæs|.

This difference between AmE and BrE has consequences for decoding the word *can't.* In BrE, the difference between the positive and negative forms *can* and *can't* is achieved with a difference in vowel quality: *can* is |kaen| and *can't* is |kaːnt| or |kaːnʔ|. British listeners often rely on picking up the difference in vowel quality to determine whether the speaker intends the negative form, even if they can't hear the final –t because of elision or glottalisation. Extract 11.5 has BrE and AmE versions of *can't.* Toby talks about climbing, and Jess talks about not being able to find time to read in her busy life.

Extract 11.5 Toby, Jess *can't*

```
BrE 01 || you CAN'T ||
BrE 02 || PUSH yourself ||
AmE 03 || CAN'T quite FINish ||
     CAN'T ... CAN'T
```

Units 01-02 are from Toby and 03 is from Jess. The last line brings the two versions of *can't* side-by-side (BrE first) so that you can hear them clearly.

In both 01 and 03, the final consonant of *can't* is realised as a glottal stop: Toby has |kɑːnʔ|, and Jess has |kænʔ|. In the BrE version, the vowel difference helps listeners perceive negation, but in AmE, where vowel difference is not utilised to signal the presence or absence of negation, the occurrence of a glottal stop in place of the fully realised |t| is insufficient for many listeners – including L1 listeners – to perceive negation. For more on this difference between BrE and AmE, cf. Windsor Lewis (2010, section 27a).

11.4   Consonants

There are three major differences between AmE and BrE as far as consonants are concerned. First the absence in AmE of |j| (known as 'yod', it represents the 'y' sound in *yes*) in words such as *new*. Second the presence, in AmE of the *r* sound in syllable-final position such as in *car* (rhoticity). Third the use, in AmE, of the alveolar tap |ɾ| which often replaces |t| in words such as *writer* and *little,* so that they sound close to, but not exactly like, *rider* and *Lidl.*

11.4.1 *New, neutral, altitude, students*

As you can hear in Extract 11.6, AmE prefers a yodless *new,* thus |nuː| not |njuː|, in contrast to the BrE *new* with yod, thus |njuː|. Jess talks about the place where she lives, Gail talks about the house that her cousin is going to move into.

Extract 11.6 Jess, Gail *new*

```
AmE 01 || in new MEXico ||
BrE 02 || live in her NEW house ||
     new ... NEW ...
```

Ying moment: in 01 *in new* sounds close to *inner* as it goes at the very fast speed of 10.0 sps. The last line brings the two versions of *new* side-by-side (AmE first) so that you can hear them clearly.

New isn't the only word where the presence or absence of yod is the main difference between the accents. Another is *students,* which we can hear in Extract 11.7. Jess talks about her university days, and Toby talks about an indoor climbing school.

Extract 11.7 Jess and Toby *students*

```
AmE 01 || MANy interNATional STUDents ||
BrE 02 || i'm TAKing some STUDents there at the MOMent ||
       STUDents ... STUDents
```

01 comes from Jess and 02 from Toby. The last line brings the two versions of *students* side-by-side (AmE first) so that you can hear them clearly.

Jess's *students* is without yod, whereas Toby's *students* contains yod. However, it is not the case that yod is absent from AmE, as we shall see with *university* below.

11.4.2 Rhoticity

We have already mentioned that AmE is a rhotic accent and BrE is a non-rhotic accent (cf. 11.1). This means that in AmE the |r| is pronounced in places where it is not pronounced in BrE, as we will hear with the words *university, other, born, start* and *year.* Extract 11.8 features *university* in AmE and BrE, with Jess and Toby speaking about their experiences as university students.

Extract 11.8 Jess and Toby *university*

```
AmE 01 || i really LIKED the university ||
BrE 02 || in his FIRST year in university ||
       uniVERSity...uniVERSity
```

01 is from Jess and 02 from Toby. Ying moments: in 01 *I really* sounds close to *ah.rill.ill* and in 02 Toby's *university* the final two syllables of *university* into one |-sti|. The last line brings the two versions of *university* side-by-side (AmE first) so that you can hear them clearly.

The two occurrences of *university* differ dramatically in the third syllable *-ver:* Jess has a rhotacized tense vowel |vɝ| resulting in |juː.nɪ.vɝ.sə.ti| and Toby has a non-rhotic long vowel |ɜː| resulting in |juː.nɪ.vɜː.sti|.

The AmE vowel |ɝ| has a weak counterpart |ɚ|, also rhotic. We can hear this AmE vowel in *other* in Extract 11.9, compared to a BrE *other* with |ə|. Jess talks about the time in her mid-teens when she worked on a ranch as a horse-wrangler – someone who takes care of horses and prepares them for their working day.

Extract 11.9 Jess and Toby *other*

```
AmE 01 || with a bunch of OTHer WRANGlers ||
BrE 02 || the the OTHer people WATCHing ||
      OTHer ... OTHer
```
01 is from Jess and 02 from Toby. The last line brings the two versions of *other* side-by-side (AmE first) so that you can hear them clearly.

The final segment of Jess's *other* is |ɚ| giving us |ʌð ɚ| which immediately precedes the |r| of *wrangler* |ræŋglɚ|. The word *wrangler* itself, of course, ends with another instance of |ɚ|, this time with the plural morpheme -*s*, resulting in |ɚz|. Toby's BrE *other,* in contrast, has a non-rhotic final segment |ʌðə|.

Words such as *born*, *start* and *year*, where the vowels |ɔː|,|ɑː| and |ɪə| are followed by *r* in the spelling provide further illustration of the rhotic/non-rhotic differences: In AmE this r is pronounced, but in BrE it is not. In fact it has not been pronounced in BrE since the eighteenth century (Wells, 1982: 218). In Extract 11.10 Jess provides a striking example of this type of rhoticity in AmE on the rising tone on *born,* which contrasts strongly with Toby's fast, non-prominent, non-rhotic *born.*

Extract 11.10 Jess and Toby *born*

```
AmE 01 || i was BORN ||
BrE 02 || i was born in HITCHIN ||
      BORN ... born
```
01 is from Jess and 02 from Toby. 01 is slow, at 3.3 sps and 02 is fast at 6.0 sps, resulting in the preposition *in* becoming almost inaudible. The last line brings the two versions of *born* side-by-side (AmE first) so that you can hear them clearly.

The rhoticity of AmE's *started* is demonstrated by Jess, who is discussing her own pronunciation. Dan's non-rhotic *started* comes as he talks about how he first came to sing in public.

Extract 11.11 Jess and Dan *started*

```
AmE 01 || i STARTed to proNOUNCE my T'S more ||
BrE 02 || it STARTed ||
      STARTed ...STARTed
```
01 is from Jess and 02 from Dan. The last line brings the two versions of *started* side-by-side (AmE first) so that you can hear them clearly.

Jess's prominent *started* at the beginning of a three-prominence speech unit enables us to hear the rhoticity of |stɑːrtɪd|. Paradoxically, however, neither the |t| of the cluster |st| nor the |t| at the end of the first syllable are clearly audible. In fact the word sounds close to a monosyllable *sard*. As we noted earlier, this is a change in soundshape which can happen early in a speech unit, even with words containing a prominent syllable (cf. Chapters 8 & 9).

Dan has a level tone beginning on the first syllable of *started*, which elongates the word so that it has a duration of 1.14 seconds, four times longer than Jess's *started* which is 0.29 seconds in duration. This elongation is very common before a pause in both BrE and AmE, and spontaneous speech of all kinds. Here it provides a very clear example of the non-rhotic BrE's |stɑːtɪd|.

Finally, the non-rhotic BrE |ɪə| in *years* and its AmE rhotic equivalent |ɪr| can be heard in Extract 11.12, featuring speech units from Jess and Toby. Jess talks about the duration of an illness of a relative, Toby about how long he worked as a builder.

Extract 11.12 Jess and Toby *years*

```
AmE 01 || for a COUPle of YEARS ||
BrE 02 || for FIVE YEARS ||
       YEARS...YEARS
```

Ying moment: in 01, *for a* are squeezed into one syllable, with *a* being almost inaudible. The last line brings the two versions of *years* side-by-side (AmE first) so that you can hear them clearly.

These units happen to illustrate a variation in rising tones – but it is not a difference between AmE and BrE, both varieties show this variation. In 01 Jess's rising tone has a steep contour, whereas in 02 Toby's rising tone has a shallow contour (cf. Chapter 4).

11.4.3   Taps and other soundshapes for *t*

Both Toby and Jess use the word *little* in their recordings, which provide us with examples of a well-known difference between AmE and BrE in Extract 11.13. Jess is talking about different types of music in the south of the USA, Toby is talking about childhood friends.

Extract 11.13 Jess and Toby *little*

```
AmE 01 || it's a LITTle bit DIFFerent STYLE ||
BrE 02 || when i was VEry LITTle ||
       LITTle... LITTle
```

01 is from Jess and 02 from Toby. Ying moment: in 02 *when i was* sounds close to two syllables. The last line brings the two versions of *little* side-by-side (AmE first) so that you can hear them clearly.

In 01 Jess has an alveolar tap instead of |t| in *little* thus |lɪɾɫ| – *liddle* – whereas in 02 Toby clearly uses |t|. Notice that Toby's *little* has a vocalised |l| at the end giving us |lɪtʊ|, a point we return to in 11.4.4 below.

Interestingly Toby and Jess have other soundshapes for *little,* which we can hear in Extract 11.14. Jess talks about the difference between residential areas in Birmingham (England) and in Santa Fe, Toby talks about his climbing equipment.

Extract 11.14 Jess *little* as *lil* and Toby *little...metal*

```
AmE 01 || there's NOT ACtually little TOWNS ||
BrE 02 || a LITTle bit of METal ||
        little ... LITTle
```

01 is from Jess, and 02 from Toby. Ying moment: in 01 *actually* has two syllables (cf. Chapter 9.6.1). The last line brings the two versions of *little* side-by-side (AmE first) so that you can hear them clearly.

Jess's *little* has no middle consonant – in fact, she omits it entirely, resulting in |lɪɫ| which, in folk spelling can be represented as *li'l.* Although this type of consonant dropping is most associated with AmE, it also occurs in BrE in non-prominent sections of speech units (squeeze zones) and we make use of this feature in classroom exercises in Chapter 18 and Appendix 4.

In 02, all of Toby's *t*'s are realised as glottal stops: his *little* is |lɪʔʊ| *bit* is |bɪʔ| and *metal* is |meʔʊ|. You might ask where the expected dark *l* symbol |ɫ| at the end of *metal* and *little* is. In fact Toby vocalises the final consonants of both *little* and *metal,* so although we might expect |ɫ|, instead they become vowel-like |lɪtʊ| and |metʊ|. This is an aspect of of BrE which we will explore further in the next section.

When Jess talks about her home city Santa Fe, she produces a very clear |t| in both *Santa* and *county* in unit 01 of Extract 11.15. However, as unit 02 shows, she does not do this consistently.

Extract 11.15 Jess *Santa Fe county*

```
AmE 01 || PART of SANta fe COUNTy ||
AmE 02 || and I came from SANta fe ||
        SANta fe ... SANta fe
```

These units come from different parts of Jess's recording. The last line brings the two versions of *Santa* side-by-side (AmE first) so that you can hear them clearly.

In 01 the word-final |t| at the end of *part* is realised as a tap, giving us |pɑːɾəf|, but of most interest are the two versions of *Santa*. While the first one is |sæntə| the second *Santa* has no |t| – Jess says |sænə|. This |t| deletion after |n| and before a vowel is very common in AmE (cf. Chapter 13).

11.4.4 Vocalised *l*

Wells (1982) reported that l-vocalisation (the use of a vowel instead of |l|), is coming into RP, we have already heard this in 11.4.3 at the end of Toby's *little*. In Extract 11.16 we hear it again in Dan's *school*, contrasted with a version from Jess.

Extract 11.16 Dan and Jess *school*

```
BrE 01|| SCHOOL CONcert ||
AmE 02|| but they were going to do it ONly for OUR SCHOOL ||
        SCHOOL ... SCHOOL
```

01 is from Dan, and 02 from Jess. Ying moment: in unit 02 the first eight syllables are in a squeeze zone (cf. Chapter 3) and go at 11.5 sps, which is very fast (cf. Chapter 7); *do it* sounds monosyllabic.
The last line brings the two versions of *school* side-by-side (BrE first) so that you can hear them clearly.

Dan's BrE *school* is |skuːʊ| compared to RP and Jess's AmE *school* which has a dark |l| |skuːɫ|. In Extract 11.17 there are even more striking examples from Toby (talking about climbing) in his pronunciations of *ankle* and *Wales* which he pronounces |æŋkʊ| rather than |æŋkɫ| and |weɪʊz| rather than |weɪɫz|.

Extract 11.17 Toby *ankle* and *Wales*

```
BrE 01 || i TWISTed my ANKle ||
BrE 02 || a LOT in WALES ||
        ANKle ... WALES
```

These units come from different parts of Toby's recording.

On this evidence one difference between AmE and BrE is that many BrE speakers have vowel-like realisations of velar *l*, but that is probably not entirely accurate, because McElhinny (1999) reports on this feature in Pittsburgh accents in the USA.

11.5 Word stress and non-prominent syllables

The differences between BrE and AmE are not confined to consonants and vowels. We will look at two types of difference that have to do with syllables: prominence placement within words, and whether or not vowel reduction occurs in non-prominent syllables.

11.5.1   Prominent syllables and word accent

In Extract 11.18 we can hear the words *translator* and *adult* which are among many words in which word stress, and therefore prominence placement, differs between AmE and BrE.

Extract 11.18 Jess *translator*

```
AmE 01 || i've ALso been a TRANSlator ||
BrE 02 || i've ALso been a transLATor ||
     TRANSlator ... transLATor
```

Unit 02 is a scripted version of 01, for the purpose of comparison. The last line brings the two versions of *translator* side-by-side (AmE first) so that you can hear them clearly.

Jess gives us an AmE version of *translator* with prominence on the first syllable, whereas BrE generally has prominence on the second syllable of thus *transLATor*. Extract 11.19 contains another example, *adults,* which comes from Karam from California talking about teaching swimming.

Extract 11.19 Karam *adults*

```
AmE 01 || though i've TAUGHT aDULTS ||
BrE 02 || though i've TAUGHT ADults ||
     aDULTS ... ADults
```

Unit 02 is a scripted version of 01, for the purpose of comparison. The last line brings the two versions of *adults* side-by-side (AmE first) so that you can hear them clearly.

Karam's AmE *adults* has prominence on the second syllable resulting in *aDULTS,* whereas BrE has prominence on the first syllable, resulting in *ADults.*

11.5.2 Non-prominent syllables

AmE and BrE differ in the amount of reduction that occurs in non-prominent syllables. In Extracts 11.20 and 11.21 we will hear examples from Jeffrey and Ashley, both from the USA, whose voices we will hear again in Chapter 13. Although their accents have a southern flavour, their versions of *cemetery* and *mandatory* in Extract 11.20 are fairly typical of AmE generally. Jeffrey is a keen photographer and he describes his favourite things to take pictures of, amongst which are the cemeteries in New Orleans.

Extract 11.20 Jeffrey *cemeteries*

```
AmE 01 || you have a LOT of CEMeteries ||
BrE 02 || you have a LOT of CEMeteries ||
```

```
      CEMeteries ... CEMeteries
```

Unit 02 is a scripted BrE version of 01, recorded for the purpose of this comparison. The last line brings the two versions of *cemeteries* side-by-side (AmE first) so that you can hear them clearly.

Jeffrey's AmE version has four syllables, with a full vowel on the third syllable, |'se.mə.te.riz|, whereas the BrE version has only three syllables |'se.mə.triz|. In effect in BrE the third syllable has been reduced to the point of non-existence by the process of compression (Wells, 2008: 173).

In Extract 11.21 Ashley talks about the history of teaching Latin in high schools in the USA. She says that it was *almost like mandatory*.

Extract 11.21 Ashley *mandatory*

```
AmE 01 || ALmost like MANdatory ||
BrE 02 || ALmost like MANdatory ||
      MANdatory ... MANdatory
```

Unit 02 is a scripted BrE version of 01, recorded for the purpose of this comparison. The last line brings the two versions of *mandatory* side-by-side (AmE first) so that you can hear them clearly.

In Ashley's *mandatory* |'mæn.də.tɔ.ri| there are four syllables, with a non-reduced vowel in the third syllable. In BrE it has three syllables |'mæn.də.tri|, although in very careful speech it could have four syllables |'mæn.də.tə.ri| with a reduced vowel, schwa |ə|, as the third syllable.

11.6   Intonation

The window on speech can be used to capture speakers choices of tone equally well in both BrE and AmE. We will compare two aspects of tone choice: uptalk, and filled pauses.

11.6.1 Uptalk

Uptalk (also known as *high rising terminal*, *upspeak* or *high rising intonation*) is a feature of speech in which rising tones occur where falling tones would normally be expected. Some people find this speech pattern irritating as they associate a rising tone with questions, for example Wells (2006: 38) writes 'using uptalk may annoy older people listening to you'. Our first example, in Extract 11.22, comes from California in which Karam explains how she became a swimming instructor.

Extract 11.22 Karam *our swim-team ... america*

```
AmE 01 || ↗ our SWIM-team ACtually RAN a PROgram ||
AmE 02 || ↗ called swim aMErica ||
AmE 03 || ↗ our SWIM-team ACtually RAN a PROgram ||
AmE 04 || ↘ called swim aMErica ||
```
Unit 03-04 are a scripted version of recorded for the purpose of this comparison.

Karam has two rising tones, both finishing very high, starting on the first syllable of *program* and the second syllable of *America*. In the non-uptalk version given in 03-04 there is a shallow rise starting on *program* followed by a fall in 04.

In Extract 11.23 we can also hear uptalk from Jacklyn (New Jersey) who is explaining why she did not choose to go to university in Boston.

Extract 11.23 Jacklyn *high school ... Boston*

```
AmE 01 || ↗ there were a LOT of people from my HIGH school ||
AmE 02 || ↗ that went to BOSTon ||
AmE 03 || ↗ there were a LOT of people from my HIGH school ||
AmE 04 || ↘ that went to BOSTon ||
```
Unit 03-04 are a scripted version of 01-02, recorded for the purpose of this comparison.

Jacklyn has high rising tones starting on both *high* and the first syllable of *Boston,* whereas in the non-uptalk version given in 03-04 there is a shallow rise starting on *high* followed by a fall in 04 on *Boston.*

Both examples of uptalk have come from females speaking AmE. However, it is neither exclusively female nor exclusively AmE: it has now spread globally to both genders of younger generations of people thanks to the influence of television programmes such as Australia's *Neighbours.* It is regarded by some older people as an unwelcome foreign influence on BrE.

In Extract 11.24 we can hear a male BrE speaker using uptalk. Dan talks about his audition for a television talent show called 'Pop Idol' (a predecessor to 'X-factor'). He is explaining the circumstances of his audition – *one* is a reference to an audition.

Extract 11.24 Dan *so they'd ... based one*

```
01 || ↘↗ so they'd FILMED the SERies ||
02 || ↗ and then they did ONE more LONdon based one ||
03 || ↘↗ so they'd FILMED the SERies ||
04 || ↘ and then they did ONE more LONdon based one ||
```

Unit 03-04 are a scripted version of 01-02, recorded for the purpose of this comparison. Ying moment: in 02 the four syllables *and then they did* sound close to *annenaydid* – they go at close to 10.0 sps.

Dan has a high-finishing rising tone starting on the first syllable of *London* and continuing over the syllables *-don based one*. This example shows that uptalk also occurs in BrE and in the speech of male speakers.

11.6.2 Filled pauses

It is interesting to compare AmE and BrE versions of the most common sounds which occur in unscripted speech – those associated with filled pauses. In writing, these sounds are often rendered *er, erm, uh* or *um*. When spoken, they can have different vowel qualities, lengths and pitch heights. Extract 11.25 contains three examples each from Jess and Toby.

Extract 11.25 AmE & BrE – Jess and Toby: filled pauses

```
AmE 01 || AHM || 02 || AH || 03 || AHM ||
BrE 04 || ERM || 05 || ER || 06 || ERM ||
```

Units 01-03 are from different parts of Jess's recording and 04-06 are from different parts of Toby's recording.

In each line the filled pauses occur in order of pitch height, from low to high. In Toby's case the differences in height are small, whereas Jess's differences in height are much greater. Toby's 05 is exceptionally long at nearly 1.4 seconds. The most striking example from Jess is 03 which is very high and has a high falling tone – all the others have level tone. Additionally, there is a difference in vowel quality, with Jess's versions close to |ɑːm| – *ahm* – and |ɑː| – *ah* – and Toby's versions close to |ɜːm| – *erm* – and |ɜː| – *er*. We might be tempted to believe that this difference in vowel quality distinguishes BrE and AmE filled pauses, but in fact there are a huge variety of vowels used for filled pauses in both accents.

11.7   Summary and what's next

This chapter has compared evidence of contemporary speakers of BrE and AmE whose accents are a reasonably close fit to RP and GenAm. Examples of the major differences included:

- BrE has |ɒ| in *odd,* AmE has |ɑː|
- BrE has |ɑː| in *class,* AmE has |æ|
- AmE is rhotic – *born* has |r|, BrE is non-rhotic – *born* is r-less
- Word stress differs: BrE *transLAtor* versus AmE *TRANSlator*
- AmE has a tap for |t|: *writer* may sound like *rider*
- BrE has yod in *new*; AmE has no yod, thus *noo*

We have also noticed that the recordings we used as evidence contained features which are exerting pressure for change on the reference models, such as Dan's and Toby's vocalised |l| and Jess's |lɪl| for *little.*

In Chapters 12 and 13 we will look at other accents from North America and from Britain and Ireland. We will see that the features which have differentiated BrE from AmE in the above comparison have a much more complex distribution. For example we will find rhotic accents in Britain and Ireland and non-rhotic accents in the USA. We will also discover that there is a feature of southern USA accents which sounds more like British RP than BrE does. Chapters 12 and 13 will also introduce the issues of identity and prejudice.

11.8   Further reading

The introductions to the major pronunciation dictionaries Wells (2008), Roach et al, (2006) and Upton et al (2001) are good sources of comparative material. Wells (1982: 279–301) and Wells (1997) are essential reading on RP, and Wells (1982: 467–490) and Labov et al. (2006) are essential reading on GenAm. For a description of AmE designed for teaching purposes (they call it 'North American English') see Chapters 3 & 4 of Celce-Murcia et al. (2010). Windsor Lewis (2010) is a comprehensive reference work for the differences between RP and AmE. Sources of information on Estuary English can be found in Rosewarne (1984), Wells (1998) and Przedlacka (2002). And lastly, for those who like the spice of prejudice, Algeo (2005) reports on the derogatory discourse that emanates from adherents of both BrE and AmE when discussing the rival varieties.

Accents, Identity and Emotion in Speech

11.9   Language awareness activities

Activity 11.1: Prepare and perform   Answer key page 239

Read the four sentences below. Look back at the relevant sections of this chapter and prepare a performance version of the sentences in both BrE and AmE. Then perform these sentences, in your own accent, and in both BrE and AmE, for a friend, colleague, or fellow teacher.

(1) My first job was as a waiter in the first-class lounge of Atlantic Airways. (2) It was a good time for me, because I met people from all over the world. (3) I can't remember how much I was paid, but I wish I'd earned as much as the passengers I served! (4) After going to night school to get the necessary exams, I went to university to study drama.

Activity 11.2: Listen and analyse   Answer key page 240

Listen to the four speech units of Extract 11.26: the units are extracted from different recordings, and are paired. Units 01 and 02 are an AmE-BrE pair containing the word *first,* and 03 and 04 are a second AmE-BrE pair containing the word *after.* Describe in detail the differences between BrE and AmE that you hear in these speech units.

Extract 11.26 AmE & BrE *first* and *after*

```
BrE 01 || well the FIRST one ||
AmE 02 || it was the FIRST ONE ||
BrE 03 || it was kind of AFTer CHRISTmas ||
AmE 04 || AFTer a LOT of ||
```

Unit 01 comes from Dan, 02 and 04 from Jess and 03 from Toby.

12   Accents of Britain and Ireland

In this chapter we will sample the variety of accents that exists in Britain and Ireland. As we do so, it will become clear that issues of social class, social stratification and prejudice arise. We begin with a survey of the terms used to describe accents, then we will look at different aspects of the relationship between personal identity and accent. We will hear two groups of accents, totalling nine in all. The first group of five will consist of one accent from each of the countries of Britain and Ireland, and the second group will feature four further accents from major cities in England. Lastly, we will hear how the accent of one individual can change over the course of twenty seconds as she speaks with an outsider about her childhood experiences.

12.1   Describing accents

The range of adjectives used to describe accents is much larger than there is space for here, so we will restrict ourselves to a quick review of the adjectives used in this chapter. An accent may be **regional** or **local**, that is it may be associated with a region, for example south-west Ireland or north-east Scotland, or a specific place, such as Birmingham or Leeds. Alternatively it may be a **social** accent, such as **Received Pronunciation,** with no regional or local trace (although it will indicate that a person is English as opposed to American), which is associated with an upper class, highly educated background. Or there may be a mixture of the regional and the social in your accent such as **Educated Scottish English**. It can be a **stigmatised** accent, one that is prejudicially associated with criminality, lack of education and even medical problems. Alternatively it can be a **prestige** accent – one that is prejudicially associated with highly-valued personal qualities such as a good education and success in life.

An accent can be **standard** – in some way official, or institutionalised, in the sense that it is a reference model for the purpose of dictionary-making and language teaching. Alternatively an accent may be non-standard, in which case it may be **broad** (or **strong,** or **thick** or **distinct**), **moderate** or **slight,** depending on its perceived distance from the standard accent.

Your accent can be **posh** or **common**. If someone says that your accent is *posh* it means that they associate your accent – and you – with a better upbringing, more material wealth, better education, pompous behaviour, or all four. If someone describes an accent as *common* then it could mean one of two things: your accent, or a feature of it, is widespread; or the opposite of posh – that your accent is associated with a bad upbringing, poverty and not a very good education. Your accent may even be so posh that it is called a **cut-glass** accent – one that is associated with royalty, the aristocracy and a very elite education.

Lastly there are joking and humorous ways of referring to accents which are expressed in deliberately non-standard English. People are encouraged to **speak proper** ('speak properly') or are described as speaking **reet posh** ('right posh' or 'truly posh') or even **dead posh** ('very posh').

12.2   Accent, identity and prejudice

We all have accents – no-one is accent-free. Our accents are an important part of our personal and social identity. They are, along with our visual appearance, a part of 'the face' that we present to the world (though it is heard, not seen). Our accent is part of us – a flavour or colouring to our voices which some groups of people will like, and other groups will dislike. Our accents are something that, most of the time, we pay little attention to. However, when our attention is drawn to our accent we discover that it is an important part of our identity. It can be upsetting when someone says 'It's cute', or laughs at it, or when someone corrects it and demands that we change it.

Brian Dakin is from the Black Country, a part of England north-west of Birmingham, where many people have an accent which is the subject of much prejudice. Brian's father told him to change his accent when he went to secondary school in the early 1960s:

> When yow go to grammar school you gotta drop your doh's, you gotta drop your cor's, becoss you cor spake like that in grammar school. (BBC, 2005b)

> In this extract *doh* means *do not* and *cor* means *can't*.

Brian tried to follow this advice but found after a while that he did not want to. He thought to him-self 'You know. I'm ... a council boy and I speak like this and I'm proud of it' and reverted to his Black Country accent. This insistence on accent change at school, and pupils' resistance to it, is not a thing of the past. It continues in the twenty-first century. Chamonix, a secondary school student from Liverpool, talks about a primary-school teacher – 'dead posh', according to Chamonix – who wanted her and her classmates not use their Liverpool accent in a singing competition:

"Don't talk like that, don't talk like yer from Liverpool," she said because we'll lose marks, it's like she was saying to us "… talk like you're from somewhere else" … It's cos she just expects us to be posh just like that when we're not. (BBC, 2005c)

Megan, Chamonix's sister, adds the comment 'It felt like she was ashamed of, of who we are and we shouldn't be ashamed of like, what our accent is or somethin'. These two sisters, like Brian from the Black Country, felt that the attempts to change their accents were an attack on their identity – they were being asked to change something about themselves which was precious to them.

The most unfortunate way that an accent might be changed is when people suffer trauma to the brain, such as a stroke. Such people can suffer from *Foreign Language Syndrome*. Linda, from Newcastle, had a stroke, and her accent changed:

My sister-in-law said that I sounded Italian, then my brother said I sounded Slovakian and someone else said I sounded French Canadian. But the latest is that I sound Jamaican, I just don't know how to explain it. (BBC, 2006)

The skill of speaking in different accents is one that is much admired in actors and comedians, but Linda Walker felt very bad about this sudden, enforced change:

I was just devastated. I've lost my identity, because I never talked like this before. I'm a very different person and it's strange and I don't like it. (BBC, 2006)

Linda resented the enforced change in her accent, but many people *want* to change their accents and, given the motivation, they can acquire a new accent deliberately and completely in a matter of weeks. It is to this topic that we now turn.

12.3   Changing an accent

People can deliberately change their accents if they are suddenly presented with the urgent need to be accepted by a new social group. Honey (1989: 28) reports that early in the twentieth century F.E. Smith (later to become Lord Chancellor) went to Oxford in 1890 'from a day school in Birkenhead … [near Liverpool] … with a marked local accent: he is said to have adapted to RP "in about six weeks" at Oxford'. In more recent times, the British Labour politician Harriet Harman is quoted as saying that her accent moved from being cut-glass to being less posh in order to fit in better with her left of centre, pro-trade union political party.

It is not clear whether F.E. Smith or Harriet Harman took classes in accent change, but there are many people offering such accent-reduction services, and there is clearly a continuing demand. But specific instruction is not always necessary to bring about change. People may, through the process of **convergence**, acquire a more moderate version of their accent without any instruction or deliberate effort on their part. They may not even notice that it is happening, only becoming aware of it after it has happened, on their return to a previous peer group. Someone from the North of England, now living in the South, made this comment:

> ... since living down south my northern-ness has mellowed. Southerners don't think that but when I go home they think I talk reet posh. (Guardian Unlimited, 29 Jan 2010)

Therefore, if someone joins a new social group, and they want to be accepted and identified as a member of that group, their accent may change so that it approximates to the norms of that group without them even being aware of it. The processes of accent change can therefore also work on a subconscious level, below the level of awareness.

Although changing your accent may result in the elimination of one accent and its replacement by another, it very commonly occurs that people develop a moderated version of their native accent so that they become bi-accented: they have two accents – their broad accent and their moderate accent. They retain their first accent for friends and family and develop another that they use in the workplace or in more formal situations. Elmes (2005) has many examples of people with regional accents also having a 'telephone voice' – closer to RP – which they use for outsiders, for people outside their circle of friends and family. In the extracts which follow, we will hear two speakers shifting between the broad and moderate versions of their accent.

12.4   Five countries, five accents

Britain and Ireland consist of five countries, England, Scotland, Wales, Northern Ireland and the Republic of Ireland. In this section, we sample one accent from each country.

12.4.1   Northern Ireland

Kim is from Coleraine in the north-east of Northern Ireland. In Extract 12.1 she speaks about the Giant's Causeway, a spectacular feature of rocks close to where she lives.

Extract 12.1 Northern Ireland – Kim

```
01 || but the CAUSEway ||
02 || DOES ACtually ||
03 || go OUT ||
04 || for about TWO MILES ||
      OUT ...OUT
      about ... about
```

The last two lines contain (in order) RP citation forms and Kim's versions of *out* and *about*.

The difference between Kim's accent and RP can be heard in her pronunciation of the word *out* in unit 03 and *about* in 04, where RP |aʊt| is close to |ɛʉt| and RP |əbaʊt| is close to |əbɛʉt|. The *u* symbol with the line through it means that this sound lies between the *oo* of *goose* and the *ee* of *fleece* (cf. Wells, 1982: xix). The |ɛ| symbol represents a vowel that is between |e| and |æ|. You can read more about the Coleraine accent in Wells (1982: 448). Interestingly, Kim's accent is quite closely related to the accent from across the sea in Scotland, from where – historically – many people came to settle in Northern Ireland.

12.4.2   Scotland

The next accent is from Glasgow, where Willie was born. He is a university professor talking, in Extract 12.2, about a visit he made to Zimbabwe.

Extract 12.2 Scotland – Willie

```
01 || OH i enJOY visiting zimbabwe ||
02 || eNORmously ||
03 || for a NUMber of DIFFerent reasons||
04 || ACtually ||
      eNORmously ...eNORmously
      DIFFerent ... DIFFerent
```

The last two lines contain (in order) RP citation forms and Willie's versions of *enormously* and *different*.

Although born in Glasgow, Willie's accent is an example of Educated Scottish English. His pronunciation of *enormously* features the |r| at the end of the second syllable which is not present in RP – his accent is thus a rhotic accent. In addition, the vowel sound in the initial segment of *enormously* is the |i| sound at the end of 'city' rather than the |ɪ| sound of 'pit', so we get |iˈnɔːr.məs.li| rather than |ɪˈnɔː.məs.li|. We can also hear a hint of Willlie's slight Glasgow accent in his pronunciation of the vowel in the first syllable of *different* which also differs from RP. It has a flavour of the |ʌ| sound found in 'cup', resulting in |dʌf.rənt|, although this is characteristic of other parts of Scotland as well (cf. Wells, 1982: 404).

12.4.3   Wales

Karen was brought up in Maesteg in South Wales. In Extract 12.3 she talks about her childhood home.

Extract 12.3 Wales – Karen

```
01 || AND at the TIME ||
02 || the HOUSE they'd BOUGHT ||
03 || ...was... ||
04 || quite diLAPidated ||
      diLAPidated ...diLAPidated
```

Ying moment: in 01 *and at* sounds like *annat*.
The last line contains (in order) the RP citation form, and Karen's version of *dilapidated*.

Karen is typical of many Welsh speakers in giving full value to the final consonants of words, as she does very clearly with the |t| at the end of *bought*. However, she demonstrates that this not an absolute rule for her because she elides the |t| at the end of *quite* due to the influence of the following |d| at the beginning of *dilapidated*. But the most striking part of this extract is the care Karen gives to the five syllables of *dilapidated* which she pronounces |dɪˈlæp.ɪ.det.ed| as opposed to the RP |dɪˈlæp.ɪ.deɪt.ɪd|. There are major differences of vowel quality on the final two syllables: a long monophthong |e| as compared with the diphthong |eɪ| in RP, and Karen pronounces the last syllable |ted| rather than the RP |tɪd|. She also gives a full value to the five syllables of this word, resulting in a rhythm (sometimes described as 'sing-song') which is characteristic of many Welsh accents, but not of RP.

12.4.4   Republic of Ireland

Liz was born in County Clare, but she now lives in Galway. In Extract 12.4 she talks about the timing of her early resignation from a job in London in order to find a job back home in Ireland, in Galway. She took a risk and resigned.

Extract 12.4 Ireland – Liz

```
01 || beFORE ||
02 || i had conFIRMED ||
03 || that i had a JOB ||
04 || in in GALway ||
      beFORE...beFORE
      conFIRMED...conFIRMED
      JOB...JOB
```

The last three lines contain (in order) RP citation forms and Liz's versions of *before, confirmed,* and *job.* Ying moment: in 03 *that i had a* go at 11.5 sps – extremely fast

This accent is rhotic, as you can hear from the second syllables of *before* and *confirmed,* where there is a distinct 'r' colouring to the vowels that in RP are |ɔː| and |ɜː| – Liz gives us |bifɔːr| and |kənfɜːrmd|. There are two other features to this accent: Liz pronounces *job* as |dʒɑːb| as opposed to RP |dʒɒb| and she pronounces the second syllable of *Galway* as |we|, as opposed to RP |weɪ|.

12.4.5   England

Our sample from England in Extract 12.5 features Toby whose voice we heard in Chapter 11.

Extract 12.5 England – Toby

```
01 || there was JUST ||
02 || a LITTle ROCK ||
03 || aBOUT ||
04 || aBOUT the size of a CABBage ||
      LITTle...LITTle
      aBOUT...aBOUT...aBOUT
```

The last two lines contain (in order) RP citation forms and Toby's versions of *little* and *about.*

As we saw in Chapter 11, people in their twenties or thirties in the south of England are more likely to speak with Toby's Estuary English accent than RP. His *little* has two features which differ from RP: the middle consonant is glottalised, and the final consonant is vocalised – he says |lɪʔʊ| in contrast to RP |lɪtɬ|. On the two occasions he says *about*, a glottal stop replaces the final consonant. He also drops the first syllable of *about* the second time he says it, resulting in |baʊʔ|.

We have now finished sampling accents of the five countries of Britain and Ireland, and we move to a brief survey of accents in four major English cities.

12.5   Accents in four cities

12.5.1   Manchester

In Extract 12.6 we will hear John, who was born and brought up in Salford, Manchester. He lived very close to Old Trafford, the home ground of Manchester United Football Club, and he is a passionate supporter. John joined the army at the age of sixteen, and had a successful career. Although he was very good at what he did (he was an instructor in climbing and other outdoor pursuits), he wasn't always happy in the army, so the army had to persuade him to stay in.

Extract 12.6 Manchester – John

```
01 || i was TECHnically DOing ||
02 || quite WELL in the army ||
03 || so they TRIED HARD ||
04 || to KEEP me IN ||
      DOing...DOing
      HARD...HARD
```

The last two lines contain (in order) RP citation forms and John's versions of *doing* and *hard*.

The second syllable of John's *doing* features |n| resulting in |dʉːɪn| compared with the RP |ŋ| as in |duːɪŋ|. This |n |for |ŋ| feature has a long history – Wells tells us that both the |n| and |ŋ| forms have co-existed since early Middle English (ca. 1450-1600). Although this feature is associated, to the point of parody, with upper-class RP (who go *huntin, shootin, fishin*), it is also often associated with non-upper-class speech across a range of regional accents (Wells, 1982:262). John's *doing* is also interesting for another reason: the first syllable does not have the same vowel as RP |duː|. Instead this vowel is close to |ʉ| something between the *oo* of *goose* and the *ee* of *fleece*.

Another noteworthy feature is that John drops the |h| of *hard* in unit 03. H-dropping is a feature of speech that has traditionally been (and continues to be) corrected by teachers: Wells (1982: 254) writes 'A London school teacher tells me he has only to look sternly at any child who drops an |h|, and that child will say the word again, this time correctly' (cf. also Crystal, 2004:411-412). It is possible that John has retained this feature because, like Brian Dakin from the Black Country, he is proud of his background, protective of his identity, and has always resisted (either consciously or unconsciously) all the pressures to change it.

12.5.2   Birmingham

Some eighty miles south of Manchester is another football ground The Hawthorns, which is home to West Bromwich Albion Football Club. Peter, our next speaker, is a passionate fan of this club. Although his team is based in the Black Country, a region north-west of Birmingham, Peter is from the city of Birmingham. Here he speaks about the organisational structure of his club.

Extract 12.7 Birmingham – Peter

```
01 || the STRUCture of the CLUB is ||
02 || BEtter than it's BEEN ||
03 || for YEARS ||
      STRUCture...STRUCture
      CLUB...CLUB
      BEEN...BEEN
      YEARS..YEARS
```

The last four lines contain (in order) RP citation forms and Peter's versions.

Peter's accent shares with many accents the vowels contained in the words *structure* and *club*. He has |strʊk.tʃə| and |klʊb|, whereas RP would have |strʌk.tʃə| and |klʌb|. His *been* has a vowel which is closer to a diphthongal |ʌɪ| rather than RP's |iː|. Unit 03 has two noteworthy features: the pronunciation of the vowel in *years* and its rising intonation. The vowel in *years* is close to |ɜː| compared with RP |ɪə|. Again this is a feature of a wide range of regional accents in Britain and Ireland. Indeed even within RP, 20% of respondents to a preference poll (Wells, 2008: 914) reported that they had this pronunciation.

12.5.3   Leeds

Nearly two hundred miles north of London and forty miles north east of Manchester we come to the city of Leeds. In Extract 12.8 we will hear Eve, a university secretary, speaking about her childhood memories of spending time on a farm. She refers to her friend's grandmother as *my mate's gran*.

Extract 12.8 Leeds – Eve

```
01 || my MATE'S GRAN ||
02 || had a caraVAN ||
03 || in the FARM ||
       FARM...FARM
```

The last line contains (in order) the RP citation form and Eve's version of *farm*.

Eve's *my* is |mə|, but this is common in many accents where *my* is non-prominent, including regional accents from all over the UK and Ireland. Her *gran, caravan,* and *farm* feature the same vowel |æ| in the prominent syllables, resulting in |græn| and |kær.ə'væn|, with her *farm* |fæm| being quite unlike the RP |fɑːm|. We will return to Eve's *farm* in Section 12.6.

12.5.5   Newcastle

Sonia is from Newcastle-upon-Tyne, a city about 100 miles further north of Leeds. She is a senior secretary who deals a lot with international students. In Extract 12.9 Sonia speaks about major events in her life and mentions two important years.

Extract 12.9 Newcastle – Sonia

```
01 || THAT was in NINEteen SEVenty ONE ||
02 || and I got MARRied ||
03 || in NINEteen SEVenty NINE ||
       NINEteen...NINEteen...
       SEVenty...SEVenty ...SEVenty
       ONE...ONE
```

The last three lines contain (in order) RP citation forms and Sonia's versions.

In this extract perhaps the most noticeable feature of Sonia's consonants concern the |t| in *nineteen,* and *seventy* which have what Wells (1982: 374) refers to as 'glottal masking' – not the same as a simple replacement of |t| by a glottal stop. Thus Sonia gives us |naɪntʔiːn|, and |sevə̃tʔi|, (where the second vowel is nasalised). But *seventy* occurs twice, and on the second occasion Sonia removes glottal masking of the |t|, resulting in |sevn̩ti|. This shift into and out of glottal masking shows that Sonia's accent varies between a broad version of her accent and a more moderate version, her 'telephone voice', in a way that is completely normal for someone of her position and background. Sonia's vowel in *one* is close to |wɔn|, a characteristic feature of her accent. Also noteworthy are her first person pronoun *I*, which is |ɑ| as opposed to RP |aɪ|, and her *nine* in which the diphthong starts mid rather than low.

12.6   Bi-accentedness

As mentioned in 12.3 above, accents change as people move from one social group to another, and we have seen Sonia's *seventy* varied between her broad accent and her telephone voice. We will end the survey with Extract 12.10 in which Eve produces three extremely different pronunciations of *farm* in the space of twenty seconds. These extracts come from a conversation about Eve's memories of moving house and moving school when she was very young – she was upset at moving because she would no longer be living near a farm which she liked to visit.

Extract 12.10 Eve *farms*

```
01 || my MATE'S GRAN ||
02 || had a caraVAN ||
03 || in the FARM || ...
04 || there was a FARM ||
05 || on the END of the STREET || ...
06 || i WANTed to be at the BACK of the HOUSE ||
07 || cos I missed the FARM ||
        FARM...FARM...FARM...
```

01-03, 04-05, and 06-7 come from different parts of the recording, but they occur within twenty seconds of each other. The last line gives Eve's three versions of *farm* side-by-side.

The second version of *farm* (04) is the broadest |fæm|, the third (07) is closest to RP |fɑːm|, and the first version is somewhere in between. Why does Eve's accent vary like this, in the space of twenty seconds? It could be that Eve is making unmotivated, unconscious choices from her accent range, somewhere on a broad-accent/moderate-accent continuum.

Alternatively, it could be that the variations in accent are not random – that they correlate with different moments in Eve's story where the focus of identification shifts from the re-creation of the childhood memory (the *farm* in 03 and 04) to explaining the significance of her choice of room directly to her

RP-speaking interviewer (the *farm* in 07). So for *farm* in 03 and 04, Eve's focus on re-creating the child-hood memory results in a broad accent choice, but for *farm* in 07, her focus on explaining to an outsider results in a moderate accent choice. Whatever the case, it is very common for people with broad and moderate versions of their regional accent to display these shifts in pronunciation.

12.7 Trends in accent change: are regional accents becoming weaker?

Some of the evidence in this chapter seems to indicate that regional accents are becoming less broad, and consequently more moderate. We have heard Sonia's Geordie accent shifting between her broad accent and her more RP-like moderate telephone voice, and we have heard Eve's Leeds accent making dramatic steps in the space of twenty seconds from her broad accent towards RP. Does this mean that regional accents will disappear? The evidence concerning national and regional changes is mixed. However, the consensus seems to be that accents are definitely not going to disappear: it is not the case that regional accents will weaken to the point of disappearing, or be replaced by Estuary English.

Although accents will not disappear, they are changing through processes prompted by social pressures of different kinds. These pressures vary from personal views of identity – not wanting to sound like the older generation, wanting to sound like the group of people who you identify with – through to the influences of modern living, such as job mobility and contact with other social groups.

It is likely, however, that certain versions of accents will disappear, simply because accents do change over time and people do not live forever. So the broadest versions of accents which are associated with older working-class men (labelled by McMahon et al, 2007 as 'traditional') will disappear, to be replaced by modern versions of the accent. These modern versions are likely to be shaped by the features of the nearest influential urban centre.

The influence of urban centres on each other will vary, according to whether they are perceived as having a friendly relationship, as in the case of Durham and Newcastle (cf. Kerswill 2003, quoting the work of Llamas & Watt, 2010), or in an antagonistic relationship, as in the case of Liverpool and Manchester, where, although geographically very close, the accents seem set to remain distinct:

> [they] are only half an hour apart but the accents remain rock solid ... there must be a lot of commuting between the two cities but they are not merging. (Paul Kerswill, quoted in Tobin & Leake, 2010)

The key to the survival of these accents is people's desire to preserve their identity by asserting through their accent 'I wish to be identified with this group, not any other group, and particularly not that nearby group just over there'.

12.8   Prejudices: a personal note

I believe everyone has prejudices about accents, although they may not express them in public. I occasionally believe myself to be free of prejudices about accents, but then I catch myself making judgements, and having private emotional reactions on hearing someone speak with a particular type of voice or accent. I do not believe these reactions will ever go away, but I do think it is important to recognise that they are present, and to keep them under control.

Every accent – including RP – excites prejudicial reactions. Although often associated with social advantage and a good educational background, RP is also regarded as less friendly, and it is a mark of a particular type of upper-class background which can be a disadvantage anywhere in Britain and Ireland where there is a strong social identity associated with the local accent. For example, Stuart-Smith (1999: 204) reports that 'RP has little status in Glasgow, and is regarded with hostility in some quarters', and Jacob Rees-Mogg campaigning as a Conservative politician in Fife in Scotland provides evidence of similar hostility:

> I gradually realised that whatever I happened to be speaking about, the number of voters
> in my favour dropped as soon as I opened my mouth (Rees-Mogg, 2012)

All accents will attract irritation, amusement or any other reaction in some group of people, somewhere. L2 speakers who have learned perfect RP may be admired and praised, but amidst the admiration from the L1 speakers, there may be those who think 'They speak better than I do, that sounds too pure to be true!'

12.9   Summary and what's next

Accents are an important part of our identity, but they are not an invariable feature. We can consciously change them, or they may change without our being aware of it, or we may add another accent to our repertoire – such as a 'telephone voice'. We have seen that there continue to exist strong social pressures from parents, teachers and peer-groups for young people to moderate their broad accents (Black

Country, Liverpool) in order to become successful in their school and working lives. However, as we heard from Brian and Chamonix, such pressures are often resented and resisted.

We, as individuals can present ourselves differently according to whom we are speaking, the context in which we are speaking and the purposes of our speech. We show different aspects of our identity, and our accents may vary when we are in the workplace, when speaking to a close friend, when speaking to a distant relative, or when travelling overseas. Circumstances can occur where someone's accent can vary from moment to moment even with the same speaker in the same context, as we have heard in the accents of Sonia (*seventy*) and Eve (*farm*).

Every accent, including the reference and upper class model (RP), is guaranteed to have one or more social groups within Britain and Ireland that have some kind of prejudice towards it. However, it must be stressed that all the accents that we have seen, and those we have not (and there are many more), are legitimate ways of speaking English. Each one of them brings its own set of colours and flavours to the sound substance of English that we have to prepare our students for. Of course we cannot provide specific preparation for all the accents of Britain and Ireland (or elsewhere), but we do need to prepare them generally for their listening encounters with the wide range of accents of English that are not a close fit to the reference models, such as RP, which are used in teaching.

In the next chapter we will turn our attention to a sample of accents of North America.

12.10 Further reading

The classic publication on accents of Britain and Ireland is Wells (1982, volume 2) and he also has a section, in volume 1, on why accents differ (1982: 93-116). The Soundcomparisons site from the University of Edinburgh is a useful collection of accents from the UK (McMahon et al 2007). The BBC Voices project (BBC, 2005a) of accents of the United Kingdom (note that this does not include the Republic of Ireland) is also extremely useful and is associated with a book by Elmes (2005). The BBC Voices project is now under the care of British Library and is available online at the URL given in the references. Lastly, the personal view of prejudice which was briefly discussed in 12.8 above is given more extensive treatment in Cauldwell (2013).

12.11   Language awareness activities

Activity 12.1: Prepare and perform

Look back at, and listen to Karen from Wales. Using the information about her accent, prepare two versions of the following units: one in her accent and one in RP. Perform them both to a friend, colleague, or fellow teacher.

```
01 || BUT at the TIME ||
02 || the HOUSE they WANTed ||
03 || ...was... ||
04 || too ANTiquated ||
```

Activity 12.2: Listen and analyse   Answer key page 240

Listen to three speech units spoken by John from Manchester. What differences do you notice between his accent and RP?

Extract 12.11 Manchester – John

```
01 || HAVing the CHANCE to DO things ||
02 || you WOULDn't be ABle to DO ||
03 || OFten ARMy things ||
```

13   Accents of North America

In this chapter we will hear a sample of some of the different accents which can be heard in North America. We will start with an accent from Toronto in Canada, and then proceed south to the USA to hear accents from New York City, Richmond Virginia, Nashville Tennessee, and Houston Texas. We will finish by hearing an African-American Vernacular English accent. As in Britain and Ireland, differences in accent excite strong reactions of allegiance and prejudice. Jess, whose voice we heard in Chapter 11, was born and brought up in New Mexico, but moved to Texas as a young teenager. We might expect that her accent would contain elements of the Texan accent, but it does not. She explains why:

> Growing up I kind of had all the stereotypical prejudice against Texans, so when I moved to Texas and all my friends were like Oh my God! I can't believe you're really moving to Texas! So I think it was partly that I was rejecting a little bit of the accent in a way that was kind of saying No I don't want to be like a Texan, I am still New Mexican ... I'm just living here for the time being.

Jess's words indicate that social forces of identification and distancing apply to accents in North America just as they do in Britain and Ireland. Although North America does not have the same degree of sensitivity to social class that Britain and Ireland have, it still has strongly demarked social stratification, and there are correlations between the social strata that people inhabit and the accents they have. However, as with the accents we heard in Chapter 12, the relationships between accent, location and social group is not a simple one.

As we proceed, we will compare the accents we hear with General American (GenAm), which we will define as that accent of American English which is given in pronunciation dictionaries such as Wells (2008) and Roach et al. (2011). Our journey starts in Toronto, Canada's largest city.

13.1   Canada – Toronto

One of the stereotypes of the Canadian accent is that *out and about* is heard as *oot and aboot* (Wells, 1982: 494), where the diphthong of the GenAm |aʊ| is realised as |ʌʊ| and is heard by many as if it were a realisation of |uː|. In Extract 13.1 we will hear the word *about* in a recording by Nick from Toronto. He is a student in his early twenties. In his late teens he drove across Canada with a group of friends – a trip of 4,500 kilometers. He talks about how long it took for him to drive from Toronto in the East to the westernmost point of Canada, Tofino on Vancouver Island.

Extract 13.1 Canada, Toronto – Nick *about*

```
01 || UH ||
02 || aBOUT ||
03 || SEVen to ten DAYS ||
      aBOUT...aBOUT
```
The last line shows (in order) the GenAm citation form of *about* side-by-side with Nick's version.

Nick's *about* is close to |əbʌʊt| rather than GenAm's |əbaʊt|. And because Nick's pronunciation of |aʊ| lies outside the standard set of GenAm realisations, and because it is strongly associated with a separate social group (Canadians), it is caricatured by those who like to tease Canadians. The technical term for this type of pronunciation is **Canadian raising,** but it is not exclusive to Canada (cf. Labov et al 2006: 221).

Before we leave Nick, we should hear his pronunciation of *Toronto* in Extract 13.2.

Extract 13.2 Canada, Toronto – Nick *Toronto*

```
|| we STARTed in toRONto ||
      toRONto...toRONto
```
The last line shows (in order) the GenAm citation form of *Toronto* side-by-side with Nick's version.

There are two things to notice: the first and second syllables of *Toronto* merge to become one – the schwa of the first syllable *Tor* is elided, resulting in the consonant cluster |tr|, followed by the vowel sound |ɒ|, and secondly we have elision of |t| after |n| resulting in |trɒnoʊ|. This type of elision is a common feature in North American accents which we will return to below.

13.2   New York

About 800 kilometres car-ride south-east of Toronto lies New York City. As with the Canadian accent, there are popular stereotypes of the New York accent, sometimes termed 'Brooklynese'. The stereotype has the vowels of *thirty-third nurse* as *toity-toid noiss* (the |ɜ| is often realised as |ɜɪ|), which William Labov has described as 'the most well known example of a stigmatized New York City trait'. (Labov, 1966: 337, quoted in Wells, 1982: 508–509).

The stereotype has a plosive |t| rather than GenAm's fricative |θ| and a closing diphthong |ɜɪ| rather than the rhotic vowel |ɝ|, resulting in |tɜɪt̬i| rather than GenAm |θɝt̬i|. This feature has an interesting history. Labov found that for those born in the two decades before the end of World War II, its use 'receded down the social scale', and Wells (Wells, 1982: 509) commented that 'it is now a highly stigmatized mark of lower-class speech'.

Bruce is a teacher in his fifties from New York, whose accent does not have this pronunciation of *thirty*. He tells an anecdote about mistaken identity, beginning – in Extract 13.3 – by setting the anecdote in time.

Extract 13.3 New York – Bruce *thirty*

```
|| about THIRTy years aGO ||
      THIRTy...THIRTy
```
The last line shows (in order) the GenAm citation form of *thirty* side-by-side with Bruce's version.

His version of *thirty* is very close to GenAm, with theta |θ|, a rhotic vowel |ɝ| and an alveolar tap |ɾ| replacing the |t| (cf. Section 11.4) resulting in |θɝɾi|. Wells comments 'For New Yorkers born since about 1950, this r-coloured variant is the usual one'. (ibid: 508).

However, the New York accent is generally thought to be non-rhotic – Labov et al state that 'r-lessness persists' (2006: 236) – and, as we hear other extracts from Bruce, we will hear non-rhotic mixed in with rhotic vowels. First, though, we will hear another feature of his New York accent, in Extract 13.4, as he explains another strand of the anecdote, which is that he loves to sing songs, and particularly showtunes.

Extract 13.4 New York – Bruce *broadway showtunes*

```
|| BROADway SHOWtunes ||
      BROADway...BROADway
```
The last line shows (in order) the GenAm citation form of *Broadway* side-by-side with Bruce's version.

Bruce's *Broadway* features a trait which is found in New York and in much of the Eastern US. He pronounces the vowel in the first syllable of *Broadway* as |ɔː| rather than |ɑː| resulting in |brɔːdweɪ| rather than |brɑːdweɪ|. Bruce's accent, unlike many that of many Americans has both |ɔː| and |ɑː| whereas many Americans have merged these two phonemes into one, |ɑː|. This is the 'cot-caught merger' (Labov et al, 2006: 58–67) which we encountered in Chapter 11.

As a result of this merger, for many GenAm speakers the vowels in the first syllables of *college* and *Broadway* are the same, |ɑː|. However, as we can hear in Extract 13.5, Bruce's versions of these words have different vowels: |ɑː| and |ɔː| respectively.

Extract 13.5 New York – Bruce *college* and *broadway*

```
01 || and SHE was going to COLLege ||
02 || BROADway SHOWtunes ||
      COLLege... COLLege
      BROADway...BROADway
```

The last two lines show (in order) the GenAm citation form of *College* and *Broadway* side-by-side with Bruce's versions.

Thus Bruce, like many New Yorkers, and many other people living in the east of the USA, produces distinct |ɔː| and |ɑː|.

Another important strand of Bruce's anecdote is that he likes to burst into song whenever an opportunity arises and, as we can hear in Extract 13.6, he has characteristic New York feature in his pronunciation of the word *songs*.

Extract 13.6 New York – Bruce *songs*

```
|| i REALLy LIKE to SING SONGS ||
      SONGS...SONGS
```

The last line shows (in order) the GenAm citation form of *songs* side-by-side with Bruce's version.

Bruce's *songs* is not the GenAm version |sɑːŋz|. He has a longer, diphthongal vowel |sɔəŋz|, which is highly characteristic of a New York accent.

Another characteristic of the New York accent is the pronunciation of the set of words that have |ɛə| for |æ|, as in the words *bad* and *after* (Wells, 1982: 510–512). We can hear this feature in *afterwards* in Extract 13.7 when Bruce has just sung a song ('Mammy, Mammy, I'd walk a million miles ...').

Extract 13.7 New York – Bruce *afterwards*

```
|| iMMEDiately AFTerwards ||
      AFTerwards...AFTerwards
```

The last line shows (in order) the GenAm citation form of *afterwards* side-by-side with Bruce's version.

As you can hear, Bruce's version starts closer to |ε| than |æ|. This kind of pronunciation occurs in a number of different regions in the US, as we will hear later. While we are focusing on *afterwards* we should note that there is no rhoticity where we might expect two instances of it – in the second and third syllables. In fact Bruce says |ɛftəwədz| rather than |æftɚwɚdz|.

There is another example of r-lessness in Bruce's *California*. In Extract 13.8 he explains that a friend of his is studying at university.

Extract 13.8 New York – Bruce *California*

```
01 || at the UNiversity of caliFORnia ||
02 || in UH ||
03 || DAVis ||
04 || DAVis CALiFORnia ||
      CALiFORNia...CALiFORNia
```

The last line shows (in order) the GenAm citation form of *California* side-by-side with Bruce's version.

His *California* is clearly r-less, it is |kæl.əˈfɔə.njə| rather than GenAm |kæl.əˈfɔr.njə|.

Bruce's accent, in common with many New Yorkers, produces a distinct |g| after |ŋ| giving clusters of |ŋg| in words such as *singing*. In Extract 13.9 we can hear this in *young* which is |jʌŋg|.

Extract 13.9 New York – Bruce *young lady*

```
|| a young LADy named ELLen ||
      young LADy...young LADy
```

The last line shows (in order) the GenAm citation form of *young lady* side-by-side with Bruce's version.

Bruce's *young lady* could be rendered jokingly into *young gladey* (where *gladey* is a nonsense word) and indeed Wikipedia ('NewYork Dialect' accessed 27/05/2010) reports that 'This variant is another salient stereotype of the New York accent and is commonly mocked with "Long Island" being pronounced *Lawn Guyland*.

Another, but less well-known, New York accent feature affecting consonants can be heard in Extract 13.10 with the pronunciation of |d| in *including*.

Extract 13.10 New York – Bruce *including*

```
|| inCLUDing the OWner ||
|| of the HOUSE ||
    inCLUDing...inCLUDing
```

The last line shows (in order) the GenAm citation form of *including* side-by-side with Bruce's version.

The |d| in *including* is close to |ð| thus |ɪŋkluðɪŋ| rather than GenAm |ɪŋkludɪŋ|.

13.3   Virginia

Driving south from New York for about 560 kilometres, through New Jersey, across the top of Delaware, then through Maryland and into Virginia we get to Richmond, Virginia. This is the hometown of Ashley. When Ashley went to college she thought she might study a modern living language, Spanish. But a number of things conspired to change her mind, the first of which was a test of her ability to study a foreign language, in which she did not do well. Extract 13.11 contains two speech units from different parts of her recording.

Extract 13.11 Virginia – Ashley *foreign* and *horribly*

```
01 || take a FOReign language aSSESSment test ||
02 || i did RATHer HORRibly ||
      FOReign...FOReign
      HORRibly...HORRibly
```

The last two lines show (in order) the GenAm citation form of *foreign* and *horribly* side-by-side with Ashley's versions.

Like Bruce in New York, and Catherine from Texas (see Section 13.4 below), Ashley's accent features the |ɔː| sound, which we can hear in |fɔːr ən| and |hɔːr əbl̩i|. Her rhoticity is very strong in these words.

In Extract 13.12, Ashley goes on to explain how the study of Latin has gained prestige over time and, as she does so, she uses the word *years*.

Extract 13.12 Virginia – Ashley *years*

```
01 || FOUR YEARS ||
02 || TWENTy YEARS ||
      YEARS...YEARS
```

The last line shows (in order) the GenAm citation form of *years* side-by-side with Ashley's version.

These are two striking examples of rhotic *years* in which the rhoticity continues over |s|, giving us |ʂ|, resulting in |jɪərʂ|. – the little hook on the bottom of the symbol tells us that the |ʂ| is r-coloured. We should also notice that *twenty* sounds like *twenny* – a topic we will come to in Section 13.4 below. Similar rhoticity can be heard in Extract 13.13, as Ashley describes one of the advantages of studying Latin in high school.

Extract 13.13 Virginia – Ashley *scores*

```
|| imPROVE your s a T SCORES ||
     SCORES...SCORES
```

The last line shows (in order) the GenAm citation form of *scores* side-by-side with Ashley's version.

The monosyllabic *scores* sounds almost bisyllabic (two syllables) as Ashley says it with level tone and lengthens it. Indeed Wells (1982: 546) describes such words ('vowel plus |r|') as varisyllabic. It is often difficult to distinguish between a centering diphthong (one that ends in schwa |ə|) and a bisyllabic sequence of vowel plus |ə-ɚ|. The accents of the Southern USA have varied in the extent to which they were rhotic both from time to time, and from social group to social group, cf. Wells (1982: 542) and Labov et al (2006: 47).

As she talks about her experience of the study of Latin in Extract 13.14, Ashley says both the word *seventies* and *twenty* with an elided |t|.

Extract 13.14 Virginia – Ashley *seventies* and *twenty*

```
01 || the SEVenties ||
02 || TWENTy YEARS ||
     SEVenties...SEVenties
     TWENTy...TWENTy
```

These two units are from different parts of Ashley's recording. The last two lines show (in order) the GenAm citation form of *seventies* and *twenty* side-by-side with Ashley's versions.

You will hear that she elides |t| in the middle of each of these words, so they become *sevennies* and *twenny*. Although this kind of elision is characteristic of her accent, it is also a feature of many accents of North America.

In Extract 13.15 Ashley describes the moment when she made the decision to try Spanish.

Accents, Identity and Emotion in Speech

Extract 13.15 Virginia – Ashley *new*

```
01 || a comPLETEly NEW LANGuage ||
02 || AND ||
03 || i CHOSE SPANish ||
    NEW ... NEW
```

The last line shows (in order) the GenAm citation form of *new* side-by-side with Ashley's version.

In 01 *new* occurs with yod |nju| not without it |nu|, as we might expect from GenAm. Although this may be as a result of the fact that Ashley was recorded in England, it is also the case that (as Wells, 1982: 489 reports) there are parts of North America where pronunciation with yod is encouraged by teachers.

Before we leave Ashley there is one other feature we should notice. In Extract 13.16 Ashley talks about Latin.

Extract 13.16 Virginia – Ashley – creak

```
01 || it's an enJOYable LANGuage to LEARN i think ||
02 || it's an enJOYable LANGuage to LEARN i think ||
```

Unit 01 is Ashley's original; unit 02 was recorded for this chapter.

Ashley's last four words *to learn I think* are spoken very low in her vocal range, and they feature a lot of creak (a low slow vibration of the vocal cords, cf. Henton & Bladon, 1988). This creak, which is becoming an increasingly common feature of female speech in many accents of the USA, indeed around the world, much to the annoyance of some people, who regard it as an unfeminine trait.

After her bad experience in Spanish class, Ashley had a negative reason for choosing Latin over Spanish. But she reasoned that if she studied Latin at college, and chose a career as a Latin teacher, then she could take school trips to Italy every year – a positive reason. In Extract 13.17 she tells us that this is what helped her finally make her decision (where *nailed* means *decided*).

Extract 13.17 Virginia – Ashley *so*

```
01 || SO ||
02 || that was what NAILED it ||
03 || for ME ||
    SO...SO
```

The last line shows (in order) the GenAm citation form of *so* side-by-side with Ashley's version.

Ashley's *so* sounds, through the creak, close to upper-class RP |səʊ| rather than GenAm |soʊ|. We will hear again this surprisingly RP-like nature of some of the features of southern accents when we listen to Jeffrey from Tennessee.

13.4   Tennessee

About 950 kilometres drive west (and a little bit south) of Richmond Virginia is Nashville Tennessee, where Jeffrey worked for a while in a very large hotel. In Extract 13.18 Jeffrey describes the hotel.

Extract 13.18 Tennessee – Jeffrey *hotel*

```
01 || the HO TEL ||
02 || had aBOUT ||
03 || i THINK it's THREE thousand ROOMS ||
        HO TEL...hoTEL
```

The last line shows (in order) the GenAm citation form of *hotel* side-by-side with Jeffrey's version.

Jeffrey gives *hotel* two prominences and the first prominence features a noteworthy southern feature, which we heard (but not quite so clearly) in Ashley's accent. We hear something very close to RP |həʊtel| rather than the expected GenAm |hoʊtel|.

Because it was such a large hotel, and because it was a popular location for conferences, there were some days when the hotel front desk was really busy, as we can hear in Extract 13.19.

Extract 13.19 Tennessee – Jeffrey *twenty, hundreds* and *five*

```
01 || TWENty FIVE HUNdred or ||
02 || TWO thousand were CHECKing OUT ||
03 || and then TWENty five hundred or TWO thousand ||
04 || were CHECKing IN ||
        TWENty...TWENty
        HUNdred...HUNdred...HUNdred
        FIVE...FIVE
```

The last three lines show (in order) the GenAm citation form of *twenty, hundred* and *five* side-by-side with Jeffrey's versions.

Jeffrey, like Ashley, elides the second |t| of *twenty*. However, unlike Ashley, he pronunces the initial vowel as |ɪ| not |e| resulting in something close to |twɪni| – *twinny*, not |tweni|.The words *hundred* occurs in both 01 and 03. They sound close to *hundered* (01) and *hunner* (03), with the final |r| segment being lengthened as the realisation of *or*. Thus *hundred or* becomes something close to *hunnerer*. Jeffrey's vowel in *five* is close to a monophthong |fɑːv| rather than the GenAm diphthong |faɪv|. This is very characteristic of southern accents, but we will hear an even clearer version if we travel further south, to Texas.

13.5   Texas

About 1200 kilometers drive south-west of Nashville we come to Houston Texas. Catherine, like Ashley, is a lover of languages. She describes being 'bowled over' by her first experience of learning French and making the decision (as a young student) to leave Houston and go to Paris to study. We heard *five* from Jeffrey, but Catherine gives us an even clearer monophthongal version of this vowel as she describes her family background in Extract 13.20.

Extract 13.20 Texas – Catherine *five*

```
|| i've GOT FIVE BROthers ||
      FIVE...FIVE
```

The last line shows (in order) the GenAm citation form of *five* side-by-side with Catherine's version.

Catherine has |fɑːv| compared to GenAm |faɪv| and this is one of the characteristics of southern accents that was picked up and made into a stereotype 'nice white rice' |nɑːs wɑːt rɑːs| Wells (1982: 537–538). Labov et al (2006: 241) refer to this as 'glide deletion'. Decades ago, the monophthong used to be a associated with a lack of education, but it has become standard pronunciation in the south amongst all groups.

Unlike Ashley, who had a bad first (and last) experience with a modern foreign language, Catherine had a very memorable first encounter with French, as she describes in Extract 13.21.

Extract 13.21 Texas – Catherine *started* and *French*

```
01 || in my SECond YEAR ||
02 || i STARTed FRENCH ||
03 || and i was SO BLOWN aWAY by it || ...
04 || were DOing a deGREE in FRENCH ||
```

```
FRENCH...FRENCH...FRENCH
```

Units 01-03 occur together in Catherine's recording, but 04 occurs separately.

The last line shows (in order) the GenAm citation form of *French* side-by-side with Catherine's versions.

Catherine's two instances of *French* are close to |frɪntʃ| – *frintch* – particularly the version in unit 04. Although characteristic of her accent, this merger between |ɪ| and |e| is spreading amongst many accents of the USA (we heard it above in Jeffrey's *twinny*), resulting in the words *pin* and *pen* being perfect rhymes for many speakers.

Historically, southern accents were described as non-rhotic but this description seems always to have been controversial and partial (cf. Wells, 1982: 542–5). However, Catherine's accent, like those of many people in the South, is rhotic, as we can hear in Extract 13.22.

Extract 13.22 Texas – Catherine *start*, *modern* and *foreign*

```
01 || i HAD to START ||
02 || a MODern foreign LANguage ||
     FOReign...FOReign
```

The last line shows (in order) the GenAm citation form of *foreign* side-by-side with Catherine's version.

Catherine's *start* is clearly rhotic – |stɑːrt| rather than |stɑːt|. In unit 02 you can hear that like Ashley's, Catherine's accent does not feature the 'cot-caught merger' (cf. 11.3.2). Catherine's *modern* has |ɑː| in the first syllable thus |mɑːdən|, and *foreign* has |ɔː| in its first syllable. In fact non-prominent *foreign* is spoken so fast that it is virtually monosyllabic: |fɔːrn| rather than |ˈfɔːrən|.

Like both Ashley and Jeffrey, Catherine's accent features an RP-like vowel in words such as *go*, as we can hear in Extract 13.23.

Extract 13.23 Texas – Catherine *go* and *to*

```
|| that i was going to GO to FRANCE ||
     GO...GO
     FRANCE
```

The last two lines show (in order) the GenAm citation form of *go* and *France* side-by-side with Catherine's versions.

Her pronunciation of *France* has a centering off-glide |fræəns| rather than GenAm |fræns|. And finally, like Jeffrey and Ashley, Catherine also drops the |t| when it is preceded by |n| and followed by a vowel, as in Extract 13.24.

Extract 13.24 Texas – Catherine *wanted* and *plenty*

```
01 || i WANTed TO ||
02 || there were PLENty of other people aROUND ||
      WANTed...WANTed
      PLENty...PLENty
```

These two units are from different parts of Catherine's recording.
The last two lines show (in order) the GenAm citation forms of *wanted* and *plenty* side-by-side with Catherine's versions.

What we hear in these two words can be represented in folk spelling as *wannid* and *plenny*.

For our final accent we are going to travel back north-east to Philadelphia in the state of Pennsylvania – a trip of some 2,400 kilometres.

13.6   African American Vernacular English (AAVE)

Tim was born in Philadelphia, and we will hear him speaking in different accents which he uses with different groups and in different geographical areas of the USA. His recording comes from Kirkpatrick (2007). In Extract 13.25 Tim talks about his family background – his mother grew up in Philadelphia but her parents (Tim's maternal grandparents) are from elsewhere.

Extract 13.25 AAVE – Tim *England*

```
|| but HER PARents ||
|| grew UP in new ENGland ||
      PARents...PARents
      ENGland...ENGland
```

The last two lines show (in order) the GenAm citation forms of *parents* and *England* side-by-side with Tim's versions.

There are two cluster simplifications here (cf. Wells 1982: 558): the |nts| of *parents* is simplified to |ns|, and the final |d| of *England* is dropped to give |ɪŋglən| (folk spelling *Englan*).

We can hear this feature again when Tim speaks affectionately of his father, who he describes as a Southerner from North Carolina (about 600 kilometres drive south). Tim talks about his father's use of the word *hand*:

> He still holds very much the Southern cadence of his speech I always laugh at him because one of his little expressions you know before we're getting ready for dinner is 'er Tim you wash your hand?' making hand ... singular ... is one of my favourite little things that he does.

Extract 13.26 gives us Tim's version of his father's speech.

Extract 13.26 AAVE – Tim *hand*

```
|| you WASH your HAND ||
     HAND...HAND
```

The last line shows (in order) the GenAm citation form of *hand* side-by-side with Tim's version.

Tim focuses our attention on the singular form of *hand*, but it is also interesting to note that Tim's imitation of his father features elision of |d| in a simplification of the cluster |nd| in hand |hæn|, just as we heard when he was speaking of his mother's background in New England.

Tim illustrates the difference between Philadelphia AAVE and the Southern AAVE of his father's side of the family by giving three different ways of saying *Are you going to go to the store*, which we can hear in Extract 13.27. There are lexical differences (*bounce to, finnin to* and *roll to*), but we will focus on his pronunciation of the word *store*, which occurs three times.

Extract 13.27 AAVE – Tim *store*

```
01 || are you GOing to GO to the STORE ||
02 || you READy to BOUNCE to the STORE ||
03 || you FINNin to ROLL to the STORE ||
       STORE...STORE...STORE
```

The last line shows Tim's three versions of *store* side-by-side.

In 01, the GenAm *store* is rhotic to the point of being almost disyllabic |stɔːr|. In 02 Tim's Philadelphia version of *store* retains the rhoticity, but it is much less obvious. However, in 03 his southern version of AAVE *store* is not only non-rhotic, but it ends with a vocalised segment, so that *store* becomes |stəuː| (folk spelling *stow*). One of the themes of Tim's recording (Kirkpatrick, 2007) is that, in his experience,

AAVE varies from region to region. He is thus somewhat in disagreement with Labov et al (2006: 297–301) who make the claim that there is 'relatively little regional differentiation' in AAVE.

13.7 Summary and what's next

In this chapter we have seen and heard six accents from North America, from Toronto in Canada to Texas in the southern United States. This has been a sample which, although it has travelled from North to South, has stayed on the eastern side of North America. We have not covered the Mid-West, the Midlands, the Plains or any West Coast accents in the USA, and we have only had one sample from Canada. There are, however, many resources on the internet (cf. Further reading) to help you fill this gap.

We have seen that although AmE is differentiated from BrE (cf. Chapter 11) by rhoticity and by yod-lessness (amongst other things), there are accents within the USA which are non-rhotic, or which feature yod. For example, Bruce's New York accent gave us some non-rhotic soundshapes (e.g. *California*), and Ashley's Virginian accent gave us an example of *new* with yod. Thus the features that differentiate the two major reference models in language teaching, RP and GenAm, do not differentiate all British/ Irish accents from all North American accents. There is an overlapping of features.

As we discussed in Section 12.3, many people are multi-accented – their accent varies according to the group of people they are interacting with. Tim provided examples of several versions of his American accent, including different versions of AAVE, that he would use in different circumstances. Just as we saw with Britain and Ireland, accents attract allegiance and prejudice in varying amounts. Although the USA regards itself as a class-less society, not having the social class systems of the United Kingdom, there is nevertheless a relationship between social stratification and accent which results in certain accents (such as New York) being stigmatised.

In the following chapter we will look at some accents of Global English, of people whose first language is not English.

13.8 Further reading

This survey of accents of North America has necessarily been very brief and there are many omissions. The contents page of the International Dialects of English Archive at the University of Kansas (IDEA, 1997) will give an idea of how many accents there are. One notable omission in this survey is

Hispanic English – the English of those millions of Americans whose accent is influenced by Spanish as a first language. However, in Chapter 14 you can hear Hector from Venezuela whose accent is influenced by his Spanish L1 background, and who has spent some time in the USA. Some of America's favourite sporting stars have such accents: Yadier Molina (born in Puerto Rico) and Albert Pujols (born in the Dominican Republic) are star baseball players at the time of writing, and their accents are influenced by their Spanish L1. The key publications to read are Wells (1982: 467-559) and Labov et al. (2006).

AAVE is a fascinating area of study, and attitudes towards it both by its speakers, and by those who do not speak it, are complex and difficult to summarise. There are resources on the web to explore, particularly at the Public Broadcasting Service website (PBS, 2012). Another resource is Lippi-Green (1997, Chapter 9), which contains illustrations of the complexity of attitudes towards AAVE, as illustrated in the media, from both European Americans and African Americans.

13.9   Language awareness activities

Activity 13.1: Prepare and perform

Listen to Bruce's New York accent in 13.2, then practise saying the following words in both GenAm and New York accents. Symbols are given to guide you.

		GenAm	New York
1	Hong Kong	ǀhɑːŋ kɑːŋǀ	ǀhɔən kɔəŋgǀ
2	young	ǀjʌŋǀ	ǀjʌŋgǀ
3	fog	ǀfɑːgǀ	ǀfɔəgǀ
4	foghorns	ǀfɑːghɔːrnzǀ	ǀfɔəghɔːənzǀ
5	afterwards	ǀæftɚwɚdzǀ	ǀɛftəwɔdzǀ
6	law	ǀlɑːǀ	ǀlɔəǀ
7	including	ǀɪŋkluːdɪŋǀ	ǀɪŋkluðɪŋǀ

Now prepare a performance of the text below in two versions, the first in a GenAm accent, the second in a New York accent. Perform them to a friend, colleague or fellow teacher.

1) I've been to **Hong Kong** five times! (2) The first when I was a **young** lad, in the navy, some twenty years ago. (3) Unusually there was **fog** as we came into the harbour. (4) So I remember hearing **foghorns** as we dropped anchor. (5) **Afterwards**, I left the navy. (6) I studied **law**, and visited on business. (7) I'd like to go as a tourist, **including** my family in the trip.

Activity 13.2: Listen and analyse   Answer key page 241

Look up and listen to the GenAm pronunciations of the following words in any pronunciation dictionary:

anybody, decided, go, I, mastery, myself, telling, wanted.

Then listen to Catherine speaking about learning French. Make notes on the differences in pronunciation that you hear between the dictionary pronunciations and what Catherine says in her Texan accent.

Extract 13.28 Texas – Catherine *for myself ... to France*

```
01 || FOR mySELF ||
02 || i WANTed TO ||
03 || UM ||
03 || i WANTed to feel CONfident ||
04 || about my MAStery of FRENCH ||
05 || so I deCIDed ||
06 || withOUT telling Anybody ELSE ||
07 || that I was going to GO to FRANCE ||
```

14   Accents of Global English

Globally there are far more L2 (second language) speakers of English than L1 speakers – the estimated figures are 1.4 billion and 400 million respectively (Jenkins, 2000:1; Crystal, 2003:67-8; Walker, 2010:2-4). The number of L2 accents of Global English is therefore huge, and we cannot possibly cover them all. In this chapter we will look at five of them: from Europe, Africa and from South America. All of the voices you will hear are professional people who operate in English and whose voices retain the accents – in varying degrees – of their first languages. Each voice will be commented upon from three perspectives: **the window on speech** perspective; an **accent reduction** perspective and the **English as a Lingua Franca** (**ELF**) perspective. The comments from the window on speech perspective are included to demonstrate the usefulness of the framework for the presentation and analysis of L2 speaker speech. The accent reduction perspective is one where an expert in pronunciation helps speakers eradicate, as far as it is possible to do so, those features of their pronunciation that do not match a given reference model such as Received Pronunciation (RP) or General American (GenAm). The reference model used below is RP. The ELF perspective is one which recognises that most interactions in English around the globe take place between L2 speakers of English, with no L1 speakers present. The ELF perspective therefore holds that any internationally intelligible L2 accent is a legitimate accent.

We begin and end the chapter with comments from Lydia, an L2 speaker of English who teaches English in Taiwan. Lydia's comments illustrate two things. First, the types of prejudice that people such as herself are the victims of, both when they visit an L1 speaker environment (in Lydia's case the USA) and back home within their own profession. Second, the reassurance that Lydia gains from feeling that she, and other L2 speakers, are supported by the central tenets of the ELF movement. These tenets include:

- most interactions in English are between L2 speakers in circumstances where no L1 speakers are present
- L1-speaker norms and notions of correctness are therefore no longer appropriate for these circumstances
- English is therefore no longer the property of its L1 speakers
- there is an emerging lingua franca core which can act as a syllabus for pronunciation for international communication

- native speakers need to respect the norms of ELF when they operate in ELF settings
- an L2 accent is a marker of identity and is as valid as any L1 accent of English
- the benchmark of acceptability for an L2 accent of English is that it should be internationally intelligible.

14.1   Lydia's feelings about her own accent

Lydia is an L2 speaker of English and a teacher of English from Taiwan. She visited the USA in order to study for professional qualifications. While there, she wrote about peoples' reactions to her accent:

> I always think of myself as very smart, but ... sometimes I feel frustrated because I look stupid here, just because I can't speak ... fluently or ... or speak with ... preferred ... pronunciation ... sometimes people are just impatient. (Golombek & Jordan, 2005: 524)

The way people react to Lydia's accent conflicts with, and damages, her sense of her own identity. She believes she is intelligent, but people treat her as if she is stupid because she speaks with an L2 accent, and this (of course) makes her feel bad. As Golombek and Jordan (2005) make clear, she also realises that people are reacting on the basis of race and her appearance. However, this kind of reaction to her spoken English happened not only during her visit to the USA, but also within her professional circles in Taiwan, where the myth of native-speaker superiority means that white L1 speakers of English often have a higher status than is warranted by their teaching abilities.

As we look and listen to each accent in this chapter, we will see how people in Lydia's position feel comforted and supported, thanks to the growing acceptance of the ELF perspective.

14.2   Richard from England

Before we embark on the five L2 accents of English, we will listen to an L1 speaker of English – Richard – from the point of view of an ELF practitioner who is concerned with international intelligibility. We are doing this because there is anecdotal evidence that L2 speakers understand other L2 speakers better than they do L1 speakers. Indeed, a conversation between L2 speakers may be flowing very well, until the arrival of an L1 speaker 'has ... a negative impact on the interaction' (Walker, 2010: 6). So we will subject the speech of an L1 speaker to some comments concerning intelligibility both from a Toastmaster (cf. Chapter 6) and from an ELF perspective.

Extract 14.1 is from a conversation about films. Richard in his late fifties and Olivia is in her early twenties – she can be heard giving response tokens in units 08 and 11.

Extract 14.1 England: Richard *engrossed in films*

```
01 || ...i've...||
02 || i've MADE some bad CHOIces seeing FILMS ||
03 || ...i'm very...||
04 || i'm VEry ERM ||
05 || ... i get very ... ||
06 || i get VEry ||
07 || enGROSSED in films ||
08 || YEAH ||
09 || ...they... ||
10 || they REAlly TAKE me IN ||
11 || MMM ||
12 || AND ||
13 || IF it's VIolent ||
14 || i get VEry upSET ||
```

This extract has a number of drafting phenomena (Chapter 6): repetitions of *i've* and *i'm very* and *i get very* in 01-06, a filled pause *erm* in 04 and a stepping stone *and* in 12. If this were extract was judged by the *ah counter* of a Toastmaster club (cf. Chapter 6), Richard would be chastised for these features of his speech, which would be viewed as faults.

From an ELF perspective, there are number of features of Richard's speech which differ from ELF norms. If this were a conversation involving Richard and L2 speakers (it isn't, it is an L1 conversation), an ELF practitioner might comment as follows:

> In 01 and 02 the reductions in *I have* |af| and *some* |sm̩| are not helpful for international intelligibility – it would be better if you gave these words clearer pronunciations, |aɪv| and |səm|.

You make some important words non-prominent and difficult to hear – for example *bad* in 02 seems important to your meaning, but it is non-prominent, so you would need to make it prominent for international intelligibility.

In 02 *seeing* is spoken so fast that it is virtually a single syllable, and this makes it less easy to understand. You have the L1 speaker tendency to make things sound 'stress-timed'. All these non-prominent syllables, while they may be perfectly natural in L1 speech, do not make for international intelligibility.

It is generally thought that the emerging varieties of English will be much more syllable timed, and you should consider producing fewer non-prominent syllables and fewer vowel reductions when you speak with L2 speakers.

As we can see from these comments, an ELF practitioner is likely to encourage L1 speakers to speak with greater sensitivity to the requirements of their international interlocutors, and to adjust their speech for the purposes of international intelligibility by using:

- fewer non-prominent words
- fewer reduced vowels
- less syllable compression (Wells, 2008: 173)
- more 'perceived syllable timing' (cf. Chapter 10).

Incidentally, Richard's use of the word *film* is an example of a final consonant cluster which some learners of English find difficult. ELF practitioners would recommend that – in cases of difficulty – learners add a weak vowel, and consequently an extra syllable, to make it easier to say and understand: thus |fɪl.əm| or |fɪl.ɪm| instead of |fɪlm|. This pronunciation is in fact one used by native speakers from the South of Ireland, but is regarded by some as a stigmatised version 'common ... among Southern Irish plebs' (Doel, 2006: 181). As we have mentioned before, every accent will have – somewhere – a social group which has a prejudice about it.

14.3   Andrzej from Poland: University Professor

The first L2 accent we will hear is from Andrzej – in his fifties – who was born in southern Poland. He has worked at a university in England for twenty years. In Extract 14.2 Andrzej talks about the difference between the winters in Poland of his childhood and those of more recent years.

Extract 14.2 Poland: Andrzej *but I guess ... used to be*

```
01 || BUT ||
02 || i GUESS that ||
03 || there (they?) MUST be SOME ||
04 || MINor climate changes ||
05 || beCAUSE ||
06 || WINTers in POLand THESE days ||
07 || are NOT as HARSH ||
08 || as they USED to be ||
```

14.3.1   Window on speech perspective

What does the window on speech help us hear in this extract? Units 04 and 08 are single-prominence units (cf. Chapter 3), with syllables after the tonic prominence. Unit 04 has a fall-rise tone starting on the first syllable of *minor* and continuing over the four syllables of *climate changes* |klaɪ.mət tʃeɪnʤ.ɪz|. Although you can still hear the word stress in these two words, the syllables are not highlighted in the way that the tonic prominence on *minor* is. Unit 08 has a falling tone starting on *used* which continues over the non-prominent syllables *to be*. Andrzej thus reveals himself to be an expert user of the relationship between prominent and non-prominent syllables to convey his meaning in real time. In 03 his *there* sounds close to *they*, but this is a normal variant of *there* as we will hear in Chapter 20.5.

14.3.2   Accent reduction perspective

An accent reduction specialist might focus on the following features of this extract:

In 02 the |s| of your *guess* is voiced as so you say |gɪzðət| rather than |gesðət|. It is a very nice assimilation, but not what RP speakers would do. Meanwhile your vowel in *guess* is closer to |ɪ| than to RP |e| but this is something a lot of L1 speakers do.

In 06 your *these* has an initial consonant which is closer to |d| than to |ð|; and the vowel is the short vowel |ɪ| rather than the long vowel |iː|. Thus you say |dɪz| not |ðiːz|. However, you can say this vowel – you do so nicely in with the |ɪ| in *winters*.

In 07 your initial consonant of *harsh* is close to the final sound of *loch*, so you say |xɑːrʃ| rather than RP |hɑːʃ|.

Using these observations an accent reduction specialist would aim to make Andrzej sound more RP-like, hoping perhaps to get as close to the RP model as the Polish speaker in Walker (2010: 162ff). However, with all the success that surrounds his life in England, Andrzej has no reason to change. In fact there are strong reasons why he should not change, as we shall see from the ELF perspective.

14.3.3   ELF perspective

ELF practitioners do not view L2 speaker accents as something to be corrected, rather they regard them as valid accents, and Andrzej's situation gives us an indication of what constitutes validity. He has lived and worked in an English language working and social environment (both in the UK and in international contexts) for more than twenty years, and has a successful career.

One of the really positive developments of the ELF movement is that it gives intellectual support to the idea that a person's L2 accent (as long as it is internationally intelligible) is a valid accent of English. Previously many L2 professionals operating in English, particularly L2 teachers of English such as Lydia, felt a sense of professional inadequacy or deficiency if they had not mastered (and of course most had not) perfect L1 pronunciation. This is why so many L2 teachers find this aspect of the ELF movement a very liberating concept.

14.4   Hector from Venezuela: Musician

Hector is a classical musician – in his thirties – from Venezuela and his first language is Spanish. He has studied and worked in both the USA and in the UK, where he had been living and working for five years at the time of the recording. In Extract 14.3 he speaks about the time when he got a scholarship to study at a music school in New York, only to realise that the value of the scholarship was too small for him to afford to live in New York.

Extract 14.3 Venezuela: Hector *then i ... to leave*

```
01 || then i reaLISED that ||
```

```
02 || it WASn't enough MONey ||
03 || for ME to be ABle to LIVE ||
04 || in SUCH a CITy ||
05 || Ok||
06 || and and GO to a SCHOOL ||
07 || SO ||
08 || i deCIDed to LEAVE ||
```

Richard gives a response token in unit 05.

14.4.1   Window on speech perspective

What does the transcript help us hear in this extract? In units 02 and 03 we have a pair of units which nicely demonstrate the difference between a double and triple-prominence unit: in 02 *enough* is non-prominent between the two prominences of *was* and *mon-*, whereas in 03 there is clearly a triple rhythm with prominences on *me, able,* and *live*. In 06 there is a repetition of the word *and* which is an entirely natural and normal feature of spontaneous speech, and in 07 we get a stepping stone (cf. Chapter 6) with a level tone on *so*. Thus, like Andrzej, Hector is an expert in using the features of spontaneous speech to convey his meaning in real time.

14.4.3   Accent-reduction perspective

An accent reduction specialist might focus on the following features of this extract:

In 01, your word stress in *realised* is |rɪə.ˈlaɪzd|. Such word stress is used by Irish speakers of English amongst others, but the RP form is |ˈrɪə.laɪzd|.

Again, in 01, the end of *realised* and the beginning of *that* has a sequence of three consonants |zdð|, the second of which would normally be dropped, which you do very nicely. However the |z| has become devoiced and it sounds like |s| so we get |ˈrɪəlaɪsðæt| rather than RP |ˈrɪəlaɪzðæt|.

In 02, your vowels in the second syllable of *enough* and the first syllable of *money* are not RP. They are closer to |ɒ| than to |ʌ|. You can say this |ʌ| vowel – in 04 your vowel in *such* is much closer to RP.

In 03 your vowel in *live* is long – you give us |liːv|, whereas RP has a short vowel |lɪv|.

In 04 your *city* sounds very American, not RP-like – we have |sɪɾi| rather than |sɪti|. We need to decide on which reference model you would like to work with, RP or GenAm.

In 07 your vowel in *so* makes it sound closer to *saw* |sɔː| than to RP |səʊ|.

14.4.4   ELF perspective

ELF's lingua franca core in general prioritises the teaching and learning of vowel length rather than vowel quality, so it is likely that an ELF practitioner would agree that remedial work should be done on *live* and *leave* (Jenkins, 2000: 144-5; Walker, 2010: 34-5).

But interestingly, L1 speakers' speech sometimes contains instances of what would count as errors in the speech of L2 speakers, but which go unnoticed in L1 speech. Hector's version of |ʌ| which sounded close to |ɒ| and his version of |ɪ| which sounded close to |iː| can be heard in Extract 14.4, where Dan – one of our BrE speakers from Chapter 11 – produces versions which are very close to Hector's.

Extract 14.4 England – Dan *to make ... comfortable*

```
|| to make PEOPle feel more COMfortable ||
```

We might expect Dan's *feel* to be |fiːɫ|, but the vowel sounds close to |ɪ|. We might equally expect his *comfortable* to be |kʌmfətəbɫ|, but the first vowel is close to |ɒ|. One could argue that this could provide justification for not tampering with Hector's accent: if native speakers can do this, and not be thought to be speaking in a faulty accent, why should Hector be?

14.5   Caroline from France: University researcher

Caroline is a researcher working at a university in England. In Extract 14.5 she talks about travelling to secondary school.

Extract 14.5 France – Caroline *my secondary ... my school*

```
01 || my SECondary school WAS ||
02 || maybe I don't KNOW ||
03 || TWENTy MINutes aWAY ||
04 || from my HOME and ||
05 || i HAD to go BACK for LUNCH ||
```

```
06 || SO ||
07 || ...i took this... ||
08 || OLD BIKE ||
09 || and CYcled to my SCHOOL ||
```

14.5.1   Window on speech perspective

What does the transcript help us to hear in this extract? Unit 07 is an incomplete speech unit (cf. Chapter 3.6), with no prominences. The three syllables are spoken at 7.7 syllables per second – extremely fast. In 08, the syllables *old bike* are delivered in a playful sing-song way which are transcribed as two successive prominent syllables. The sing-song is present in the recording, but absent from the transcription – this is one of the limitations of any transcription system (cf. Chapter 5) – it cannot represent everything that happens in speech. Again, as we saw with Andrzej and Hector, Caroline expertly uses the features of spontaneous speech to present her meanings in real time.

14.5.2   Accent reduction perspective

French learners of English often have difficulty with |h| and |ð| (cf. Swan & Smith, 2001: 54), but Caroline does very well with these sounds in *home* (04) and *this* (07). However, an accent reduction specialist might focus on the following features of this extract:

In 01 the last two syllables of your *secondary* are American-like, with an unreduced vowel in the penultimate syllable. RP speakers would probably compress these syllables into one, you say |sek.ən.de.ri| rather than the RP |sek.ən.dri|.

In 01 the vowel quality of *was* is not RP-like. You say something close to GenAm |wɑːz| rather than RP |wɒz|. We need to choose which reference model to work with, RP or GenAm.

In 03 your second vowel in *away* is not RP – it is a single sound |e| and it needs to be more of a diphthong |eɪ|.

In 05 your vowel in *lunch* is not RP. It is close to |ɜː| rather than RP |ʌ|.

In 09 your vowel in *school* is too short and the quality not quite RP |skuːl|.

In Caroline's extract, the accent reduction specialist is confronted with a dilemma. Being British and RP-oriented, the specialist would like to teach her to sound more British, but the Americanisms in her speech would seem to indicate that GenAm would be a more suitable reference model for her. If the specialist is one who is prejudiced against all non-RP accents, but particularly prejudiced against American accents (as some are), then the work would be focused on changing Caroline's accent towards RP.

14.5.3   ELF perspective

The ELF movement's argument is that any internationally intelligible L2 accent is a valid one, and would view the accent reduction specialist's anti-American stance as an irrelevance. Caroline's four-syllable version of *secondary* – with no compression, and less vowel reduction than RP – would probably win her approval from the ELF perspective.

14.6   Mohamed from Sudan: University professor

Mohamed is a university academic from Sudan, in his late forties, and his first language is Arabic. He is speaking to a native speaker he knows fairly well. In Extract 14.6 he talks about his ambition to study French.

Extract 14.6 Sudan – Mohamed *after that ... and the culture*

```
01 || AFter that i WENT to FRANCE ||
02 || i ALways WANTed ||
03 || TO ||
04 || to do FRENCH ||
06 || and I ||
07 || thought the BEST way to do FRENCH ||
08 || UM ||
09 || WAS ||
10 || TO ||
11 || go and ACtually LIVE in the country ||
12 || AND ||
13 || JUST ||
14 || AS it were imMERSE myself ||
15 || in in in in the LANGuage and the CULture ||
```

14.6.1 Window on speech perspective

What does this transcription help us hear in this extract? Mohamed uses a very common pattern of a series of stepping stones (cf. Chapter 6) which buy him some planning time (units 08-10; 12, & 13), followed by double-prominence speech units (11 & 12) which contain the results of his planning. In Unit 15, he begins with four repetitions of *in,* which in the careful speech model would be viewed as a disfluency (cf. Chapter 6), but which sound to me very dignified and professorial. As with the other speakers, Mohamed makes expert use of the features of spontaneous speech to present his meanings in real time.

14.6.2 Accent reduction perspective

An accent reduction specialist might focus on the following features of this extract:

> In 01 you should be consistent with your pronunciation of the 'bath vowel', and pronounce *after* as |ɑːftə| and not |æftə|. You can certainly produce the 'long a' sound, because you do it very well in *France* |frɑːns|.

> In 09 your pronunciation of *was* is not entirely RP-like – a it sounds a bit American |wɑːz|, but the RP pronunciation is |wɒz|

> In 14 *immerse* is very attractive, it is something close to |ɪmeɚs| but it is not RP. The RP version is the *nurse* vowel |ɪmɜːs|.

14.6.3 ELF perspective

It is possible that an ELF practitioner might agree with the accent reduction specialist in the case of the vowel |ɜː|, (often referred to as 'the nurse vowel') because ELF places particular importance on this vowel. The reason being that there is research evidence which shows a significant number of occasions of communication break down in cases where this vowel was mispronounced (Walker, 2010: 34).

14.7 Silvia from Romania: Clerical assistant

Silvia was born in Romania not far from the capital, Bucharest. She is in her mid-twenties. At the time of the recording in Extract 14.7 she had been in England for three years, and was helping newly-arrived students settle in England.

Extract 14.7 Romania – Sylvia *they also ... a week*

```
01 || THEY ||
02 || ... Also ... ||
03 || they RENTed a CAR ||
04 || mmHMM ||
05 || ERM ||
06 || they HIRED a CAR FOR ||
07 || FEW ||
08 || DAYS ||
09 || probably a WEEK ||
```
Unit 04 is a response token from Richard.

14.7.1 Window on speech perspective

What does the transcription help us hear in this extract? Unit 09 is a single-prominence speech unit (cf. Chapter 3.1), in which *probably* occurs with two syllables not three – Wells (2006) tells us that in casual speech it is sometimes |prɒb.li|. But in my experience the two-syllable version is very frequent in spontaneous speech. Interestingly, as well as dropping the weak second syllable, Silvia makes the final consonant |b| of the first syllable virtually inaudible, so that *probably* sounds close to *prolly* (rhyming with *brolly*). Dropping of a mid-word consonant in this way is something we observed in Chapters 8 and 9, and is something we will make use of in teaching in Chapter 18. As Silvia moves from the final vowel of *probably* towards the word *week* the indefinite article *a* sounds something like a short *oo* (rhyming with boot'). These three syllables are going at 7.5 syllables per second, which is very fast (cf. Chapter 7). Sylvia makes expert use of the features of spontaneous speech as part of communicating her meanings in real time.

14.7.2 Accent reduction perspective

If Silvia wanted to make her accent sound more British, an accent reduction specialist would probably focus on the following features of this extract:

> In 01, 03 and 06 your first consonant in *they* is closer to |d| than RP |ð|. This is an important feature of RP pronunciation, so we need to work on it together.

> In 03 and 06 your *car* |kɑr| has a rhotic quality to it, which sounds American rather than RP |kɑː| so we have to choose whether to use RP or GenAm as our reference model.

Your *probably* only has two syllables: you say something like *prolly*. You should use the three-syllable version |prɒb.əb.li| as much as possible, so do not use the two-syllable version |prɒb.li| too often.

You produce three rising tones on *car* (03) *days* (08), and *week* (09), where we might expect falling tones. These are examples of uptalk. You should be aware of Professor Wells's advice in relation to this: 'using uptalk may annoy older people listening to you'. (Wells, 2006: 37-38).

14.7.3   ELF perspective

ELF practitioners would probably approve of Silvia's rhotic accent (cf. Walker, 2010: 32). And they almost certainly not work to improve her pronunciation of |ð|. This is because one of the (more controversial) suggestions of ELF is that the dental fricatives |θ| and |ð| should not be insisted upon in pronunciation teaching because they are difficult to produce, teaching is ineffective and they are not essential for intelligibility (Jenkins, 2000: 137; Walker, 2010: 29-30). ELF practitioners argue further that even L1 speakers start life unable to pronounce these two sounds and substitute them with |f|, and some L1 accents do not include these sounds (for example Irish, New Jersey and Jamaican). ELF does not specify what should be taught in their place, but practitioners mention |d̪| and |t̪|, or |f| and |v| as possible versions for |θ| and |ð| respectively, which are more easily learned.

14.8   Summary and what's next

It is one of the great strengths of the ELF movement that it provides academic support for the achievements of language learners who get to the point of international intelligibility. It celebrates individual and group attainments, and provides a timely counterbalance to the point of view that the goal of pronunciation is to match the perfection of the native speaker reference models.

L2 accents are heard not just from tourists and students visiting countries where English is the L1: they are heard from people who are resident, have citizenship, and who are successful professionals in those countries. They include musicians, university professors and researchers, medical consultants, teachers and politicians.

But most importantly, L2 accents are also heard in circumstances where no native speakers are present, and the ELF movement has provided an academic impetus for a change in attitudes towards L2 accents in these situations. Lydia, our teacher from Taiwan mentioned in 14.1 above, is grateful for this impetus:

> ... we do need [researchers'] articulation to arouse the public awareness since people tend to prefer expertise to the protest of nobodies. (Golombek & Arnold, 2005: 525)

Lydia feels supported in her position by the arguments of academics against the power of, and the prejudices associated with, native speaker norms, but even so she realises that prejudices against L2 speaker accents still exist and remain influential.

In this chapter we have looked at five accents of Global English. There are, of course, a huge – close to uncountable – number of such accents. All of them contribute to the colours and flavours of the sound substance of speech which our students need to become familiar and comfortable with.

In Chapter 15 we will look at a different kind of colouring that speech can have – the emotional colouring that speakers communicate when they are feeling angry, surprised, etc. We will take a close look at the relationship between prosodic phenomena and the expression of attitude and emotion in spontaneous speech.

14.9   Further reading

The continuing existence of prejudices against L2 accents is revealed in Kang & Rubin (2009). Lippi-Green (1997) documents prejudice against L2 accents in the USA and Honey (1989) is a source of historical information on prejudice in the UK . Derwing & Munro (2009: 483) describe some of the more outrageous approaches to accent reduction, give definitions of **accentedness**, **comprehensibility**, and **intelligibility** and report research findings that show they are separately measurable (ibid. 478-479). An annotated reading list by the same authors (Derwing & Munro, 2008) provides an excellent starting point for research.

Swan & Smith (2001) is a reference work which is an important diagnostic tool to help people who want to change their accents. For more on ELF, the best places to start are Walker (2010) and Jenkins (2000). Doel (2006) is interesting for the way he captures a wide variety of native speaker opinions of Dutch accents and Osimk (2009) is an early example of research into intelligibility which takes account of the ELF perspective. Jenkins et al (2011) provides a summary of the research and attitudes towards the ELF movement. For more academic treatments of accents Edinburgh University Press has a series entitled 'Dialects of English' which provides up-to-date documentation for varieties of English from around the world.

14.10 Language awareness activities

Activity 14.1: Prepare and perform
Choose two of the five extracts of global accents, listen carefully to them and prepare a performances of them, both in your own accent and in the accents of the original speakers. Perform them for a friend, colleague or fellow teacher.

Afterwards, consider the following questions: Which of the two accents were you more comfortable with, and why? Which accent would you be happiest to listen to, and why? Can you think of people who would have negative opinions of these accents? If so, what would the negative opinions be? What would be the advantages and disadvantages of speaking in such accents (a) in groups where everyone else is an L1 speaker and (b) in groups where there are no L1 speakers?

Activity 14.2: Listen and analyse   Answer key page 241
Extract 14.8 features Anke, from Germany. Before you listen, read the extract and predict what the features of her pronunciation might be focused upon by an accent reduction practitioner who specialises in RP. Use the following information from Swan and Smith (2001: 38-40) concerning the differences between German-accented English and RP to make your predictions.

[1] |v| and |w| may be confused – listen for *village* in 02
[2] |θ| and |ð| are often realised as |z| – listen for *the* in 06
[3] |e| and |æ| may be confused – listen for *had* in 04, 06, & 08; and *Dad* in 05
[4] |ʌ| and |a| may be confused – listen for *bus* in 09

Now listen to Extract 14.8 and check whether or not your predictions were correct. Then consider whether the accent reduction specialist might focus on anything else in the recording.

Extract 14.8 Germany – Anke

```
01 || but we COULDn't go OFTen to the CINema ||
02 || because WE were in a SMALL VILLage ||
```

```
03  || my PARents ||
04  || had ONly ONE car ||
05  || and my DAD ||
06  || HAD the CAR ||
07  || for GOing to WORK ||
08  || so so OFTen WE had ||
09  || could ONly USE a BUS ||
10  || to GET to the NEXT CIty ||
11  || WHERE you could GO to CINema ||
```

15   Emotion in speech

In this chapter we look at the relationship between how speakers say something and the emotional or attitudinal meanings that their listeners perceive.

We can ask a question ('What do you mean?') or even say a single word ('Yeah') with different tones, making each version sound happy, sad, angry, irritated, rude, disgusted or delighted. We might therefore claim that what we do with our voices causes the change of emotional meaning. We might also claim that anyone doing the same would produce the same changes on future occasions. Thus we could conclude: 'That goes to show that a high-falling tone means surprise, and a low-falling tone means sadness'. Indeed, where research into these emotions has involved acted speech, strong connections between tone choice and emotional meanings are found. However, research into spontaneous speech shows that the relationship between how you say something and emotional meanings is much more complex.

In this chapter we will look at, and evaluate, some influential statements which have shaped our knowledge and understanding of the relationship between the expression of emotion and the sound substance of speech. Our principal aim will be to understand how these meanings are conveyed in spontaneous speech.

15.1   The labelling problem

A great deal of research has focused on what have been termed the 'big six' emotions: 'anger', 'sadness', 'surprise', 'happiness', 'fear' and 'disgust'. However, a moment's reflection will tell you that these six labels are insufficient to describe the wide range of human emotions and attitudes. In fact many more labels are used by researchers: Stibbard (2001: 10) lists ninety-four (from 'admiration' to 'yearning') and Douglas-Cowie et al (2000: 41) counted 300 labels in just two publications. Researchers agree that having so many labels is a problem. In this chapter we will focus on just two emotions – 'surprise' and 'anger' – introducing other labels as we need them.

It is not simply the number of labels which is a problem. Each label overlaps with others, and it is very difficult to define each label so that it is sufficiently distinct to provide a basis for scientific investigation.

For example, it is very difficult to define 'surprise' in ways which exclude 'shock', or to define 'anger' in ways which exclude 'irritation' and 'indignation'. Each researcher tends to use a preferred set of labels which, unfortunately, do not correspond to the labels of other researchers. So there are problems with the proliferation of labels, with their definitions and with the lack of consistency of their use.

For the purposes of this chapter we use the terms **emotion/emotional meaning** and **attitude/attitudinal meaning** interchangeably to include both the big six emotions and their derivatives ('irritation', 'fear', 'anxiety'), as well as attitudes such as 'tentative', 'reserved' and 'challenging'.

We use the term **vocal effects** to refer to the full range of effects with which the vocal apparatus (lungs, vocal tract, glottis, tongue, lips, etc.) colours the sound substance of speech. These effects include tone (cf. Chapter 4), and all the terms of the prosodic systems (e.g. loudness, tempo, rhythmicality, etc.) and paralinguistic systems, (e.g. breathiness, creak, laugh, etc.) as listed and described by Crystal (1969: 177). We use the term **kinesics** to refer to movements of the face, and other body language.

15.2   The assumption of a causal connection

The general view is that there is a causal relationship between the choice of vocal effect and attitudinal meaning. For example if you have a particular sentence type – such as a statement or question – the view is that you can change the attitudinal meaning by changing the tone. This view underlies Halliday's (1970: 27) explanation of the meaning of tones in *wh*-questions, as demonstrated in Extract 15.1.

Extract 15.1 Attitudinal meanings in *wh*-questions

```
01 || ↘ WHAT'S the TIME || neutral
02 || ↗ WHAT'S the TIME || tentative or deferential
```
Note this is not Halliday's original recording. It has be re-created for this chapter.

Unit 01 has a falling tone on the word *time*, which Halliday (1970: 27) tells us conveys a neutral meaning (where 'neutral' means 'conveying no emotion or attitude'), whereas in unit 02 the rising tone gives a 'tentative or deferential' meaning.

There are three problems with this type of demonstration. First, it is incomplete because it only allows for three attitudes – 'neutral', 'tentative', and 'deferential'. It is possible (because we are human beings) to both feel, and to express, any attitude at any time whatever we are saying, but Halliday provides no explanation of other attitudes which might be conveyed in *wh*-questions. The second problem is that only two (fall and rise) of the five tones (fall, fall-rise, rise-fall, rise and level cf. Chapter 4) are mentioned here and, to be satisfactory, an account of the relationship between questions and tones would need to include the effects of using all five tones. These two problems are in principle easily remedied, but the third is not.

The third problem is that the causal relationships said to exist between tone and meaning are demonstrably untrue. You can, by adding vocal effects such as tenseness, reverse the apparent relationships between attitudinal meanings and tones. For example, you can make a supposedly neutral falling tone on a *wh*- question sound quite 'non-neutral' – even 'angry' – by changing the accompanying vocal effects and, by the same means, you can make a rising tone sound 'angry', as you can hear in Extract 15.2.

Extract 15.2 Attitudinal meanings in *wh*-questions

```
01 || ↘ WHAT'S the TIME || angry
02 || ↗ WHAT'S the TIME || angry
```

In 01 the falling tone is spoken with tenseness in the voice, making this tone, which is supposedly 'neutral' in a *wh*-question, sound angry. Similarly in 02, the rising tone is supposedly 'tentative', but the accompanying vocal effect helps make the speaker sound 'angry' – a completely different meaning. The fact that we can reverse the meaning while still using the same tone, demonstrates that it is not the falling or rising tone that conveys the meaning, but – it would seem – other vocal effects such as tenseness.

Extract 15.3 brings the four versions of the *wh*-question side-by-side, demonstrating that falling tones can occur both with 'neutral' and with 'angry' meanings, and that rising tones can occur both with 'tentative/deferential' and with 'angry' meanings.

Extract 15.3 Attitudinal meanings in *wh*-questions

```
01 || ↘ WHAT'S the TIME || neutral
02 || ↘ WHAT'S the TIME || angry
03 || ↗ WHAT'S the TIME || tentative or deferential
04 || ↗ WHAT'S the TIME || angry
```

The problems underlying much of the research and teacher-training in this area have been that:

- the focus is on rising, falling (and other) tones, to the exclusion of other vocal effects and contextual considerations
- the co-occurrence of an emotion and a particular vocal effect is mistaken for causation
- the evidence has often been taken from acted speech rather than spontaneous speech.

Note that up to this point, all our examples have been acted, isolated sentences of the type traditionally found in ELT materials.

15.3   Inhibiting learners

Despite the demonstrable flaws in the statements about the relationship between tone and attitude, the assumption that there is a direct link lives on: 'We do this by tone,' writes Wells (2006: 11) about the expression of attitudes and emotions. It is understandable that the belief in a direct cause continues to survive: the careful speech model prefers concepts which are rule-governed even though they are somewhat fictional.

However, the careful speech model approach to tone and attitude can have some negative side-effects. The impression given is that every tone and tune, in association with sentence type, carries with it an attitudinal meaning ('angry', 'disdainful', etc.). Adherents of the careful speech model approach seem to suggest that the student of English must learn to use these tunes correctly, otherwise 'misunderstandings and possible embarrassment' or worse, will result (O'Connor & Arnold, 1973: 2). This results in learners becoming inhibited in their speech because they are afraid that they might sound intentionally bored or rude if they get the tune wrong. We shall return to this issue in Section 15.6 below.

15.4   The mystery of disappearing anger

Up to this point we have been considering scripted examples of acted speech. We now turn our attention to examples from spontaneous speech.

The two questions in Extract 15.4 are taken from a dinner-table conversation involving parents and children. Later you will hear the questions in the context in which they originally occurred.

Extract 15.4 Two questions in isolation

```
01 || ↘ WHAT do you MEAN ||
02 || ↘ WHEN ||
```

These two questions come from different parts of the recording. These are two *wh*-questions with a falling tone, which Halliday would say are attitudinally neutral. However, I expect that you will agree with me (and many others have – cf. Cauldwell, 2002) that there is a negative attitudinal colouring to these examples which could be characterised as 'angry' or 'irritated'. (You absolutely need to hear the recording.)

As we have seen in Section 15.2 above, the tones on their own cannot help with an explanation, but perhaps (we might speculate) the accompanying vocal effects are causing this perception. For example we might seek for explanations in the field of voice quality research (e.g. Gobl & Ni Chasaide, 2000) – perhaps there is an added tension, or terseness, in the voice which makes the speaker sound angry. But before we go too far in our search for an adequate description of the vocal effects in this extract, we should hear the speech units in the context in which they originally occurred.

Extract 15.5. is from a conversation at a dinner table between Matt (aged two years and seven months), his brother Patrick (13), and his parents Dad (42) and Mum (38). Matt is describing an incident in the family car at which he and Mum were present, but which Dad knows nothing about. The incident involved the car getting stuck in mud in a car park, but Matt refers to the mud as *snow*. Matt begins the extract with an enthusiastic non-lexical noise – he is playing with a toy – which is transcribed as *miao bumma*. The two *wh*-questions from Extract 15.4 occur in units 18 and 21.

Extract 15.5 Two questions in context

```
01-05 || miAO BUMMa || [chuckle] || ...ME...|| HEY || ...HEY... ||
06-07 || ...WHEN it... || ...when...||
08-10 || when when WHEN it when it SNOWS ||... we can ... || DRIVE ||
11    || AND / what were you going to SAY || [overlap]
12-13 || YEAH || YEAH yeah / Dad || [overlap]
14-15 || and OUR car || got STUCK ||
16-17 || ... our ca wha wha ... || ... WHAT ... ||
18       || WHAT do you MEAN ||
19-20 || OUR car got STUCK || in the SNOW ||
21       || WHEN ||
```

```
22-24 || well WHEN it SNOWED || it got STUCK in the MUD || ONCE ||
25-26 || AT the NATure centre || DIDn't it ||
```
Note there is more than one speech unit per line in this transcript due to reasons of space.

The 'anger' that was perceived when the questions were heard in isolation is no longer perceived when they are heard in their original context (cf. Cauldwell, 2000). So what has happened? Where has the 'anger' gone?

The answer is that the 'anger' went nowhere. In fact it was never in the sound substance of the speech units in the first place: it was not in the wording, nor in the falling tones, nor in the vocal effects. The 'anger' was perceived anger *heard in the minds of the listeners.*

To understand what happened, we need to use the concepts of **normal vocal settings** and **normalisation**. The normal vocal settings for a speaker are the parameters of volume, degree of contour of tone, pitch range and other vocal effects which they use when speaking. The vocal settings themselves vary with context: who the addressees are, the time of day and the nature of the accompanying activities, etc. For example, if you are sitting in a quiet garden talking to a friend, your normal vocal settings will be different from those when you are talking across a table of noisy party goers, or answering a question in a classroom.

Normalisation is the process by which a listener in a particular context very quickly attunes to the normal vocal settings for the speaker. The listener then has a baseline of expectations of what constitutes 'normal' for the speaker in that context. When the speakers make a noticeable departure from the baseline associated with them – their current settings for normal – the listener will evaluate whether these departures are cueing the presence of non-neutral attitudinal meanings.

In the case of the isolated *wh*-questions of Extract 15.4, listeners have no contextual information and no prior experience of the speaker's voice. This means they do not have sufficient time to attune to the speaker's current normal range and the process of normalisation cannot take place. In a situation like this, the listener makes judgements based on their past experience of similar voices in familiar contexts.

Therefore the reason for the listeners' perception of 'anger' in these *wh*-questions lies in the fact that the speech units have characteristics of speed and tenseness which, when *heard in isolation*, mark them as outside the normal vocal settings for an average adult male voice.

However, when the *wh*-questions are heard in context there is enough preceding speech for listeners to normalise (very quickly) their perceptions of the speaker's vocal settings, and realise that the vocal effects associated with the *wh*-questions lie well within the current setting of normal for this speaker.

In this example, 'anger' initially appeared to be present but in fact it was not. We will now look at examples where various emotions are undeniably present.

15.5   Emotional involvement

We will hear two extracts, both of which feature high falling tones but which have different attitudinal meanings.

15.5.1   High fall *why have ... thank you*

First, some context. Patrick passed his UK driving test at the age of eighteen. Learning to drive and passing the test do not require any experience of driving on motorways, so Patrick was given a lesson on motorway driving by his father. Extract 15.6 comes from a moment in the lesson when Patrick is joining a motorway and is simultaneously being overtaken by another car, which is also joining the motorway. This understandably causes him some alarm and anger.

Extract 15.6 Patrick *Why ... thank you*

```
01 || ↘ WHY have you been trying to over↑TAKE me ||
02 || ↘ what are you ↑DOing ||
03 || ↘ THANK you ||
```

In units 01 and 02 Patrick's voice is very high in his vocal range and he speaks very fast. In a short space of time (under four seconds) there are reactions to this event for which we might use the following labels: 'alarm', 'anger', 'indignation' and 'anxiety'. The other driver then changes his mind about overtaking and allows Patrick to join the motorway, at which point Patrick says – much lower in his vocal range – *thank you* in a way which we might label as 'sarcastic'.

The contours of his high falling tones (starting on *take* and *do*) are short and shallow, and not clearly defined (cf. Chapter 4). However, it is not the tones alone which cue the presence of emotions. There are a great many other factors which include: the cultural context of knowledge of the rules of driving in the UK, particularly those about overtaking on motorways; the context of this being a new driver inexperienced in dealing with the behaviour of other drivers; the context suggested by the words *why have you been* which are often used to introduce a rebuke; and the fact that the total range of Patrick's vocal effects (speed, near-falsetto, etc.) constitutes a noticeable departure from the settings for normal for a male voice.

15.5.2 High fall – *I really liked it*

In Extract 15.7 Richard asks Toby about the work he did on a building site prior to going to university. He asks whether he did this work out of interest, or simply to pass the time.

Extract 15.7 Toby *I really liked it*

```
01 || ↘ did you FIND that INTeresting ||
02 || → or was it JUST ||
03 || → TO ||
04 || ↘ i ↑REALly ↑LIKED it ||
05 || ↘ i LIKED doing PRACTical STUFF ||
06 || ↘ i STILL like doing ||
07 || ↗ PRACTical STUFF ||
```

Richard asks a question (which he doesn't finish) in 01-03. Toby answers in 04-07.

Toby goes high in his vocal range in unit 04, using high key on the two prominences, with a steeply contoured falling tone starting on *liked*. The high choices clearly constitute a noticeable departure from his current settings for normal. But of the meanings that were relevant for Patrick in Extract 15.5 ('alarm', 'anger', 'indignation', 'anxiety'), only one seems relevant here: 'indignation'. One could argue that the high key choices signify an indignant denial of Richard's apparently erroneous assumption that Toby might not have found building work interesting. If the notion of 'indignation' seems a bit too strong for this extract, we can find a milder, but related, description in Brazil's explanation (1997: 41-49) that the high key choices constitute a 'contradiction of an assumption'.

In discussing Extracts 15.4 and 15.5 we have used the following labels for the emotions which are associated with the high falling tone: 'alarm', 'anger', 'indignation', 'anxiety' and 'contradiction'. Crystal (1975: 38; 1997: 173) also suggests that more positive emotions such as 'surprise', 'warmth', and 'excitement' are associated with the high fall. Clearly there is a wide range of meanings that can be linked with this single type of tone. And if we also take into account the fact that context, kinesics, and words are powerful influences on the conveying and perception of emotions, it then becomes obvious that any intonational feature (such as a high fall) can mean anything, depending on the context.

We have therefore established that, in spontaneous speech, the co-occurrence of a feature (e.g. tone) and a specific meaning (e.g. 'surprise') cannot be generalised to all occasions and all contexts. The most that one can safely claim is that where there is a noticeable departure from the current settings for normal (whether it be in tone choice or any other vocal setting), this departure is likely to be signalling the presence of a relevant attitude or emotion, or a level of emotional commitment or emotional involvement (Crystal, 1975: 38; 1997: 173). One cannot be more specific than that.

Another complication of the relationship between vocal effects and emotion is that there is no necessary connection between the feeling of an emotion and its expression. Many people can feel an emotion and yet refrain from expressing it, or moderate its expression in a way that is socially appropriate for the culture and context in which it occurs. Research shows that people express their emotions in different ways: some cry when they are experiencing extreme happiness and some laugh hysterically in the face of bad news.

15.6   Inadvertently rude?

In the previous sections we have dealt with the relationship between attitudinal meanings and vocal effects, but the question still remains: 'Is it possible to be unintentionally rude by making a wrong intonation choice?' The answer is *Yes*, but the risk of it happening is very low. L2 speakers will not be heard as being rude if they break the rules of the careful speech model, and (for example) ask a *yes-no* question with a falling tone. If they are smiling, cooperative and attentive when listening, when it comes to their turn to speak, people will interpret what they say, and the way that they say it, in the way that they intend it. However, if L2 speakers suddenly make noticeable departures from their normal vocal settings which are (to the listener) unwarranted by the context, or are culturally inappropriate, then they might be heard as being 'grumpy', 'rude' or 'indignant'.

15.7   Acclimatisation

One of the implications for language learners is that they need to acclimatise to what is culturally acceptable in terms of vocal settings for normal for the groups of speakers with whom they want to interact.

15.8   Summary and what's next

There is no one-to-one relationship between vocal effects and attitudes. Instead there is a 'many-to-many relationship': any single vocal effect can occur with many different attitudes and any single attitude can occur with many different vocal effects. It is therefore incorrect to say that vocal effect 'x' conveys 'y' attitude because there is no generalisable direct causal relationship. Stibbard (2001: 201) ends his evaluation of a major research project into emotion in speech with the following statement:

> ...the sounds of speech do not alone carry systematic, reliable cues to differentiate emotions, and ... phonetic investigation alone ... is not sufficient to produce a model for their simulation or recognition. (2001: 206)

In combination with contextual factors and the choice of words, a noticeable departure from the normal settings for vocal effects will signify that there is something for the listener's powers of interpretation to work on. The emotions and attitudes reside somewhere in the context of interaction, in the social and psychological context that includes both the speaker's and listener's knowledge of each other, each others' vocal norms and the purpose of their talk.

It may not be immediately apparent how the content of this chapter is relevant to the teaching of listening. The relevance is that these are facts about the sound substance of speech which are consistently misrepresented in English language teaching because of its adherence to the careful speech model. In order to be effective teachers of the sound substance, for both listening and pronunciation purposes, we need to have a model of the sound substance which is as accurate and as true-to-life as possible.

This chapter therefore contributes to our spontaneous speech model, and our comparison of it with the careful speech model (cf. Appendix 1). The area of emotional and attitudinal meanings is one in which the difference between the rules of the careful speech model and the unruliness of the spontaneous speech model is perhaps at its greatest.

This chapter brings to an end Part 3. We have used the window on speech framework to help us explore issues associated with accents from Britain and Ireland, North America and Global English, and the relationship between vocal effects and emotional meanings in speech. In Part 4 we look at the implications of all the issues raised in Parts 1 to 3 for the teaching of listening.

15.9   Further reading

The best critique of recent research can be found in Stibbard (2001, Chapter 8). Cowie et al's (2003) special issue of *Speech Communication* will give you a flavour of the type of research in this area. For a long time, some of the most interesting research has been done by Klaus Scherer and his colleagues in Switzerland. You can see a list of his publications at Scherer (2012).

15.10   Language awareness activities

Activity 15.1: Prepare and perform
Halliday (1970: 27) tells us that a rising tone on a *yes-no* question has a neutral meaning (cf. 01), and that with a falling tone it will sound forceful and impatient (cf. 02).

```
01 || ↗ ARE you SATisfied ||
02 || ↘ ARE you SATisfied ||
03 || ↘↗ ARE you SATisfied ||
04 || → ARE you SATisfied ||
05 || ↗↘ ARE you SATisfied ||
```

Prepare a performance of two versions of each of the five speech units above: one which sounds neutral, and one with an attitudinal meaning chosen from the following list: 'anger', 'sadness', 'surprise', 'happiness', 'fear' and 'disgust'.

Perform your ten speech units to a friend, colleague or fellow teacher. Ask them if they can tell which meanings you intend and then discuss what this exercise tells you about the relationship between tone choice and attitudinal meanings.

Activity 15.2: Listen and analyse   Answer key page 242
In Extract 15.8 Richard talks to Toby about his favourite hobby, climbing, which Toby does both outdoors and indoors. Using the evidence contained this extract, evaluate the following 'rules' of intonation:

- High falling tones mean 'emotional commitment', 'surprise', 'anger', 'warmth', 'alarm', 'indignation', 'anxiety', 'contradiction' and 'emphasis'
- Rising tones mean 'uncertainty' and 'incompletion'

Extract 15.8 Toby *it's very interesting indoors*

```
01 || ↘ i i CAN'T conCEIVE ||
02 || ↘ that it could be INTeresting to do INdoors ||
03 || ↘ ↑OH ||
04 || ↘ it's ↑VEry interesting indoors ||
05 || ...beCAUSE ... ||
06 || ↗ you can REALLy PUSH yourself ||
07 || ↗ because it's REALLy SAFE ||
```

References for Part 3

Algeo, J. (2005) Language Myth #21: Americans are ruining English. PBS. Available online at http://www.pbs.org/speak/ahead/change/ruining/ [Accessed 3 March 2011].

BBC (2005a) BBC Voices. http://www.bbc.co.uk/voices/ [Accessed 16 Feb. 2011].

BBC (2005b) BBC Voices: West Midlands, Dudley, Brian Dakin. https://sounds.bl.uk/Accents-and-dialects/BBC-Voices/021M-C1190X0005XX-0201V0 at 51:16 minutes into the recording [Accessed 15 Oct. 2012].

BBC, (2005c) BBC Voices: Merseyside, Garston, Chamonix. https://sounds.bl.uk/Accents-and-Dialects/BBC-Voices/021M-C1190X0022XX-0301V0 at 43:36 minutes into the recording. [Accessed 15 Oct. 2012]

BBC (2006) Stroke gives woman foreign accent. [BBC News website article] http://news.bbc.co.uk/1/hi/england/tyne/5144300.stm [Accessed 24 Feb. 2010].

Brazil, D. (1997) The Communicative Value of Intonation in English. Cambridge: Cambridge University Press.

Cauldwell, R. (2013) Lord Rant: A personal journey through prejudice, accent, and identity. Speak Out!, 48, 4-7.

Cauldwell, R. T. (2000) Where did the anger go? The role of context in interpreting emotion in speech. In Cowie, R., Douglas-Cowie, E. and Schroeder, M. (eds.) Proceedings of the ISACA Workshop on Speech and Emotion, 127–13. Newcastle: Northern Ireland.

Celce-Murcia, M., Brinton, D. M. and Goodwin, J. M. (2010) Teaching Pronunciation: A Course Book and Reference Guide, [2nd edition]. New York: Cambridge University Press.

Cowie, R., Douglas-Cowie, E., and Campbell, N. (2003) (eds.). Special issue on speech and emotion. Speech Communication, 40.

Crystal, D. (1969) Prosodic Systems and Intonation in English. Cambridge: Cambridge University Press.

Crystal, D. (1975) The English Tone of Voice. London: Edward Arnold.

Crystal, D. (1997) The Cambridge Encyclopedia of Language, [2nd edition]. Cambridge: Cambridge University Press.

Crystal, D. (2003) English as a Global Language, [2nd edition]. Cambridge: Cambridge University Press.

Crystal, D. (2004) The Stories of English. London: Penguin.

Derwing, T. M. and Munro, M. J. (2008) Putting accent in its place. [Reading list]. Available at http://www.sfu.ca/~mjmunro/DandMHandout.pdf [Retrieved 2 March 2011].

Derwing, T. M. and Munro, M. J. (2009) Putting accent in its place: Rethinking obstacles to communication. *Language Teaching*, 42/4, 476-490.

Doel, Rias van den (2006) How Friendly are the Natives? An Evaluation of Native-speaker Judgements of Foreign-accented British and American English. Utrecht: LOT.

Edinburgh University Press. (2007-) *Dialects of English.* [Series]. http://www.euppublishing.com/series/DIOE

Elmes, S. (2005) Talking for Britain: A Journey through the Nation's Dialects. London: Penguin.

Gobl, C. and Ní Chasaide, A. (2000) Testing affective correlates of voice quality through analysis and resynthesis. Cowie, R., Douglas-Cowie, E. and Schroeder, M. (eds.) *Proceedings of the ISACA Workshop on Speech and Emotion* (pp.178–183). Newcastle Northern Ireland.

Golombek, P. and Jordan, S. R. (2005) Becoming "Black lambs" not "Parrots": A poststructuralist orientation to intelligibility and identity. *TESOL Quarterly*, 39/3, 513-533.

Guardian unlimited. (2012) Harriet Harman's Accent. http://www.guardian.co.uk/commentisfree/2010/jan/29/harriet-harman-accent [Accessed 13 November 2012].

Halliday, M. A. K. (1970) *A Course in Spoken English: Intonation.* London: Oxford University Press.

Henton, C. and Bladon, A. (1988) Creak as a Sociophonetic Marker. In Hyman, L.M. and Li, C.N. (eds.). *Language, Speech and Mind: Studies in Honour of Victoria A.* Fromkin, 3-29. London: Routledge.

Honey, J. (1989) *Does Accent Matter? The Pygmalion Factor.* London: Faber and Faber.

IDEA (1997) *International Dialects of English Archive.* [Website] [Accessed 16 Feb. 2010]. http://web.ku.edu/~idea/ University of Kansas: Lawrence, Kansas.

Jenkins, J. (2000) *The Phonology of English as a Lingua Franca.* Oxford: Oxford University Press.

Jenkins, J. (2004) *English as a Lingua Franca: Attitude and Identity.* Oxford: Oxford University Press.

Jenkins, J., Cogo, A., and Dewey, M. (2011) Review of developments in research into English as a lingua franca. *Language Teaching*, 44/3, 281-315.

Kang, O. and Rubin, D. (2009) Reverse linguistic stereotyping: Measuring the effect of listener expectations on speech evaluation. *Journal of Language and Social Psychology*, 28/4, 441-456.

Kerswill, P. (2010) http://www.timesonline.co.uk/tol/news/uk/article6973975.ece

Kerswill, P. (2003) Dialect levelling and geographical diffusion in British English. In Britain, D. and Cheshire, J. (eds.). *Social Dialectology. In honour of Peter Trudgill*, 223–243. Amsterdam: Benjamins.

Kirkpatrick, A. (2007) *World Englishes.* Cambridge: Cambridge University Press.

Labov, W. (1966) *The Social Stratification of English in New York City.* Washington, DC: Center for Applied Linguistics.

Labov, W., Ash, S. and Boberg, C. (2006) Atlas of North American English Phonetics, Phonology and Sound Change. Berlin: Mouton de Gruyter.

Lippi-Green, Rosina (1997) English with an Accent: Language, Ideology and Discrimination in the United States. New York: Routledge.

Llamas, C. and Watt, D. (2010) *Language and Identities*. Edinburgh: Edinburgh University Press.

McElhinny, B. (1999) More on the third dialect of English: Linguistic constraints on the use of three phonological variables in Pittsburgh. *Language Variation and Change*, 11, 171–195.

McMahon, A., Maguire, W., and Heggarty, P. (2007) Accents of English from around the world. [Website]. http://www.soundcomparisons.com/ [Accessed 16 Feb. 2011].

O'Connor, J.D. and Arnold, G. (1973) *Intonation of Colloquial English*. Harlow: Longman.

Osimk, R. (2009) Decoding sounds: An experimental approach to intelligibility in ELF. *Vienna English Working Papers*, 18/1, 64-89. Available here: http://anglistik.univie.ac.at/staff/osimk/ [Accessed 05 July 2012].

PBS. (2012) *African American English: When worlds collide*. Webpage http://www.pbs.org/speak/seatosea/americanvarieties/AAVE/worldscollide/ . [Accessed 10 Sept 2012].

Przedlacka, J. (2002) Estuary English? A Sociophonetic Study of Teenage Speech in the Home Counties. Bern: Peter Lang.

Rees-Mogg, J. (2012) Jacob Rees-Mogg. Wikipedia. http://en.wikipedia.org/wiki/Jacob_Rees-Mogg [Accessed 29 Oct. 2012].

Roach, P., Setter, J. and Esling, J. (eds.) (2011) *Cambridge English Pronouncing Dictionary*. Cambridge: Cambridge University Press.

Rosewarne, D. (1984) Estuary English. *Times Educational Supplement*, 19.

Scherer, K. (2012) [Publications]. http://www.affective-sciences.org/publications/author/scherer. [Accessed 13 July 2011].

Stibbard, R. (2001) Vocal expression of emotions in non-laboratory speech: An investigation of the Reading/Leeds emotion in speech project annotation data. [Doctoral dissertation]. University of Reading.

Stuart-Smith, J. (1999) Glasgow: Accent and voice quality. In Foulkes, P. and Docherty, G. (eds.) *Urban Voices: Accent Studies in the British Isles* pp. 203–222. London: Arnold.

Swan, M. and Smith, B. (eds.). (2001) *Learner English: A Teacher's Guide to Interference and Other Problems*, [2nd edition]. Cambridge: Cambridge University Press.

Tobin, D. and Leake, J. (2010) Regional accents thrive against the odds in Britain: It's baffling up north as city accents spread. http://www.timesonline.co.uk/tol/news/uk/article6973975.ece [Accessed 16 Feb 2011].

Upton, C., Kretschmar, W. A. Jr. and Konopka, R. (2001) *The Oxford Dictionary of Pronunciation for Current English*. Oxford: Oxford University Press.

Walker, R. (2010) Teaching the Pronunciation of English as a Lingua Franca. Oxford: Oxford University Press.

Wells, J. C. (1997) Whatever happened to Received Pronunciation? In Medina Casado, C. and Soto Palomo, C. (eds.) *Il Jomadas de Estudios Inglese*, 19–28. Universidad de Jaén. http://www.phon.ucl.ac.uk/home/wells/rphappened.htm [Accessed 14 February 2011].

Wells, J. C. (1998) [Web documents relating to Estuary English]. http://www.phon.ucl.ac.uk/home/estuary/home.htm [Accessed 9 Sept 2012].

Wells, J. C. (1982) Accents of English. Cambridge: Cambridge University Press.

Wells, J. C. (2006) English Intonation: An Introduction. Cambridge: Cambridge University Press.

Wells, J. C. (2008) Longman Pronunciation Dictionary. Harlow: Pearson Education.

Windsor Lewis, J. (2010) The General American and General British pronunciations of English. http://www.yek.me.uk/gavgb.html [Accessed 9 Sept 2012].

Part 3 Answer Key

Chapter 11

Activity 11.1: Prepare and perform

The syllables in which AmE would be likely to feature rhoticity (cf. 11.4.2) are shown in bold.

> (1) My **first** job was as a wait**er** in the **first**-class lounge of Atlantic **Air**ways. (2) It was a good time **for** me, because I met people from all ov**er** the **world**. (3) I can't rememb**er** how much I was paid, but I wished I **earned** as much as the passen**gers** I **served**! (4) Aft**er** going to night-school to get the necessary exams, I went to univ**er**sity to study drama

Mentioned below, sentence by sentence, are the other main differences with references to the relevant sections in the chapter.

(1) AmE *job* |dʒɑːb|, BrE |dʒɒb| (cf. 11.3.1)

(1) AmE *waiter* |weɪɚ|, BrE |weɪtə| (cf. 11.4.3)

(2) AmE *all* |ɑːɫ|, BrE |ɔːɫ| (cf. 11.3.2)

(3) AmE *can't* |kænt|, BrE |kɑːnt| (cf. 11.3.3)

(4) AmE *after* |æftɚ|, BrE |aːftə| (cf. 11.3.3)

(4) AmE *school* |skuːɫ|, BrE |skuːʊ| (cf.. 11.4.4)

(4) AmE *necessary* |ˈnes.ə.ser.i|, BrE |ˈnes.ə.sri| (cf.. 11.5.2)

(4) AmE *university*, |juːnivɝsəri| BrE |juːnivɜːsəti| (cf. 11.4.3).

Activity 11.2: Listen and analyse

Extract 11.26 AmE & BrE *first* and *after*

```
01 || it was the FIRST one ||
02 || well the FIRST ONE ||
03 || it was kind of AFTer CHRISTmas ||
04 || AFTer a LOT of ||
```
Unit 01 comes from Dan, 02 and 04 from Jess, 03 from Toby.

In unit 01 *first* is rhotic, in 02 it is non-rhotic. Note also the fate of the two |st| consonant clusters before *one*. In 02, Jess simplifies the cluster by omitting |t| thus |fɜ·s wʌn|, whereas in 01 Dan just about keeps the |t| – although it is difficult to hear. Dan's *one* is close to |wɒn|, which is a very common variant pronunciation normally associated with accents from the Midlands and the North of England, but Dan is from the South. Wells (2008) reports a preference poll showing that 30% of respondents reported using |wɒn|, but with younger people using it more than older people.

In 03 Toby's *after* |ɑːftə| is non-rhotic, whereas in 04 Jess's *after* |æftɚ| is rhotic. Jess's first vowel in *after* is |æ|, as opposed to Toby's which is |ɑː|. Note also that Toby simplifies the consonant cluster |nd| in *kind,* even though it is preceding the vowel in *of,* and we might therefore expect |kaɪndə|, but we get |kaɪnə|. His pronunciation of *Christmas* |krɪsməs| with the omission of the |t| is the normal pronunciation for this word. Jess's *lot* has AmE |ɑː|, rather than BrE |ɒ| and the level tone which starts on *lot* and continues over *of* results in the vowel in *of* becoming a lengthened schwa. Interestingly, we might expect Jess to produce an alveolar tap at the end of *lot* |lɒɾə|, but she produces a glottal stop instead, |lɒʔə|. This is possibly because she lives and works in England and her accent may have converged on RP.

Chapter 12

Activity 12.2: Listen and analyse

In 01 there are three differences to notice. First John drops the *h* and gives us an *n* at the end of *having* so we get |ævɪn| compared to RP |hævɪŋ|. We then get *chance* as |tʃæns|, compared to RP |tʃɑːns|. Finally *do* has a somewhat fronted vowel so we get |dʉ| compared to RP |duː|.

In 02, we get the same pronunciation of *do* again |dʉ| compared to RP |duː|.

In 03 John pronounces the *t* sound in *often* so we get |ɒftn̩| compared to RP |ɒfn̩|. Interestingly, Wells (2008: 560) writes: 'Many people use both the form without |t| and with it'. And he reports a preference poll in which 73% of British people report using the form without |t|.

Chapter 13

Activity 13.2: Listen and analyse
The following table summarises the differences between GenAm pronunciation, and Catherine's.

		GenAm	Catherine
01	myself	|maɪself|	|maːself|
02	wanted	|waːntɪd|	|waːnɪd|
05	decided	|disaɪdɪd|	|disaːdɪd|
06	telling	|telɪŋ|	|telɪn|
06	anybody	|enibaːdi|	|inibaːdi|
07	go	|goʊ|	|gəʊ|
07	France	|frænts|	|fræənts|

Chapter 14

Activity 14.2: Listen and analyse
In 02 the |v| of *village* is RP-like: Anke does not confuse |w| and |v|.

In 06 *the* is spoken non-prominently between *had,* and *car* and is RP-like.

In 04 the vowel in *had* is closer to |hed| than to |hæd|, but it is spoken non-prominently and Anke's version would be a normal variant in RP.

In 05 the vowel in *Dad* is diphthongal – it starts as |e| and changes to |æ|.

In 06 *had* is between |hed| and |hæd|, and very close to RP.

In 08 *had* is very fast and non-prominent and is RP-like.

In 09 *bus* sounds like |bas| rather than |bʌs|, but Anke can produce |ʌ| very clearly, as she does in 04 on one |wʌn|.

The accent reduction specialist, being oriented to RP, might also offer to correct the American rhotic pronunciations of *car*.

Chapter 15

15.2: Listen and analyse

Extract 15.8 Toby *it's very interesting indoors*

```
01 || ↘ i i CAN'T conCEIVE ||
02 || ↘ that it could be INTeresting to do INdoors ||
03 || ↘ ↑OH ||
04 || ↘ it's ↑VEry interesting indoors ||
05 || ...beCAUSE ... ||
06 || ↗ you can REALLy PUSH yourself ||
07 || ↗ because it's REALLy SAFE ||
```

No negative attitudes

There are high falling tones on *Oh* in unit 03 and on the first syllable of *very* in unit 04. Given that this is a conversation about hobbies, and we know that Toby is very passionate about his hobbies, we can for contextual reasons consider that the negative meaning of 'anger' is unlikely.

'Emphasis'

One could also argue that the high falling tone means emphasis, but it is not the tone choice which is of importance here. It is the fact that *very* is prominent and *interesting indoors* is non-prominent which is conveying emphasis.

'Surprise'

It is unlikely that Toby, would be surprised – of course he knows everything about his personal experience of climbing – but it could be argued that he is projecting 'surprise' as an appropriate emotion for Richard to have: It's not *moderately* interesting, it's not *fairly* interesting, it's not *sort of* interesting, it's not *rather* interesting, it's not *sometimes* interesting, its none of those – it's *very* interesting. So for the purposes of this explanation, let us assume that some form of 'surprise' is contextually present in units 03-04.

Changing key and tone

To continue with our evaluation, we can also experiment with changing the key and the tone, to see whether the meaning changes. If we take out the high key, and perform the speech units with mid key falling tones, very little changes, as we can hear in Extract 15.9. The most that one can say is that the level of emotional commitment is a little lower.

Extract 15.9 Toby *it's very interesting indoors* – no high key

```
03a || ↘ OH ||
04a || ↘ it's VEry interesting indoors ||
```
If we change the tone of 04 so that it becomes a fall-rise, we get

Extract 15.10 Toby *it's very interesting indoors* – fall-rise tone

```
04b || ↘↗ it's ↑VEry interesting indoors ||
```

but making this change from falling to fall-rise does not bring about a change in the 'surprise' meaning – it is still there. In fact it is inherent in all contexts where one person is telling another person something that they do not know. In such contexts 'surprise' is a readily available meaning, within easy reach, because of the very strong associations that it has with suddenly getting to know something that you did not previously know. In such getting-to-know-something-new contexts, any departure (faster, louder, higher pitch, steeper contours, etc.) from the current settings for normal is likely to cue the interpretive search for relevant meanings.

Rising tones

There are two possible explanations for the use of rising tones in units 06-07. First, that they are examples of uptalk (cf. Chapter 11.6), which is becoming a feature of the speech patterns of younger British people. If it is a normal feature of Toby's speech, then these rising tones would be heard as being within the current settings for normal, and therefore would not cue any attitudinal meanings. The second possible explanation is that they are excursions from the current settings for normal (i.e. they are unexpected because falling tones would be expected), and will therefore activate a listener's interpretive process of determining what meaning is being cued here.

PART 4

Teaching listening

Part 4:   Teaching listening

In Part 4 we review current practice in the teaching of listening and suggest a variety of activities – both low-tech and hi-tech – through which students can best engage with the sound substance to improve their learning of listening. Rost (2001: 13) wrote: 'listening is still often considered a mysterious "black box" for which the best approach seems to be 'more practice'. Much work needs to be done to modernise the teaching of listening.' These chapters aim to open up Rost's 'black box', and to modernise how we teach listening.

Each chapter ends with two activities for you to do: *Reflect on Learning* and *Reflect on teaching*. The aim of these activities is to encourage you to consider how your learning of listening would be, or would have been, different if you were to be involved in these activities, and to encourage you – if you are a teacher – to experiment with the suggested activities with your students.

Chapter 16 *Issues in teaching listening* describes problems with current approaches to listening. There is an over-reliance on osmosis; recordings (of all types) are under-used; we use the wrong model of speech; teachers are unaware of the blur-gap and the decoding gap, and goals are not sufficiently distinguished from activities.

Chapter 17 *Goals and mindset* argues that we need to accept that the messiness and unruliness of spontaneous speech is completely normal. We look at a goal for teaching listening and at metaphors for describing speech.

Chapter 18 *Vocal gymnastics in the classroom* describes ways in which teachers' and students' voices can be used to create pronunciation activities which serve the goal of listening.

Chapter 19 *Rebalancing listening comprehension* looks at the traditional listening comprehension exercise and suggests ways in which it can be adapted to maximise the learning opportunities that recordings – even scripted recordings – present.

Chapter 20 *Hi-tech solutions and activities* looks at how computer software, and tablet and smartphone apps, can be used to improve the teaching of listening.

Remember you need the recordings. Download them from www.speechinaction.com.

16   Issues in teaching listening

We begin this chapter with angry memories of a listening class from Anna:

> ... I've hated the underuse of the material. I've ... answered three silly questions ... then someone tells me patronisingly (it IS bloody patronising) that the rest doesn't matter. Well it does if I want to learn the language! *(personal communication)*

Anna is complaining about the traditional listening comprehension exercise in which questions are set, students listen to a recording, answer the questions and then the teacher gives the answers and moves swiftly on to another activity. In Anna's opinion there is something missing from this pattern – namely teaching 'the language' that is contained in the recording. She could mean a number of different things by 'the language': new vocabulary, known vocabulary used in new ways, grammar points or decoding problems. However, the thing that makes her most angry is the fact that the recording was underused.

In this chapter we will see that this underuse happens for reasons which include: the inherent difficulties presented by the sound substance itself, an over-reliance on **osmosis** and a lack of recognition of two gaps: **the blur gap** and **the decoding gap.** Our ultimate aim is to improve learners' listening abilities in relation to spontaneous speech, but much of the argument of this chapter applies also to those scripted recordings which – although closer to the careful speech model – might be described as natural, authentic or genuine.

16.1   An omission in teacher training

The **conventional listening lesson** is full of good things to do, which many of us are well trained in doing. These include making the students feel good about themselves as learners of listening, contextualising the recording, pre-teaching vocabulary (or not), reviewing the questions that they are required to answer and encouraging prediction. These things are often found in the first part of a listening comprehension exercise, the pre-listening phase. The while-listening phase then involves listening to the recording and answering questions, and the post-listening phase involves checking the answers, doing vocabulary work with the transcription and then moving on to another activity, leaving a great deal of the learning potential of the recording untapped.

Most teachers have become expert in fostering the development of strategies such as predicting and guessing (cf. Mendelsohn, 1998). We are also expert in the methodology of fitting listening activities into a sequence of communicative tasks so that there is a flow to the lesson – a momentum which drives the class on to the next activity. It is therefore possible, indeed common, for what counts as 'a good listening lesson' to involve no engagement with the sound substance itself. It is almost as if we deliberately *avoid* engaging with the sound substance. However, the truth is that it does not occur to most of us to do so, simply because we are not trained to do so.

This omission happens because, as we have seen in Parts 1 and 2, there are inherent difficulties in getting to grips with the sound substance of speech in a way to make it easily teachable: it is invisible, it is transient and it is far less easy to describe than the written language, even for teachers who have training in phonetics. In fact phonetic training may be of little help as Brown (1990) tells us:

> ... the stretches of obscure acoustic blur often no longer permit any representation on a segment-by-segment basis. (Brown 1990: 7)

Therefore in order to engage with the sound substance we need the knowledge and skills to enable us to grasp a substance which is inherently ungraspable. We need to handle the transient so that students can 'get their fingers dirty' with a substance which leaves no trace. We also need to do this without misrepresenting the essential transient nature of speech.

If and when we do engage with spontaneous speech, we are then confronted with the fact that it does not obey the rules of the careful speech model. Explaining this to students and answering their questions therefore becomes rather challenging, even for the most experienced teacher. It is natural for us to prefer classroom activities in which we can easily answer questions about what is happening so that we can remain secure in our role as reliable providers of accurate information and answers. We feel uncomfortable about being asked something which is beyond our professional knowledge and therefore beyond our capacity to explain.

16.2   Students' reactions to listening

Decoding speech (of all kinds, not just spontaneous speech) is a private, non-observable mental process. It happens inside the head of the individual. Social elements can be added to the learning of listening in which students co-operate during activities and discuss what they have heard, but essentially the process of listening takes place in a private, unobservable dimension.

When students encounter speech which is challenging for them (spontaneous or scripted), they are often horrified (Thorn, 2009: 8), and a happy, active class can be reduced to a silent awkwardness by the isolating effect of needing to work in this private dimension (Field, 1998a: 14). In addition, students very often feel bad about themselves as listeners. They attribute this to a failing in themselves – a personal failing – when it is, in fact, a weakness in the field of language teaching, which *Phonology for Listening* aims to redress.

The horrified reaction in the students can take many forms: puzzlement, discomfort, or even frustration. We teachers find this difficult, because for many of us, it is important for students to be busily working on something, or cheerfully co-operating on communicative tasks which produce a happy atmosphere in the classroom. Rather than dwell on the difficulties, and rather than delving into the recordings, we prefer to move on to other activities which have a better chance of generating these public observable behaviours. And often, these other activities become the focus of the lesson, at the expense of listening. Listening activities are often used to serve other goals.

16.3   Listening activities vs listening goals

It is important to distinguish between activities and goals. In the classroom, an **activity** is an observable behaviour – what we might call 'a doing' – so that an observer sitting at the back of the class could say 'they are doing a reading activity' or 'they are doing a listening activity'. A reading activity involves students looking at a piece of writing, and a listening activity involves input of sound substance – typically from teacher-talk or from an audio or video recording.

A **goal** is a purpose for learning – a learning target which students strive towards. This goal is what the students are referring to when they say 'I want to improve my listening.' This difference between a listening activity and a listening goal is referred to by Wilson (2008: 135) when he distinguishes between 'the listening lesson' and 'listening in the lesson'.

In principle any activity may serve any goal, as there is no fixed relationship between activity and goal. For example, it is common for a reading activity to be used with the goal of writing a particular type of text, such as a job application. Therefore it may be that the activity an observer witnesses ('they are doing reading') may be in pursuit of a goal of another skill – 'they are reading the transcript of a recording in order to improve their listening'.

It is a common fate for listening in the classroom to be principally an activity in pursuit of another goal. For example a survey by White (1987, cited in Anderson & Lynch 1988: 66) found that teachers valued listening materials for reasons such as 'good for starting discussions', 'amusing' and 'consolidates language'. Nowhere in the survey of reasons was there recognition from teachers that listening activities could have listening goals.

16.4   L1 listening vs L2 listening – stresses and osmosis

Anna was also angry about one of the standard pieces of advice given in listening classes: 'Listen for the stressed content words, do not strain after every word, do not worry about every word'. Here is Anna's reaction to this advice:

> It's no good telling learners not to worry about every word. How are they to know which words to worry about, if they only capture about a quarter of those that were uttered?

The justification for the advice 'listen out for the stressed content words' comes from research into first language listening which tells us that L1 listeners do not attend to every word when listening. L1 listeners report the meanings that they understood, but they cannot report accurately the words that they heard. The sound substance is decoded subliminally, below the level of attention.

This finding has been wrongly applied to L2 learners. They are asked to behave like an L1 listener, when, as we see from Anna's quote, they simply do not have the decoding abilities to do so. Learners are expected to acquire these decoding abilities through **osmosis**, that is by listening to a lot of material (Rost's 'more practice' 2001: 13), and focusing on meaning.

Osmosis is the process of exposing students to speech, and for them gradually to acquire the ability to decode it as they focus on trying to understand. It is a model of learning which involves acquisition through contact. The assumption is that if large amounts of the sound substance wash over the students, they will eventually acquire L1-level decoding abilities. This is not teaching – this is a surrender in the face of difficulty. The belief seems to be that decoding cannot be taught but, by focusing on understanding, the ability to decode the sound substance of speech will be acquired 'automatically and unconsciously' (Buck, 1995: 123). One consequence of this view is that it takes a long time – students need to listen to a lot of language so that their 'natural learning processes' (ibid) will eventually give them the decoding abilities required to master the sound substance.

The challenge for us therefore is to devise teaching and learning activities which can work faster than osmosis.

16.5   Two models revisited: careful speech and spontaneous speech

Another reason for the lack of engagement with the sound substance is that the more a recording contains the features of spontaneous speech (as described in Part 2), the less it conforms to textbook rules and our students' expectations. These rules and expectations are powerful, and they come from the careful speech model which is based on the guidelines for pronunciation and speaking that appear in dictionaries and textbooks (cf. Chapter 1.4 and Appendix 1). It acts as a model of the best type of speech that students are happy to emulate in their own speech, and it is based on pedagogic guidelines of proven effectiveness for learning pronunciation.

However, we need a different model of speech – the spontaneous speech model – to help with the plight of the listener who has to deal with the unruliness of the speech which they encounter outside the classroom. This model is one which regards the facts of everyday speech – such as those we saw in Part 2 – as completely normal, not as deviant. Of course we need to allow the careful speech model to continue its role in giving guidance for pronunciation work. But to improve the teaching of listening, we need to use the spontaneous speech model to engage with the sound substance of spontaneous speech on its own terms as an object of study, an object of teaching and learning goal.

However, we need to be careful not to treat the spontaneous speech model as if it is an emulation model (cf. Chapter 1.4). We have to treat it not as *something to get right* but as *something to get used to* – this point is developed further in Chapter 17.

16.6   Authenticity

With the acceptance of the existence and status of the spontaneous speech model comes the issue of whether or not the recordings that are used in the listening classroom should be **authentic**. One definition of an authentic recording might be that it consists of a sound-grab of real-world speech of interactions between L1 speakers who are surreptitiously recorded as they go about their daily lives. Another might be that it is any recording that is not specifically made with language learning in mind. Yet another that the recording should be unscripted. Some listening enthusiasts argue that for listening classes to be effective, they should consist principally or entirely of work on recordings of authentic speech.

However, the notion of authenticity has been the subject of a great deal of debate (Rost 2011: 165-7), and it is difficult to come up with a definition of authenticity which has universal acceptance. The word has acquired a variety of meanings which range from 'genuine spoken language as used by native speaker' (Rost, 2011: 166) to 'anything that is in the target language that [the students] want to listen to' (ibid: 167). The terms have become heavy with connotations: 'authentic' connoting 'good' and 'inauthentic' connoting 'bad'. In effect the two terms 'authentic' and 'inauthentic' have become over-extended – bloated with the good and the bad things that have become associated with them, and they can now be taken to mean virtually anything.

Rost usefully introduces the notion of **genuineness** which 'refers to features of colloquial style of spontaneous planning that are characteristic of everyday spoken discourse' (ibid: 166), which means that any recording which has the features of spontaneous speech can be considered as genuine. These features include those covered in Part 2. In practice, any type of recording (or indeed any type of activity) which helps students towards mastery of decoding and understanding spontaneous speech will serve our purposes.

16.7   The blur gap revisited

Another reason for the lack of engagement with the sound substance of speech is that we do not sufficiently differentiate between L1 perceptions of speech and the contents – the physical properties – of the sound substance. This is **the blur gap** that was first mentioned in Chapter 1.3.

L1 listeners and expert L2 listeners hear traces of words in the acoustic blur and yet they perceive something close to full citation forms in these traces. For example the acoustic blur may contain a rush of three syllables going at 750 words per minute 'weatherwuh', but L1 listeners will believe that they hear 'where' followed by 'there', followed by 'were' in soundshapes which are close to the citation form. L1 listeners are deaf (and I include myself) in this special way – deaf to the fact that much of the sound substance consists of very small traces of words which we successfully reconstruct and decode. We do not hear the acoustic blur of the sound substance which reaches our ears. Instead we hear the results of an extremely rapid automatic decoding process which matches the mere traces of words to their citation forms. This is an expert skill which operates subliminally, below the level of awareness and attention.

L1 teachers are at a disadvantage here – the very expertise we have as L1 listeners is an obstacle to the effective teaching of listening. L2 teachers may therefore have the advantage in teaching listening, because they have worked through the difficulties which their students face. On the other hand, there is a chance that they may have become so expert at subliminal decoding that they have forgotten about the difficulties that faced them as they were learning.

One of the consequences of the blur gap is that we L1 teachers may insist too much on what we thought we heard, rather than on what was actually there in the sound substance. For example we may insist, wrongly, that the sound substance contained the full forms of the words, |weə.ðeə.wɜː|, whereas it consisted of the traces |we.ðe.wə|. The consequence of such an insistence is that we are likely to add to the discomfort of our students: they will feel bad about themselves as learner listeners if they cannot hear what we believe (erroneously) to be present in the sound substance. The blur gap is therefore something we must guard against.

16.8   The decoding gap

The blur gap concerns the difference between *the teacher's perceptions*, and *the realities of the sound substance*. There is another gap that we need to take account of: the one that lies between *the teacher's perceptions* and *the students' perceptions* of the sound substance, which we will refer to as the **decoding gap**. Students do not have the ability to decode the traces contained in the acoustic blur. Brown, (1990: 60) writes of students experiencing 'a devastating diminution of phonetic information at the segmental level when they encounter normal speech'. This results in Ying's dilemma (cf. Chapter 1) – students not recognising words that they know, even the most frequent forms which are part of their active vocabulary (Field, 2008a). L1 teachers may be unaware of their students' predicament, and unable to comprehend why students do not perceive the same full forms that they, the teachers (think they) do. This creates a mismatch in the classroom, which often results in teachers failing to investigate what their students actually perceive in the sound substance of a recording. This is regrettable because the place to start teaching decoding is with the students' initial perceptions – with what they believe they have heard.

16.9 Listening comprehension is testing

Listening comprehension exercises are more to do with testing than teaching. These exercises require students to act as if they are – to assume the role of – L1 listeners, without teaching them the fundamental prerequisite for acting as L1 listeners do: the ability to decode the sound substance.

Listening comprehension is a testing activity because there are things for the students to get right or wrong. Meanwhile the teacher – in the role of the tester – knows the answers and gives them to the students at what he or she judges to be the appropriate time. Listening comprehension exercises have value in that they provide brief opportunities for the process of osmosis to work. They also provide opportunities for students to practise coping strategies in that they give students – working at their current level of competence – the opportunity to extract meanings from a recording.

In Chapter 19 we will see that listening comprehension activities can easily be modified to provide opportunities for engaging with, and learning about, the sound substance.

16.10 Summary and what's next

In learning to read it is a fundamental requirement that students master the substance of graphic symbols on page or screen so that they can recognise letters and words. Similarly, in learning to listen it is a fundamental requirement that students master the sound substance of speech so that they can decode it and then process it for meaning.

However, current listening methodology omits direct engagement with the sound substance. Instead it is dominated by testing, listening comprehension practice, training in compensatory strategies and a reliance on the fact (or hope) that osmosis will work in the long term.

So we have to find a way in which we can help students grasp a substance which is inherently ungraspable. We need to train them to handle the transient – to 'get their fingers dirty' – with a substance which leaves no trace. And we need to do this without mis-representing the invisible transient nature of speech.

Buck (1995) suggests four ways in which we might set about this task:

- sensitizing the students to the problem
- consciously discussing it
- explaining how pronunciation changes
- giving examples

The aim of Chapters 17-20 is to demonstrate ways in which these four things can be done.

16.11   Further reading

John Field (1998, 2003, 2008, 2009) gives extensive critiques of the listening comprehension approach and suggestions for the adaptation of listening comprehension exercises. Mendelsohn (1998) writes on the role of strategies in listening training. Vandergrift (2006) summarises different approaches to listening research and listening instruction. His section on lexical segmentation describes work by Hulstijn (2003) which brings students into intensive contact with short extracts of the stream of speech. Thorn (2009) suggests specific ways in which teachers can use authentic recordings which go beyond the limitations of the traditional listening comprehension approach.

16.12   Learning and teaching activities

Activity 16.1: Reflect on learning

Look at Anna's two angry statements about how she was taught to listen. Think about your own experiences of learning to listen in a foreign or second language. How did you feel about listening lessons? Did you feel there was something missing? Talk to a friend, colleague or fellow teacher about your experiences. Summarise your thoughts, and the gist of your discussions, in your notebook.

Activity 16.2: Reflect on teaching

Consider some of the listening lessons that you have taught, or that you have observed. What proportion of the time in the listening lesson has been spent on teaching the sound substance? How much time was spent on contextualising the recording, explaining the questions, checking the answers and training in the use of strategies? Talk to a fellow teacher, colleague or friend about your experiences. Summarise your thoughts, and the gist of your discussions in your notebook.

17   Goals and mindset

In order to be effective teachers of listening we need both to be clear about the goal of teaching listening, and to have the right mindset in order to teach towards this goal. This requires being comfortable with the implications of using the spontaneous speech model. This chapter describes these implications, starting with a goal for learners. We will then look in turn at a goal for teacher-training, some metaphors which will help us distinguish between careful and spontaneous speech, how we can best cope with the blur gap and the decoding gap and how we can deal with the discomfort and frustration that our students often feel in listening activities.

17.1   A goal for learners

The goal of teaching listening can be formulated as follows:

> To make learners familiar and comfortable with the sound substance of spontaneous speech so that they can decode and understand speech of all kinds, with increasing expertise.

The words 'familiar and comfortable' show that the goal talks about something that has to become accustomed to, not something that has to be emulated and copied. Although the main emphasis in *Phonology for Listening* is on *decoding*, there is specific mention of *understanding* as well. The reason for the emphasis on decoding is that work on it is frequently absent from teaching listening (cf. Chapter 16), but it would be a mistake – and probably impossible – to leave out any consideration of meaning. This is because the main shapers of the stream of speech are the speaker's moment-by-moment decisions of how to communicate meanings to listeners (cf. Parts 1-2).

17.2   A goal for teachers

The goal of teacher training for the effective teaching of listening can be formulated as follows:

To equip teachers with the knowledge, skills and tools which will enable them to plan and teach activities which will instruct their students in the patterns of the sound substance of speech so that they can decode this sound substance and achieve their listening goals.

The knowledge, skills and tools include both conceptual tools such as the *window on speech framework* (Part 1) and the evidence about spontaneous speech that we have seen emerge from using the framework in Parts 2-3. The goal includes reference to the fundamental fact that *there exists something to be taught* – the sound substance of speech – and that it *should* be taught. Considerable amounts of time in the classroom should be devoted to instruction and guidance by the teacher. The acquisition of the ability to decode is simply too important to be left to osmosis. The skills and tools include methodological competence, classroom management and learner training, as well as the teacher's own vocal skills (cf. Chapter 18) and computer skills (Chapter 20). Currently the teaching of compensatory strategies dominates time in the listening classroom at the expense of teaching decoding (cf. Chapter 16). Training in the use of such strategies needs to continue, but more room needs to be made for decoding activities.

17.3   Two models, five metaphors

Throughout *Phonology for Listening* we have seen that there are major differences between the *careful speech model* and the *spontaneous speech model* (summarised in Appendix 1).

We need to sensitise our students to the difference between the clear intelligible speech that we want them to emulate and the other wilder forms of speech that they will have to cope with while listening in the real world. We need to do this systematically and regularly. One way of doing this is to introduce a striking metaphor which reflects the differences between a tidy, rule-obedient model on the one hand and a messy, unruly model of speech on the other hand.

One such metaphor is *The greenhouse, the garden and the jungle*, which can be introduced both verbally and with pictures. The pictures can be displayed in strategic places in the classroom so that in subsequent lessons you need only to move to stand next to the pictures, or point to them, in order to let the students know which model of speech is the focus of attention. As you will see below, each model involves different expectations and behaviours.

17.3.1   The greenhouse

The words we learn in the classroom are like plants that we grow in a greenhouse. They are carefully chosen and there are no weeds. They grow in neat rows, a suitable distance from one another, they have a wide range of colours and they are healthy and whole. The speech we use to model the correct pronunciation of new vocabulary and slow careful speech is usually like greenhouse plants. This is the domain of citation forms.

17.3.2   The garden

The sentences we learn in the classroom contain words which come into gentle orderly contact with each other. Words are joined together to make pleasing patterns of colours in sentences. These words-in-sentences are like flowers-in-flowerbeds, where flowers of different types and colours are placed next to each other and seem to flow together in an orderly way. This is the domain of assimilation, elision, linking and connected speech rules.

17.3.3   The jungle

The words-in-speech units that we hear outside the classroom are like the vegetation of a jungle. Everything seems to be of random size and in a random arrangement. There are some plants that we would never see in the greenhouse or the garden. Sometimes the growth of plants is so dense that it is impossible to tell where one finishes and another starts. The spontaneous speech that we hear from L1 and fluent L2 speakers is like these plants in the jungle. This is the domain of unruly, messy, spontaneous speech.

These metaphors are not the only ones that can be used. You can make up your own – the only requirement is that there should be two extremes, and a middle ground in between. One extreme needs to be very tidy, disciplined and organised and the other extreme needs to be messy, unruly and disorganised. It is a good idea to have striking images that can be displayed at the front of the classroom so that you can step from one world (orderly correctness) to the other (disorderly mess) and to the middle ground very rapidly.

17.3.4   Savouring

We will also use metaphors involving the senses of taste and touch to describe aspects of the teaching and learning the sound substance. We need these metaphors to add to the rather limited vocabulary that exists to describe activities in which our students interact with the sound substance of speech. We will refer to short sequences of speech units as being **savoured** as if they were a liquid being tasted, and moved around the mouth, back and forth over different sets of taste-buds, so that as many of their qualities as possible can be sensed, appreciated and described before being swallowed. Short sequences of speech units provide mouthful-sized amounts of material to work with and learn from.

17.3.5   Handling

We will also speak of students **handling** short stretches of speech, as if they are cupping water from a stream in their hands so they can observe its colours, freshness, and temperature before it runs away through their fingers. We will be looking at ways in which we can get students to savour and handle auditorily – with their ears – the sound substance of speech by manipulating it and interacting with it in a variety of ways.

17.4   Letting go of the careful speech model

As well as making a physical space in the classroom for the spontaneous speech model, we need to let go – temporarily – of certain ideas and rules which are deeply embedded in language teaching. These ideas are the rules and expectations of the careful speech model, which are an obstacle to the achievement of listening goals, because spontaneous speech does not follow these rules and expectations. For example, in Part 2 we have seen that:

- words have a wide variety of soundshapes
- past tense endings may be inaudible
- syllable-final consonants may be inaudible
- syllables may be dropped
- entire words may be dropped
- definite and indefinite articles may sound the same

We need to be prepared to recognise these facts, and others like them, when they occur in the recordings, and not discount them as 'abnormal'. They *are* normal, but they do not comply with the careful speech model. We also need to be able to recreate features of the spontaneous speech when instructing our students on the nature of spontaneous speech (cf. Chapter 18), just as we model correct pronunciation for our students.

If we deny the unruliness of spontaneous speech, we will perceive it through the filter of the careful speech model. The danger of this is that it will predispose us to hear things in the sound substance which *may have been intended* by the speaker, or *required by the grammar*, but which are *not actually there* in the sound substance. We will have fallen victim to the blur gap.

17.5   Neutralising the blur gap

The *blur gap* (cf. Chapters 1.3, 16.7) is the gap between what is actually present in the sound substance and the reconstructed version of speech that L1 and expert listeners perceive. This gap is something we need to be continually on our guard against. It is my personal experience that when I am working with a recording of spontaneous speech, I have to make a great effort to neutralise my expert-listener processes, to get to a point when I can notice what is, and (crucially) what is not present in the sound substance. I do this by taking short extracts of speech and then isolating, and copying and pasting words and clusters of words into other sound files where they can be compared to their citation forms. If I fail to do this, then I will perceive past tense endings (for example) as actually present in a recording – because the past tenses were the speaker's intention – when they are in fact not audible in the sound substance. Words and their important endings (past tense, negatives) may be intended but they are often inaudible. It is not helpful for us to insist that they are intended – really meant – without also recognising that they are absent or inaudible. To do so will create or magnify our students' feelings of discomfort and personal inadequacy in relation to listening.

There is therefore a continual need for those of us who are L1 teachers, and expert L2 teachers, to remind ourselves of the blur gap. A very effective way to do this is to record a short stretch of fast spontaneous speech, and edit it in a computer programme such as Audacity. You then identify and isolate individual words by inserting a short pause between each word. Following this you compare these words, or traces of words, with their citation forms.

It is probable that in some cases it will be virtually impossible to separate one word from another. For example an attempt to separate three first words of 'of what i WASn't GOing to do' (Cauldwell, 2012) in Extract 17.1 would probably result in a failure to come up with three reasonable chunks – the words run into each other in such a way that the properties of all three words seem to blend into one indivisible burst of the stream of speech.

Extract 17.1 Bob *of what i*

```
01 || of what i WASn't GOing to do ||
02 || of what i ||
```

```
OF ... of... WHAT ... what ... I ... i
```
Unit 03 gives the different soundshapes for *of*, *what* and *i* side-by-side with their citation forms.

This kind of analysis demonstrates the blur gap very clearly, and alerts us to the challenges of the learning task that our students face.

17.6   Dealing with the decoding gap

The decoding gap (cf. Chapter 16.8) is the gap between what learners hear and what an expert listener would hear. This decoding gap reveals the extent of the teaching and learning task. The decoding goal is to hear what the expert listener would hear. The starting point is revealed by what our students report that they hear.

Our students' processing of spontaneous English speech is – by definition – not at an expert level. They have not yet acquired the ability to match the fragments and traces of words in the sound substance of speech with words and phrases that are part of their active vocabulary – they are suffering from Ying's dilemma (Ying is the learner from Chapter 1 who 'couldn't catch' words that she knew when they were used in speech). In addition, their initial perceptions and their reports of what they hear may well be affected by the phonological characteristics of their first language

Our task as teachers is to plan a route from the starting state – where our students are – to the target state – the listening goal. We want them to be able to reconstruct the traces of words into full words, and then reach an understanding of what they mean. Both for the purposes of constructing a good listening activity (one which is directed towards the goal stated in Section 17.1), and for the purposes of learner training (minimising discomfort and self-blame), it is important to respect our students' initial perceptions, their first attempt at decoding which provides the starting point for learning. We must therefore find out what their starting state is, and we will see how to do this in Chapters 18 and 19.

17.7   Questions and answers

The primary objection to listening comprehension exercises is that students are not *taught* the language (cf. Anna's complaint in Chapter 16), instead they are *tested* on it. There is too much focus on understanding and insufficient focus on decoding. Too much classroom time is spent on giving our students practice in coping at their current level, and insufficient time is spent on teaching them what they need to know about the sound substance of speech. In Chapter 19 we will see how listening comprehension exercises can be re-balanced so that there is appropriate focus on both understanding and decoding. Two points need to be made in advance of Chapter 19 – the first in relation to questions and the second in relation to answers.

Typically, listening comprehension questions address the level of understanding. However, for the purpose of teaching decoding, questions can be given an additional purpose – that of a focusing device. Questions can be used to draw attention to a speech unit, or a group of speech units, which contain useful examples of the sound substance which will form the basis of learning. The consequence of giving this additional function to questions is that the giving of answers at the level of meaning constitutes the beginning of learning about the sound substance. In other words, the giving of answers should not be the end of the listening comprehension exercise. We will also be teaching students like Anna something about the language that is the focus of the question, about the sound substance of speech.

17.8   Questions from students

Students often ask questions which are difficult to answer, and when unruly events happen in spontaneous speech, it is (sometimes) impossible to account for them using a system of rules. We therefore need to give up our desire to find an explanation, or a rule, for everything that happens. In dealing with spontaneous speech it is useful to take the point of view that 'anything can happen', and that it can happen for no obvious reason. We need to have the confidence to say either 'I don't know', or 'In the jungle, anything can happen, for no obvious reason.'

17.9   The value of short extracts

It is generally believed that the best way to learn to listen is to practise a lot, doing extensive listening to long extracts – minutes in length – in the expectation that osmosis will eventually work. Buck writes of the need for learners to pass 'lots of meaningful language through their language processors' (1995: 123).

However, in order to encourage our students to get to grips with the sound substance we have to be prepared to focus on extracts that are as short as a speech unit, or a group of speech units – extracts that are between two and ten seconds long. It is at this level that the moment-by-moment choices which speakers make are observable, it is at this level that words are squeezed into the new shapes which cause

Ying's dilemma. If a recording is three minutes long, then it is difficult to get to grips with all of it for the purposes of focusing on the sound substance at the level of detail that our listening goal requires.

So teaching decoding requires working with short extracts. It is then possible to focus on soundshapes of words in the stream of speech. Whenever we use a recording, we should use the *window on speech*, or similar, framework, to identify short extracts to help us teach decoding.

17.10 No one right way …

In Part 2 we saw that words have a wide variety of soundshapes, and that speech units have a variety of relationships to sentences, clauses and phrases. The *careful speech model* promotes the idea that there are correct and incorrect ways to pronounce words and say sentences, but in the spontaneous speech model there is no one right way to say anything: any word, or group of words, may be said in a multitude of different ways.

The learning task is therefore to master a sufficiently wide sample of this great variety so that decoding can be effectively taught and learned. In order for this to happen we need to accept that – in the jungle – there is no one right way to say anything.

Having accepted this, the task then is to find a way of giving our students experience of 'the same words in a wide range of contexts and voices' (Field, 2008: 166). It is currently beyond the abilities of spoken language corpora to provide materials that give all the possible variations of the soundshapes of words. However, it is possible for teachers and students, as vocal gymnasts, to do so by comparing actual occurrences with other ways of saying the same words, as we shall see in Chapters 18-20.

17.11 Learners' discomfort and frustration

One of the reasons that listening pedagogy is relatively unsuccessful is that materials writers have been too considerate of learners' sensitivities (Cauldwell, 2002). Textbook recordings are created which learners can manage at their current levels of language development. Alternatively if the recordings are regarded as too difficult for the level, then the task is adjusted so that learners can easily cope. The focus is on *what learners can cope with* rather than teaching them to become *comfortable with the realities* of spontaneous speech.

Even with these relatively easy recordings or tasks, the conventional listening lesson creates learners who feel that they are not good at listening. They tend to blame themselves for not being able to decode as well as they feel they should. Listening activities need to take learners beyond their current level, and this will probably mean that they will feel temporary discomfort at their lack of ability to decode or make sense of a particular set of speech units.

We therefore need to accept that our students may experience discomfort, and even frustration, as they first get to grips with the sound substance of a recording. The classroom skills we use must therefore include the ability to support them through this temporary discomfort and frustration, to ensure that they do not blame themselves for the fact that they cannot decode immediately. We must not avoid this discomfort and frustration, rather we need to recognise that it is the starting point for learning. Our students need to be reassured that the difficulties of listening do not lie with them – it is not their fault that they cannot hear what an expert listener would hear. One good tactic to prevent students blaming themselves is to explain the fact that their difficulties result from the very nature of spontaneous speech itself, and simply make a joke of it: 'That's the jungle for you!'

17.12   Summary and what's next

In order to teach listening effectively we need to let go (for the purposes of the listening lesson) of the idea of correctness, and of the idea that there are rules and explanations for everything that happens. We need to accept that the sound substance of spontaneous speech should be, and can be, taught. We need to neutralise the effects of the blur gap, and use the decoding gap to find out the starting point for learning. We teachers, as listening experts, need to manage, not avoid, the discomfort and frustration that our students may feel in the early stages of the listening lesson and seize the opportunities for learning that such frustration offers us.

In Chapter 18 we will look at the way in which the teachers' and the students' voices can be used in activities which address the listening goal.

17.13   Further Reading

Field (2009) argues for qualitative work on listening processes in preference to osmosis. Cauldwell (2002) gives an alternative metaphor for teaching decoding – he writes about 'grasping the nettle' of fast speech. The mindset towards spontaneous speech, as described in this chapter, although necessary, is not in itself sufficient to deliver a good series of listening lessons. To get an overview of the types of listening class methodology inside which this mindset needs to operate, you need to read the works of Buck (1995), Harmer (2001), Scrivener (2005) and Thornbury (2006). All of them provide methodological guidance which will supplement the contents of this and the other chapters of Part 4.

17.14 Learning and teaching activities

Activity 17.1: Reflect on learning

Look back at *A goal for learners* given in Section 17.1 and consider it in relation to your own language learning experiences. Do you feel yourself to be 'familiar and comfortable' with the sound substance of a language that you have learned as an L2? Do you feel that you now have an expert ability to decode this L2, or do you still have some progress to make? Talk to a friend, colleague or fellow teacher about your experiences. Summarise your thoughts, and the gist of your discussions, in your notebook.

Activity 17.2: Reflect on teaching

Look back at *A goal for teachers* in 17.2 and consider the range of knowledge, skills and tools listed in this chapter. How comfortable would you feel as a teacher in dealing with questions about the recording that have no easy answers? How comfortable would you feel dealing with looks of discomfort and frustration on your students' faces as they listen to a recording of spontaneous speech for the first time? Talk to a friend, colleague or fellow teacher about your thoughts and experiences. Summarise your thoughts, and the gist of your discussions in your notebook.

18   Vocal gymnastics in the classroom

As we have seen, words have a wide variety of soundshapes in spontaneous speech, and our goal is to help our students become familiar and comfortable with this variety so that they do not suffer from Ying's dilemma. Her dilemma, you will recall from Chapter 1, is that she cannot catch words that she knows when they are spoken:

> I believe I need to learn what the word sounds like when it is used in the sentence. Because sometimes when a familiar word is used in a sentence, I couldn't catch it. Maybe *it changes somewhere when it is used in a sentence.* (Goh, 1997: 366) [Emphasis added]

In this chapter we are going to explore ways in which teachers' and students' voices can be used in the classroom to create, savour and handle the changes which the soundshapes of words are likely to undergo in the sound substance of spontaneous speech.

In doing so we are going to follow the advice of two experts in the field of listening research: Field (2008: 166), who advises giving learners 'the same words in a wide range of contexts and voices'; and Buck (1995), who has suggested four ways in which we can help by:

- sensitizing the students to the problem
- consciously discussing it
- explaining how pronunciation changes
- giving examples

In Chapter 20 we will look at hi-tech ways in which these things can be done, but in this chapter we will look at ways in which the teachers' and the students' voices can be used to create these different soundshapes. We can become better teachers of listening, and our students can become better learners of listening, by becoming vocal gymnasts.

Our voices can create multiple examples of words spoken in different ways. We can then demonstrate to our students the many different soundshapes that words can have, and then get them to use their own voices to savour the soundshapes of these words.

We will start by doing some easy vocal gymnastic exercises which add sound substance to speech units, first by lengthening syllables and creating stepping stones, and second by adding drafting phenomena (of the type seen in Chapter 6). Then we will look at more challenging exercises in which we speed up and squeeze words of all kinds into a variety of soundshapes (of the type seen in Chapters 7 & 8).

18.1   Stepping stones

We saw in Chapter 6 that speakers often dwell on words and sounds such as *and*, *so*, *um*, and *er* (or indeed any word or filler) in order to buy themselves planning time while they decide what to say next. The speaker dwells on a syllable with a level tone so that it is much longer than would be the case if their speech was fully planned. We have referred to these drawn-out syllables as stepping stones. The vocal gymnastic skill involved here is a slow one to get us started. It is one which simply requires us and our students to say a given syllable on a level tone, at any pitch we choose, thus creating a stepping stone.

For example, let us take this textbook sentence, (Cunningham & Moor, 2005: 27) *It's the second biggest city in my country I think*. We create a tidy, garden version (cf. Chapter 17.3) of this with four prominences and a falling tone starting on *country* to act as our reference point, which we can see and hear in Extract 18.1.

Extract 18.1 Garden version *it's the ... i think*

```
|| ↘ it's the SECond BIGgest CITy in my COUNtry i think ||
```
The symbol for the falling tone is given at the beginning of the speech unit, but it starts on the underlined syllable.

We then create a slightly messy version as in Extract 18.2. We treat the first three of the first four words as stepping stones: with level tones at high, mid and low heights (*it's, the* and *biggest*); and one falling tone on *second*. However, as we have also seen, such stepping stones are often followed with a rapid burst of speech. We will therefore end with a fast double-prominence speech unit with five words, and a falling tone starting on the first syllable of *country* which continues over its second syllable and the words *i think*.

Extract 18.2 Stepping stone version *it's the ... i think*

```
01 || → ↑ IT'S ||
02 || → THE ||
03 || ↘ SECond ||
04 || → ↓ BIGgest ||
05 || ↘ CIty in my COUNtry i think ||
```

As you listen, notice that the level tones are at different pitch heights: on *it's* there is a 'high key' level tone, on *the* a 'mid key' level tone, and there is a 'low key' level tone on *biggest* (for more on tone and key cf. Chapter 4). Note that there is a falling tone starting on the first syllable of *second*. You can either model this yourself, asking students to repeat it after you, or use the recording as the model for them to repeat as a whole class. Then let students say these units aloud, first imitating the model in Extract 18.2, then varying the pitch height ('key') of the level tones.

We can then set up a pair-work activity where one student says the four-prominence garden version (Extract 18.1), and the other student – simultaneously – says the stepping-stone version as in Extract 18.2. The stepping stone version will take longer to say than the four-prominence garden version: the idea is that both members of the pair should repeat their respective parts until they finish together, as in Extract 18.3. This is a vocal gymnastic exercise in which both students are speaking at once. The pairs repeat this a few times and then the individuals in each pair change roles. As they proceed, the student saying the stepping stone version keeps varying the pitch height and the length of the level tones.

Extract 18.3 Pairwork version *it's the ... i think*

```
A || ITS || THE || SECond || BIGgest || CIty in my COUNtry i think ||
B || it's the SECond BIGgest CIty in my COUNtry i think ||
```

We can then give each pair another sentence and ask them to create a tidy, garden version, and a stepping-stone version of it. We then ask them to prepare to perform their sentence in front of the rest of the class. Here are four more tidy speech units which can be converted into stepping stone versions.

```
01 || he RAN all the WAY to the STAtion ||
02 || it's the most BEAUtiful PLACE in the WORLD ||
03 || it's RIGHT in the CENtre of LONdon ||
04 || WHEN would he LIKE to VISit us ||
```

18.2   Drafting phenomena

In Chapter 6 we saw that filled pauses (*um, er, uh,* etc.), and other drafting phenomena such as *I mean* and *you know*, together with vague language such as *kind of like* are very common features of spontaneous speech. To make our tidy garden sentence more natural and jungle-like we can add these phenomena to the sentence, as in Extract 18.4.

Extract 18.4 Drafting phenomena version *it's the ... i think*

```
01 || → UM ||
02 || → i mean IT'S ||
03 || ↗ you KNOW ||
04 || → THE ||
05 || → SECond ||
06 || → kind of like BIGgest ||
07 || ↘ CIty in my COUNtry i think ||
```

In Extract 18.4, five of the seven units have level tones: the exceptions are unit 03 *you know* which has a short, sharp, rising tone on *know* (as it usually does in *you know*, cf. Chapter 6.7); and unit 07, which has a falling tone starting on the first syllable of *country* and continuing over *i think*. As with the stepping stones activity, we can model the example in our own voice and then ask students in pairs to do the same with their voices, before going on to add drafting phenomena to other sentences.

18.3   Word squeezer

In the previous two sections we have taken tidy garden versions of a sentence and changed them so that they resemble normal spontaneous speech. However, we have left the soundshapes of words largely intact. In this section we will look at how our voices and those of our students can be used to create markedly different soundshapes for the words in a sentence.

Our task is to say a sentence in many different ways, with the goal of producing as many different soundshapes as possible for the words it contains. This may result in some versions of a sentence which are difficult to contextualise, but it is useful for the purposes of our listening goal to behave as if all versions are possible. This is because our goal is a decoding goal, not an understanding goal.

We will use a slightly-adapted sentence from a textbook for demonstration purposes. It comes from *New Cutting Edge* Intermediate (Cunningham & Moor, 2005: 108): *I realised that I'd left my purse at home.*

The tidy garden version of the sentence is likely to be given as a quadruple speech unit, as in Extract 18.5.

Extract 18.5 Tidy version *i realised ... at home*

```
||  ↘ i REALised that i'd LEFT my PURSE at HOME ||
```
The symbol for the tone is given at the beginning of the speech unit, but it starts on the underlined syllable.

However, as we have seen in Chapter 3, this sentence can be broken up into speech units of different sizes. For the purposes of this section we will use the double-prominence speech unit only. This will enable us to make the maximum number of syllables non-prominent, as we shall hear.

The sentence could be rendered into two double prominence speech units:

Extract 18.6 Two-unit version *i realised ... at home*

```
01 ||  ↗ i REALised that i'd LEFT || 02 ↘ my PURSE at HOME ||
```
The symbol for the tone is given at the beginning of the speech unit, but it starts on the underlined syllable.

However, this allows for four syllables to be prominent and it still retains the garden clarity when, for our purposes, we need to create a range of spontaneous speech versions which feature a normal lack of clarity. We therefore have to take this tidy sentence out of the garden and make it more jungle-like.

The vocal gymnastics required here are for us to make just two syllables prominent, and all the others non-prominent. We will deal with the details of the fate of non-prominent words in the next section, but first we will simply focus on varying the position of the prominences. Remember our focus is not on possible meanings, but on possible soundshapes. So we are going to apply, strictly, the rule that this sentence is going to be performed with only two prominences. In Extract 18.7 there are prominences on the first syllable of *realised* and on the word *purse*.

Extract 18.7 Two prominence version *i realised ... at home*

```
||  ↘ i REALised that i'd left my PURSE at home ||
```

The skill is to make sure that the prominent syllables – in upper case letters – are said louder and longer than the other syllables, that they are clear; and that there is a falling tone which starts on *purse* and then continues over the syllables *at home*.

Placing the speech unit in the five columns of a double-prominence speech unit (cf. Chapters 2-3) will enable us to make some useful generalisations. Notice that the columns are numbered in reverse order, with the prominent syllables in columns 4 and 2, and the falling tone starting in column 2. From now on, we will refer to tables with five columns as the five-part pattern.

Table 18.1: Extract 18.8 The five-part pattern *i realised ... at home*

5	4	3	2	1
i	REA	lised that i'd left my	PURSE	at home

The prominent syllables are allocated one column each: columns 4 and 2. It is helpful to think of columns 4 and 2 as protected zones, where the syllables are spoken as if they are part of a citation form, with all segments fully preserved (this is not absolutely true, because the final segments are often altered or dropped, but it is a useful pedagogic fiction for our purposes). In contrast, columns 5 and 3 should be thought of as *squeeze zones* (cf. Chapter 2) where syllables will be subjected to all kinds of reductions, which may even cause them to vanish altogether. Column 1 is a semi-protected zone, where the syllables – though non-prominent – are slowing down before a pause. Although these syllables are non-prominent, they are not subjected to the same level of squeezing as they would be in columns 5 and 3.

To sum up: we are aiming for correctness for the prominent syllables in columns 4 and 2, slightly less correctness in column 1, and we are aiming for unruliness and messiness in columns 5 and 3. Remember, this is a vocal gymnastic activity with a listening goal.

It is possible to get very technical about the destructions which could happen, and we will do so later. To start with, we should simply think of making prominent syllables louder, longer and clearer and non-prominent syllables softer, shorter and less clear. It is helpful to start by exaggerating this difference, by using extremes of volume and clarity, and then gradually bring the differences down to normal limits. We must make sure that none of the non-prominent syllables become prominent, and that the speech unit has no pauses – that it is one single rhythmic flow. It need not be fast, but it must be continuous – all syllables flowing into one another – as in Extract 18.9.

Table 18.2: Extract 18.9 The five-part pattern – loud and soft *i realised ... at home*

5	4	3	2	1
i	REA	lised that i'd left my	PURSE	at home

We can then speed up slowly and model three different speeds (as in Extract 18.10): slow, medium, and fast, becoming more and more careless about the syllables in the squeeze zones (columns 5 and 3).

Table 18.3: Extract 18.10 The five-part pattern – three speeds *i realised ... at home*

	5	4	3	2	1
SLOW	i	REA	lised that i'd left my	PURSE	at home
MEDIUM	i	REA	lised that i'd left my	PURSE	at home
FAST	i	REA	lised that i'd left my	PURSE	at home

The role of the students is first of all to listen and repeat, and then in pairs for one of them to produce the different versions, with the other monitoring to ensure that (a) there are only two prominences, (b) there are no pauses and (c) it is spoken as a single rhythmic flow.

Until now, we have kept the location of prominent syllables constant – on the first syllable of *realised* and on the word *purse*. However, in order to mimic the most extreme effects of the type of squeezing that happens in spontaneous speech, we can now place the prominences on the first and last syllables of the sentence, as in Extract 18.11.

Table 18.4: Extract 18.11 The five-part pattern – prominences on *I* and *HOME*

	5	4	3	2	1
SLOW		I	realised that i'd left my purse at	HOME	
MEDIUM		I	realised that i'd left my purse at	HOME	

FAST		I	realised that i'd left my purse at	HOME	

We are now asking students to produce speech units with the longest possible column three – a squeeze zone – and with prominences on the first and last syllables (in columns 4 and 2). This can result in a lot of enjoyment and laughter.

Up to this point we have not gone into the detail of sound substance of the non-prominent syllables. We have simply had the holistic aim of making them quieter, less careful, continuous sounds. As you will have heard, however, it is possible to achieve a high degree of correctness of pronunciation (particularly in the slow versions) even when syllables are non-prominent. But for our listening goal (to make learners familiar and comfortable with the sound substance of spontaneous speech) we need to ensure that the squeeze zones – columns 5 and 3 – feature the reduced forms of words and syllables which are likely to occur in spontaneous speech.

18.4   Reducing words and syllables in the squeeze zones

For some of us, a holistic approach to the squeeze zones is sufficient. We are able to make an appropriate mess of the non-prominent syllables in an intuitive way, which would provide our students with a reasonably realistic representation of what can happen in normal speech. However, many people prefer to receive specific advice on how to reduce citation form soundshapes into plausible reduced non-prominent versions. We will now demonstrate this using the fast version of the sentence from Table 18.4 in Extract 18.12.

Extract 18.12 Focus on non-prominent syllables *realised ... at*

`|| ↘I realised that i'd left my purse at HOME ||`

In this speech unit there are eight non-prominent syllables from *rea-* to *at* (remember that *realise* has two syllables not three, even in the citation form |rɪə.laɪz|). We shall now take each of the non-prominent syllables in turn and give advice on how they can be reduced to form an acoustic blur:

- make the diphthong of the first syllable of *realise* |rɪə| a monophthong based on its first element |ɪ|, so that the first syllable of *realise* sounds like *rill*
- make the diphthong of the second syllable of *realise* |aɪ| a monophthong based on its first element |a| so that the whole syllable sounds like *lazz*, rhyming with *jazz*

- remove the past tense ending of *realised* so that it sounds like *realise*
- remove the initial consonant of *that* so that |rɪə.laɪzd.ðæt| becomes |rɪ.laɪz.æt|
- make the final |t| of *that* into a glottal stop, giving us |æʔ|
- make the diphthong of first person pronoun *i* |aɪ| a monophthong based on its first element |a|
- remove the past tense ending of *i'd*
- remove final |t| from *left* which becomes *lef*
- make the diphthong of *my* |maɪ| a monophthong based on its first element |a|
- do not make a full closure for the stop consonant |p| in *purse* so that it sounds half way to *furss*
- make the final |t| of *at* into a glottal stop |æʔ|

If we apply all these guidelines we will get versions of this sentence which are given in units 02 and 03 in Extract 18.13. Unit 01 preserves the segments of the citation forms; Unit 02 applies the reductions, but it slow; and Unit 03 is at a normal, fast speed.

Extract 18.13 Focus on non-prominent syllables *realised ... at*

```
01 || I realised that i'd left my purse at HOME ||
02 || I rillaz zaʔ a lef ma furss aʔ HOME ||
03 || I rillaz zaʔ a lef ma furss aʔ HOME ||
```

By using the advice on reductions we have created runs of non-prominent syllables of the type we find in the squeeze zones of speech units of everyday spontaneous speech. When students are engaged in these activities, they will be doing pronunciation activities for a listening goal, during which they are savouring and handling the realities of spontaneous speech. The purpose of activities like these is to help them become familiar and comfortable with the sound substance of spontaneous speech, which is our goal for listening. We should not worry too much about getting the reductions correct – there is no 'right' form in these circumstances. In fact a wide variety of reductions can occur in the non-prominent syllables in squeeze zones and we did not cover all the possibilities for the above sentence. For example we could have reduced *realised* still further by making the |l| inaudible, which would have resulted in something close to 're-ice'. For a more comprehensive list of guidelines see Appendix 4 *Creating an obscure acoustic blur*.

18.5   Seeking amusing alternatives – mondegreens

As we worked through the example in the previous section, we made a number of statements about what various syllables could sound close to. We can devise more directly playful activities out of this process of reducing and squeezing non-prominent syllables by asking our students for real or nonsense words which would help with the act of reduction. (Remember we are devising pronunciation activities in pursuit of a listening goal, which will provide our students with opportunities to savour and handle the stream of speech.) The rules of the game would allow non-English words, but they must have one or two traces of the original words. The rules would prohibit rude words.

The teacher can write up a speech unit and invite students to suggest real and possible words which have some resemblance to the sounds of the non-prominent syllables, as with Extract 18.14.

Extract 18.14 *back to see Battersea*

```
|| he CAME back to see his FAMily ||
|| he CAME battersea his FAMily ||
```

In the second version the non-prominent syllables *back to see* become *battersea* – the name of an area of London.

The suggestion here is that teachers and students should together deliberately create what are known as **mondegreens**. This is the name given to mishearings of words normally associated with song lyrics, for example 'Scuse me while I kiss *this guy*' being a mishearing of 'Scuse me while I kiss *the sky*'.

18.6   Sequences of frequent forms

Similar activities can be done using sequences of frequent forms. As we have seen in Chapter 7, these are forms which are often run together extremely fast, and even though they consist of words that are supposedly known, they are often not successfully decoded even by advanced learners (cf. Field 2008a). They therefore need special attention in the listening class.

We have already seen and heard the first three words of in Extract 18.15 which occur in the squeeze zone of a double-prominence speech unit. They appeared in the demonstration of Ying's dilemma in Chapter 1. In Extract 18.15 these three words appear at three different speeds, starting with the slow version which preserves the features of the citation form, (even though the words are non-prominent), and ending with the fast version where the three words are greatly reduced.

Extract 18.15 *where there were ... lights*

```
SLOW         || where there were STREET LIGHTS ||

MEDIUM       || where there were STREET LIGHTS ||

FAST         || where there were STREET LIGHTS ||
```

In the fast version the three words *where there were* occur extremely fast, and sound like *weatherwuh*. The diphthongs in the full forms of *where* and *there* have lost their final elements. Meanwhile the long vowel of the full form of *were* has become shortened and its quality has changed to schwa.

You can coach the class as a whole in producing both the slow and the fast versions, making it clear that one is greenhouse/garden-tidy, and the other is jungle-messy. The class can then be divided into two halves, with one half repeating three words *where there were* in citation form, slowly, while the other half repeats, very quickly, the fast version, as you can hear in Extract 18.6, which is presented in Table 18.5. The numbers of the columns represent a rhythm of three quavers (3/8), which is repeated three times. So there are three musical (actually rhythmic) bars. The citation forms (middle row) each take one bar to say, while the three syllables of the fast version (bottom row) occur one to each beat of each bar.

Table 18.5: Extract 18.16 Different rhythms for *where there were*

1	2	3	1	2	3	1	2	3
WHERE			THERE			WERE		
wə	ðə	wə	wə	ðə	wə	wə	ðə	wə

You can conduct this so that the repetitions get successively louder and then, on a given signal, all the class can shout the two prominences *STREET LIGHTS* to bring the activity to an end.

As a follow up activity, students can be asked to search through the transcripts of recordings, (or reading passages) to find other clauses which begin with word clusters – that is runs of three frequent forms (e.g. '*when I was* twenty two' or '*that I got* last year') which can be turned into similar activities. A list of word clusters is given in Appendix 3.

18.7   Teaching new vocabulary

An ideal time to teach a variety of soundshapes is when teaching new vocabulary. Typically, learning a new word involves only one soundshape – the citation form – but, given the activity types which we have looked at in this chapter, it is easy to set up some short activities which will exemplify a range of soundshapes for each new item of vocabulary. Let us take the word *anomalous* as an example. It is a word often used in the reporting of scientific findings. Its citation form has four syllables, with word-stress on the second syllable, as you can hear in Extract 18.17.

Extract 18.17 Citation form *anomalous*

|əˈnɒm.ə.ləs|

In order to demonstrate some of the soundshapes that this word can have, we need some words which typically go before and after it. One source is a dictionary which contains example phrases and sentences, such as 'The Longman Dictionary of Contemporary English' (LDOCE). This gives us the noun group *a highly anomalous situation*. Another source is an online corpus such as the 'Michigan Corpus of Academic Spoken English' (MICASE) which gives us *this was hardly an anomalous sort of thing*.

We will use the LDOCE collocation. We can create a tidy version, with three prominences:

Extract 18.18 *a highly ... situation*

```
SLOW        || a HIGHly aNOMalous situAtion ||
MEDIUM      || a HIGHly aNOMalous situAtion ||
FAST        || a HIGHly aNOMalous situAtion ||
```

You can then say this at different speeds and, while taking care to retain the three prominences, make the following reductions to the non-prominent syllables:

- make the vowels of two syllables -*ly.a*- sound like the diphthong |ɪə|
- make the four syllables -*a.lous.si.tu*- have weak vowels only
- make a single |s| out of the final consonant of *anomalous* and the initial consonant of *situation*.

We can then move to the five-part pattern, with a double-prominence speech unit, placing *anomalous* in a non-prominent squeeze zone. This gives us a run of seven non-prominent syllables in column 3 in Table 18.6.

Table 18.6: Extract 18.19 *Anomalous* in a squeeze zone

5	4	3	2	1
a	HIGH	ly anomalous situ	A	tion

To create the acoustic blur for part three:

- drop the first syllable of *a.nom.a.lous* (this is a negative prefix which is often inaudible), which leaves us with three syllables *nom.a.lous*
- drop the third syllable of *a.nom.a.lous* (it is weak, and in such circumstances is often inaudible), which leaves us with two syllables *nom.lous*

Alternatively we can search for a mondegreen and use the word *omelette* in place of *anomalous*, as in Extract 18.20.

Extract 18.20 A mondegreen for *anomalous*

```
01 || a HIGHly anomalous situAtion ||
02 || a HIGHly an.omelette situAtion ||
```

The soundshape of *omelette* has two syllables |ɒm.lət| in careful speech and, if we put the indefinite article *an* in front of the first syllable of *omelette* we get something very close to the first two syllables – |ən.ɒm | – of *anomalous*. Also, the final syllables of both words (whose tidy versions are |lət| and |ləs| respectively), are likely to become much more like each other. This is, because the final |t| of *omelette* is likely to soften and become 's-like' before the |s| of situation.

We can then set up pair work in which the first student repeats each version, the original and the mondegreen, carefully making the differences between them very clear. As the student continues repeating them, she or he should gradually make the two versions as similar as possible, and lastly identical to each other. The task of the second student is to identify the moment when the two become identical. The point of savouring and handling the sound substance in this way is to help students realise that things which should sound different in the careful speech model often sound identical in spontaneous speech.

18.8   Summary and what's next

All of the activities suggested in this chapter are aimed at getting students to savour and handle the sound substance of language by creating and playing with differences in soundshapes of words, using vocal gymnastic exercises which are designed to improve their decoding abilities. Although we have used *pronunciation activities* to handle the acoustic blur, we must remember that these activities are *in pursuit of a listening goal* - to make students familiar and comfortable with the sound substance of speech.

18.9   Further Reading

This chapter has made use of the evidence of spontaneous speech presented in Part 2, Chapters 6-10, and used this evidence to create classroom activities. Appendix 4 *Creating an obscure acoustic blur* contains a more extensive list of guidelines for creating plausible non-prominent syllables. Shockey (2003) contains detailed descriptions of what happens to words in casual speech and her vulnerability hierarchy (14-15) is particularly useful. Underhill (2005: 171ff) has a variety of classroom exercises which bridge the gap between careful speech and spontaneous speech.

18.10   Learning and teaching activities

Activity 18.1: Reflect on learning

Think back over your own experience as a language learner. Have you ever practised producing non-prominent syllables in the ways suggested in this chapter to help you learn to listen more effectively? If yes, how did it help? If no, would it have helped you? Talk to a friend, colleague or fellow teacher about your experiences. Summarise your thoughts, and the gist of your discussions, in your notebook.

Activity 18.2: Experiment in teaching

Take one of the exercises suggested in this chapter and try it out in the classroom, making sure that you tell your students that it is to help with their listening. Ideally present it in the framework of the metaphors of the greenhouse, the garden and the jungle as outlined in Chapter 17. Report on your students' reactions to a friend, colleague or fellow teacher. equipment and software give teachers in your notebook.

19   Rebalancing listening comprehension

For many teachers, teaching listening is synonymous with doing listening comprehension. However, the traditional listening comprehension exercise typically focuses on testing students' understanding at their current level of ability to decode, thereby giving them an opportunity to learn and apply compensatory strategies. It does not teach the sound substance, nor does it aim to make learners 'familiar and comfortable' with the realities of spontaneous speech.

Recent listening materials (e.g. Thorn, 2011) have incorporated exercises which focus much more on the sound substance of recordings, and teacher trainers such as Scrivener (2005) urge approaches to teaching listening which go beyond the traditional listening comprehension. However, listening comprehension remains the bedrock of listening pedagogy so it is worth looking at the implications of the preceding chapters for classes in which listening comprehension occurs.

In this chapter we will examine the assumptions, structure and methodology of the traditional listening comprehension. We will then seek to re-balance the listening comprehension class so that it includes teaching of the sound substance, thereby developing our students' ability to decode the stream of speech. We will see that this process need not rely on osmosis. Instead it can be accelerated by being made the object of conscious, deliberate instruction.

19.1   Listening comprehension: a particular point of view

If we examine the features of the traditional listening comprehension approach, we will see that it embodies a particular view of how listening skills are acquired. The very name – comprehension – indicates a bias towards understanding. The focus of attention is on understanding meanings, and on techniques and strategies that help learners *cope in the absence of decoding skills* rather than in *purposefully helping students learn to decode.*

19.2 The value of short extracts

As we have seen in Parts 1 and 2, we and our students need to focus on short sections of speech – speech units of two seconds or less – in order to witness the forces that create the different soundshapes which are both contained within, and constitute, the sound substance of speech. Unlike listening comprehension practice, work on the sound substance of speech therefore requires attention being paid to extracts which are seconds, rather than minutes. in length.

However, in order to understand the context in which speakers make their moment-by-moment decisions, short extracts are not sufficient. We have to work with a recording of a minute or more in length. It is recordings of this length and longer which contain sufficient information to understand the reasons why speakers have said things in the way that they did. This is why it is necessary to work both at the level of a seconds-long extract and a minute-long (or longer) recording. We need to be able to zoom in to details of the recording to focus on the sound substance, and to zoom out to consider the whole recording in order to understand the reasons behind the choices speakers have made.

19.3 Preparing for listening: identifying short extracts

There are several ways of deciding which parts of the recording to zoom in on.

19.3.1 Clusters of frequent forms

The transcript of the recording is likely to contain clusters of two, three or more frequent forms, such as *where there were* or *of what I was going to do* as these can often be rushed together in ways which cause Ying's dilemma. (There is a list of word-clusters in Appendix 3.) The transcript is also likely to contain content words which occur more than once in the recording and it is very likely that these words will have different soundshapes.

19.3.2 Listen and follow the transcript

We can listen to the recording and follow the transcript to identify patterns of sound substance which are typical of spontaneous speech. When we follow the transcript while listening to the recording there will often be a mismatch between the speed at which our eyes are travelling over the words and the speed at which the recording goes, particularly when the recording is of spontaneous speech. Such mismatches are likely to be useful locations in the recording to work on because the recording is very likely to be slowing down or speeding up. These moments of deceleration and acceleration can provide useful sources of sound substance to concentrate on.

19.3.3   Soft focus listening

We can also use the listening technique which we first encountered in the Introduction and in Part 1. It requires turning off the process of understanding, and listening beyond the meanings to the sound substance of a recording. The idea is that we attend to the substance of the stream of speech – its changing speeds, its rhythms, short bursts of frequent forms and so on. Listening in this way helps us identify where polysyllabic words are spoken quickly and become mondegreens (e.g. *occasionally* often sounds like *ok jolly*), or where there is a clear alternation between prominent and non-prominent syllables. We can also hear where there are long gaps between prominent syllables, or where a set of stepping stones (cf. Chapter 6) is suddenly followed by a fluent burst of fast speech. In general terms, the idea is to identify extracts where the recording is closer to the unruliness of spontaneous speech, rather than the careful speech model.

Having identified such an extract, we will now see how it can be used within the traditional structure of a listening comprehension lesson – the three stages of pre-listening, while-listening and post-listening.

19.4   Pre-, while-, and post-listening

The very names of the three stages of a listening comprehension exercise are problematic because they imply a strict sequence of three events – before, during and after – in only one of which listening takes place. They also imply a single sequence, where there is no returning to the recording. For those teachers who feel insecure about direct encounters with the realities of spontaneous speech, this pattern offers two temptations. First to minimise time working with the recording and second, to maximise the amount of time spent doing other activities. These other activities might well be useful, but they allow little time for direct instruction about the sound substance and other interesting points in the recording. In pre-listening these useful things include advice on using strategies, activities to activate schemata and explanations of key vocabulary. In post-listening they include switching to other activities – discussion, writing or reading. It is only in the while-listening stage that any listening takes place. Going through the pre-while-post-listening sequence in this way therefore results in few encounters with the sound substance and little, if any, help for learners with the decoding gap. As we saw in Chapter 16, Anna's anger was caused by a teacher who behaved in such a way.

We need to guard against rigid interpretations of this sequence and its temptations and instead adopt a flexible approach which allows for repeated access to different parts of the recording so that the listening goal remains the focus of attention throughout.

19.5 Handling and savouring the sound substance

We will use the terms 'savouring' and 'handling' (cf. Chapter 17.3) to refer to those activities in which our students learn about the sound substance, and improve their decoding skills, by repeating, changing, manipulating and interacting in a variety of ways with the sound substance.

19.6 The question as a focusing device

Questions (or items such as true-false statements) most often perform a testing-of-understanding function – the students' task is solely to listen and extract meaning from the sound substance. We need, however, to treat the sound substance not simply as something that is mined for meaning, but as something to be learned about. The temptation of the testing structure of questions and answers is to believe that the activity is finished when the answers are given. However, if we treat the recording as an opportunity for learning as well as testing, then we need to add a further dimension to the questions that are set. They can be formulated in such a way that focuses attention on those extracts of the recording which are fruitful for learning. For example an intensive listening exercise in Cauldwell (2012) begins with the following pre-listening introduction to a recording:

> When she was eighteen, Emily finished school and went to South Africa, where she worked in a large secondary school. Before she started teaching, she went to a staff meeting where she was given a job to do.

The following question is given, with a choice of three answers:

At the first staff meeting, what job was Emily given?

A. Head of English   B. Head of technology C. Head of maths

Extract 19.1 shows the speech units which were the focus of the question:

Extract 19.1 Emily *they said ... of technology*

```
01 || they SAID uh ||
02 || RIGHT ||
03 || we DON'T have a techNOLogy ||
```

```
04 || TEACHer ||
05 || we don't have ANy technology teachers ||
06 || SO um ||
07 || so NOW you're HEAD of techNOLogy ||
      we DON'T have...we don't have ANy
```

In unit 03 the words *we don't have* go at 8.5 syllables per second and in unit 05 they go at 12.8 syllables per second – extremely fast (cf. Chapter 7).

As can be seen from Extract 19.1, getting the right answer for the question is easy, and experts who write listening comprehension exercises may well complain that it is too easy to be a good test item – the word *technology* is mentioned three times, and there are no indications whatsoever that *English* or *Maths* might be possibilities. However, in this case, the question is not functioning as a test item. Instead it is functioning as a device to focus attention on the extract on which students will go to work. This extract from the recording was chosen because it features repetitions and different soundshapes for *technology* and also because it features, in units 03 and 05, repetitions of the word cluster *we don't have* with different soundshapes. It is rich in real-life features of normal speech.

The purpose of the question, therefore, is to focus on this learning-rich area of the recording, so that it can be made the object of handling activities during which teachers and learners hear, inspect, compare and savour the relationship between the squeezed traces of words and their more carefully spoken forms.

19.7   Handling different soundshapes

The key purpose of handling and savouring activities is to exemplify how the short extracts of the sound substance could have been different. In particular the handling needs to involve comparing the soundshapes of words that actually occurred with other soundshapes that the words could have had, then getting students to handle and to savour the different versions. This can be done both using hi-tech activities (cf. Chapter 20) or the techniques outlined in Chapter 18. Below are two further examples.

19.7.1   From squeezed to clear, and back

The speech unit in Extract 19.2 is tidy in the sense that it is a single clause contained in a single speech unit, but it is a single-prominence speech unit (cf. Chapter 3) which goes at 7.0 syllables per second (sps), with a falling tone starting on *any*.

Table 19.1: Extract 19.2 Emily *we don't have ... teachers*

3	2	1
we don't have	AN	y technology teachers

In a single-prominence speech unit, the squeeze zone occurs before the tonic prominence in column 3. This contains three syllables which go much faster than the rest of the speech unit – 12.8 sps – resulting in an obscure acoustic blur of the type that typically causes Ying's dilemma. The seven non-prominent syllables after the tonic prominence go much more slowly at 5.8 sps. We want our students to savour the different ways in which the syllables in the squeeze zone can be shaped.

We can do this by creating different soundshapes for this clause. Extract 19.3 shows a stepping stone version (cf. Chapter 18.2).

Extract 19.3 Stepping stone version *we don't ... teachers*

```
01 ||  → WE ||
02 ||  → DON'T ||
03 ||  → HAVE ||
04 ||  → ANy ||
05 ||  ↘ techNOlogy TEACHers ||
```

This version begins with four speech units with a level tone, with the tonic syllable lengthened and every segment of each word spoken very clearly until the double-prominence speech unit at the end.

Alternatively we can create a series of double-prominence speech units, in which the tonic prominence stays in the same place – the second syllable of *technology* – and the first prominence is located in turn on each of the first three syllables, as in Extract 19.4.

Extract 19.4 Double prominence versions *we don't ... teachers*

```
01 ||  WE don't have any techNOlogy teachers ||
02 ||  we DON'T have any techNOlogy teachers ||
03 ||  we don't HAVE any techNOlogy teachers ||
```

In these three units, each of the first three words takes it in turn to be clear and prominent, and the other two less clear, in that they are squeezed and non-prominent.

Finally, we can get students to savour single-prominent versions at different speeds, as in Extract 19.5.

Extract 19.5 different speeds *we don't ... teachers*

```
01 || we don't have ANy technology teachers ||
02 || we don't have ANy technology teachers ||
03 || we don't have ANy technology teachers ||
```

The focus in this exercise is to get the first three syllables sounding increasingly squeezed.

19.7.2   From clear to squeezed

Extract 19.1 ends with a triple-prominence speech unit, repeated below in Extract 19.6. Again this is a complete clause.

Extract 19.6 Emily *so now ... technology*

```
|| so NOW you're HEAD of techNOlogy ||
```

We can then create activities, of the type we saw in Chapter 18, with the same words in the five-part pattern, but with two prominences rather than three, as shown in Table 19.2.

Table 19.2 Extract 19.7 Double prominent versions *so now ... technology*

	5	4	3	2	1
01	so now you're	HEAD	of tech	NO	logy
02	so	NOW	you're head of tech	NO	logy

Because parts 5 and 3 are squeeze zones, there is the opportunity to have fun reducing the syllables which are non-prominent. In the case of unit 01 we can squeeze the three syllables *so now you're* making them close to *snouyer* |snaʊjə|. In the case of 02 we can squeeze the four syllables towards *your red of tech* |jəredəftek| or *your rid of tech* |jərɪdəftek| or *yuhefftek* |jəheftek| or *yuhefftik* |jəheftɪk|. This gives us the possibility of the mondegreens *now you're rid of technology* and *now you're hefty nology* (where 'nology' is a nonsense word).

We can see how the giving of the answers can be a preliminary step – a springboard to learning about the stream of speech using handling activities such as repeated listening, comparison with citation forms or clear speech, comparing different occurrences of the same word or groups of words in the same recording, and using vocal gymnastics (cf. Chapter 18) to savour how a given group of words can be said in different ways.

One word of warning: vocal gymnastics, like ordinary gymnastics, can very quickly lead to mental and physical exhaustion. They should therefore be used as short, frequent intensive activities rather than long, extended activities.

19.8   Respecting our students' perceptions

Students can succeed in answering listening comprehension questions correctly, despite having failed to decode stretches of speech (Field, 2003: 326). Therefore after checking the answers, and before looking at the transcript, it is a good idea to ask them what they thought they had heard, either by giving a short dictation, or by asking 'What words did you hear which led you to this answer?'

To illustrate the value of checking with students in this way, we will look at Extract 19.8. This was chosen as the focus of a listening comprehension question because it contains features of the Birmingham (UK) accent for a group of students who needed to familiarise themselves with this accent. There was to be a particular focus on the words *made* and *become*.

Extract 19.8 Helen *i thought … p A*

```
01 || i THOUGHT i KNOW i've MADE it ||
02 || when i've BECOME ||
03 || a CHAIRman's p A ||
```
In unit 03 'p A' is the acronym for 'Personal Assistant' with a prominence on the letter 'A'.

After checking what the students thought they had heard (by giving a short dictation) it became clear that some had heard the word *married* instead of *made it*, so there was clearly a decoding gap (cf. Chapter 16).

It is difficult to make sense of the word *married* in this context as it seems to result in nonsense: 'I will know I'm married when I've become...' However, as research by Field (2003: 325; 2008:165) has shown, learner-listeners can hold apparently illogical and contradictory opinions on the relationship between what they perceive and the sense they can make of speech.

Such perceptions, no matter how funny or outlandish they may seem, must be treated for what they are: honest attempts to decode sound substance and instances of a decoding gap. We must remember that wherever there is a decoding gap, there is something to teach and learn. In this case the dictation has acted as an exploratory device to find a decoding gap.

To turn it into a handling activity, we start by listing the number of versions of the sound substance that are relevant. In this case there are three versions of these two syllables to work with: the Birmingham-accented version of *made it*, which sounds like *mide it* |maɪdɪt| compared with RP *made it* |meɪdɪt|, and the students' perception of *married*, RP |mærɪd|:

Extract 19.9 Birmingham accent *made it*

```
01 || i've MADE it ||
02 || i've MIDE it ||
03 || i've MARRied ||
```

Students can be asked to savour the three versions by saying each one in turn, first by making them as different as possible and then by making them as similar as possible. They can then be asked to do pair work. One student chooses one of the three versions and says it out loud, and the other student has to say which of the three versions it was. They then change roles. A variation on this is for one student to say one of the speech unit numbers e.g. 'One' and the other student has to say that version aloud, and so on with the other versions – chosen randomly, and with increasing speed. The pair then swap roles. Activities like these are a fun way of getting students to savour and handle the variety of soundshapes that words can have.

19.9   Using the transcript

With any recording that is used in the listening class, an essential learning tool is the transcript. A key moment in any listening lesson comes when students see the transcript – or selected extracts of it – for the first time. When this happens their memories of the transient traces of the sound substance are matched up with the non-transient written forms.

There is no single best time for showing the transcript, but it is best not to show it straight away. It is a good idea to get students to work on the sound substance of speech on its own terms – that is as a transient, plastic (cf. Chapter 1), speedy phenomenon – before revealing the transcript. The time we give them without the transcript should be just long enough to get them to work constructively on their memory of what they heard, but not so long as to frustrate them completely. We need to be prepared to tolerate looks of small amounts of puzzlement and frustration on the faces of our students – after all, these are symptoms of learning – but not too much. When we do reveal the transcript (and the timing is an art, not a science), the matching of unrecognised acoustic traces in the sound substance with the familiar written substance is an important moment in the lesson. This is because the moment of revealing the transcript to the students may be followed by exclamations of surprise or realisation such as 'Oh it was that!'. We should listen out for such responses, and follow them up, by asking questions such as 'You look surprised. What were you expecting to see?' or 'What did you think you heard?

Alternatively, just as the teacher may have done in preparing the lesson, students can follow the transcript as the recording plays and mark moments where their eyes cannot keep up with the speed of the recording, or where there are mismatches between what they hear and what they read. They can be asked to mark as they listen where these clashes come. These parts of the recording can then either be dealt with immediately, as above, or returned to in future classes.

It is also useful to consider asking students to follow the transcript as they listen, and to ask them to consider the following questions, (all of which focus on sound substance rather than meaning), and ask them to underline those parts of the transcript relevant to the questions:

- Can you find nonsense words?
- Can you find something which sounds like a word in your language?
- Can you find something really rhythmic?
- Can you find something really fast, or really messy?
- Can you find a really loud and clear frequent form?

Having identified short extracts using these questions, the handling and savouring exercises that have been suggested above and in Chapter 18 can be used to demonstrate how the soundshapes of words can vary in the sound substance of speech.

19.10 Impromptu dictations

Both Field (2008) and Thorn (2009) advocate using 'the last four words' dictations in which the teacher stops the recording and asks the class to write down the last four words that have occurred in the recording. The reasoning for choosing four words is because this is approximately the number of words that can be held in short term memory. Their 'four words' suggestion can be used randomly at any moment while the recording is playing, but I feel it is far better done in a planned way, so that you have time to plan what teaching/learning events can take place.

Although 'the last four words' is a good guideline for the size of this short dictation task, it is also worth considering doing it with speech units of different sizes. Alternatively you can target the drafting phenomena, and other features of spontaneous speech which we have encountered in the earlier parts of *Phonology for Listening*. The reason for focusing on speech units rather than number of words is that the speech unit is the stretch of the sound substance of the stream of speech which has the biggest effect on the soundshapes of words.

When conducting a dictation activity in the service of a listening goal we must not be tempted into making it a test of spelling. We should accept variant spellings for the purpose of the dictation if they are reasonable attempts to represent the sound substance that students perceive in the stream of speech. In giving the answers, of course, we can diplomatically correct the spelling. And having given the answers, the opportunity exists for creating handling exercises of the type described earlier.

19.11 Summary and what's next

In listening comprehension activities explicit instruction about the sound substance, and the use of savouring and handling activities to promote decoding skills need to become equal partners with work on understanding. Vocal gymnastic activities should be also used to help with the listening goal.

We need to re-design the traditional listening comprehension exercise so that we can use it to check with our students to find out what they believe they have heard so that we can find the decoding gaps. Questions should not always be used simply to check understanding. Instead they should also be seen as focusing devices, and the checking of answers should be seen as the start of a pedagogic engagement with the recording in pursuit of the learning goal of becoming familiar and comfortable with the realities of spontaneous speech.

Many of the recommendations of authors such as Field and Buck point towards the need for using hi-tech approaches and materials and we shall turn to this topic in the next chapter.

19.12 Further reading

Field (2009) argues for focused practice using short activities and (1998) also argues for the systematic introduction of the features of natural speech in micro-listening exercises. Thorn (2011–12) is an important contributor to the argument for working with unscripted materials at all levels of learning and to the argument for examining and listening closely to authentic recordings as a way of learning about the sound substance. Cauldwell (2002) gives an account of how to manage learner frustration and puzzlement in the listening class so that learners finish the activity in a reasonably happy state. And Cauldwell (2012) contains twenty-four 'Hotspot' exercises (intensive listening) which are very short extracts that students can listen to repeatedly, compare with other versions, and savour.

19.13 Learning and teaching activities

Activity 19.1: Learning

Look again at Anna's angry evaluation of the listening comprehension classes that she attended, which is repeated here from Chapter 16.

> ... I've hated the underuse of the material. I've ... answered three silly questions ... then someone tells me patronisingly (it IS bloody patronising) that the rest doesn't matter. Well it does if I want to learn the language!

Do you think that Anna would have been happier if her teacher had used some of the techniques suggested in this chapter? Would you have been happier (or more angry) if your listening classes had contained activities of the sort described in this chapter? Discuss these questions with a friend, colleague or fellow teacher. Summarise your thoughts, and the gist of your discussions, in your notebook.

Activity 19.2: Experiment in teaching

Read through the transcript of a listening comprehension exercise in a textbook which you are familiar with. Underline any three-word or longer runs of frequent forms (e.g. *where there were*), and underline content words that occur more than once. Now go to those underlined sections in the recording itself and (using Audacity or another digital audio editor) copy and paste those extracts into another soundfile and judge whether (a) these words show any sign of the squeezing that we associate with non-prominent sections of speech units (b) they have different soundshapes compared to the other occasions when they occur and (c) whether they have soundshapes which differ markedly from the citation form. Report on your findings to a friend, colleague or fellow teacher. Summarise your thoughts and experiences in your notebook.

20   Hi-tech solutions and activities

The written form of the language is easy to navigate, explore and exploit for use in the classroom. As teachers, we have a wide variety of text-processing techniques at our disposal. We can search for words and phrases in single documents, and in millions of documents in corpora, and we can create teaching materials from the results of the search. Text can be highlighted in colour, cut and pasted and assembled in a different order.

This chapter explores the extent to which such text-processing techniques can be applied to the sound substance of speech to make it as easy to visualise, navigate, search and manipulate as the written language. In the era of computers and hand-held smart devices which can record and edit sound, this ought to be easy to do, but in practice, it is difficult. Digital recordings which are published and used on CD are not easy to navigate around, and therefore activities such as collecting small samples and zooming in and out of parts of the recording, are problematic. However, the situation is gradually improving: more and more software is being developed which allows teachers and students to navigate quickly around a recording with relative ease. They can then assemble and manipulate short extracts for teaching and learning purposes.

For the purposes of this chapter 'hi-tech' refers to programmes that are found on computers and on mobile devices such as smartphones and tablets. It does not include tape recorders and audio CD players. Where specific software is mentioned, it is because it exemplifies a particular functionality which is useful for our purposes. By the time you read this chapter, the software mentioned may have been superseded by other software that performs the same functions in better ways. So in this chapter, the focus is on functionality rather than on specific pieces of software.

The particular functionality we are interested in is that which will enable us to follow the advice of Field (2008: 166) who advises giving learners 'the same words in a wide range of contexts and voices' and of Buck (1995) who suggested giving examples of the way pronunciation changes as a way to improve listening.

20.1   Resources on the Internet

There is an infinite number of listening resources on the Internet: news channels have video and audio content, YouTube has videos made by individuals and organisations for every topic, interest and hobby that it is possible to imagine. These are excellent sources for listening practice, but this kind of resource is not the concern of this chapter. Our focus is not on extensive listening to lots of different texts, but on focused, intensive listening to short extracts – of using hi-tech solutions to savour, handle, and teach the patterns of spontaneous speech. In this way we can maximize exposure to multiple examples of words spoken in different ways.

20.2   Copyright

Whatever recordings you use, it is essential to respect the rights of the copyright holders of the recordings. You should always check what your obligations are if you are going to use recorded material produced by other individuals and organisations.

20.3   Digital audio editors

One of the biggest challenges of the sound substance of speech is that it is transient and invisible. It is therefore useful to be able to capture it and visualise it, and the best-known tool for visualising speech is the digital audio editor. There are many editors, with Audacity being the most widely-used free version. Digital audio editors display sound substance as a series of vertical lines of varying heights above and below a centre-line. Below is an image of the phrase 'where there were street lights' (Brazil, 1994) which we used to illustrate Ying's dilemma (Chapter 1).

Figure 20.1: Extract 20.1 *Where there were...* Extract 20.1

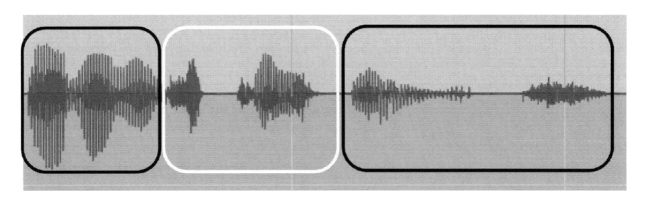

This screenshot was taken from the Amadeus digital audio editor.

The non-prominent words *where there were* are shown inside the left-hand rectangle, prominent *street* is shown in the white rectangle, prominent (and tonic) *lights* is contained in the black rectangle on the right-hand side. The gaps in the waveform for *street lights* indicate the brief closure (and therefore no signal) for the consonant |t| which is the second and last segment in |stri:t| and the penultimate segment in |laɪts|.

In Figure 2 below you can see the three non-prominent words *where there were* with a 0.2 second gap between them.

Figure 20.2: Extract 20.2 *Where there were...* with pauses

The waveform provides a graphic metaphor for the sound substance and is useful for language awareness exercises which help us (teachers) combat the blur-gap, the gap between what we believe we hear and what is actually present in the sound substance (cf. Chapters 1.3; 16.7). As far as students are concerned, they can be given one or two speech units from a recording of spontaneous speech and asked to identify where words begin and end, adding a short silence between each word. Exercises of this type are invaluable in drawing our students' attention to how the soundshapes of words can vary dramatically from their citation forms in a stream of speech, and how multiple words are often squeezed into one acoustic blur.

20.4 Pronunciation dictionaries

Pronunciation dictionaries such as Wells (2008) and Roach et al (2011) come with CDs which contain soundfiles. These soundfiles are, of course, citation forms, but they give two forms of each word, one in British English (Received Pronunciation, or BBC English), and one in American English (General American, or North American English). Such dictionaries and general dictionaries with their phonetic transcriptions provide an authoritative source of citation forms which can be used as a point of comparison when working on recordings of more natural speech.

General dictionaries also provide both British and American soundshapes for each word and some have the facility to 'play word automatically' while you are browsing the Internet, or using your computer. However, such dictionaries will only play the headword and not any inflected forms. Therefore users hear the singular form of nouns, not plurals, and the root form of the verb. For example, if you click on the word *dictionaries* you will hear *dictionary*, or if you click on the past participle *clashed* you will hear *clash*, the base form of the verb *clash*.

20.5 Dictionary examples

The *Longman Dictionary of Contemporary English* (*LDOCE*) application, for iPad and iPhone includes not only headwords in both UK and US English, but also – very usefully – example phrases and sentences read by actors.

For the word *there* symbols and soundfiles are given for both UK and US citation forms, followed by seven example sentences, all of which are recorded and available – at the touch of a button – to be streamed to your device. The examples for *there* are:

> Is there any milk left?
> There are a few things we need to discuss.
> There must be easier ways of doing this.
> There seems to be a lack of communication.
> There remain several questions still to be answered.
> Suddenly there was a loud explosion.
> They were all laughing when there came a knock at the door.

These examples are spoken very naturally by the standards of radio drama or radio news and although they are scripted, they are an excellent source of examples of the same words spoken in different sentences. (You will recall that the purpose of this chapter is to identify precisely this functionality – the same word in many different contexts). All instances of *there* in the examples are non-prominent, as might be expected. The examples also contain other natural features of spontaneous speech. For example, the tone in the *yes-no* question *Is there any milk left* is a falling tone and the soundshape of *there* in the last example is close to *they* – a commonly occurring soundshape for this word.

The *LDOCE* has a large resource of recordings, admittedly not as messy as spontaneous speech can be, but with a variety of speeds, and these are a very useful source of material for listening projects. For example, we can ask students, either singly or in small groups, to use the LDOCE to explore the sound-files of the examples for new vocabulary. They can then report back on their listening successes and difficulties, and what they notice about the soundshapes of words in the example sentences.

20.6 Text to speech

Computers can now read aloud. In Apple's operating system, for example, teachers can select text and choose a voice to read it out. The software does a reasonable job of creating an imitation of the stream of speech. We can create different versions of a sentence, at different speeds, with different voices. At the time of writing, Apple's 'Alex' is one of the best-sounding voices. Alex can be set to speak at different speeds and with different intonation patterns. Alex's slow-normal speed-range is of better quality than his normal-fast range, which becomes somewhat choppy. Intonation can be varied by the use of punctuation marks. A full stop between each word gives a citation form with a falling tone, a comma will give a fall-rise tone and a question mark will give a rising tone.

We can give students the task of producing computer-speech versions of speech units from spontaneous speech. For example, we can give them a short extract (a few speech units) of a recording, and ask them to create other versions with Alex (or any text-to-speech programme) which are as close as possible to the speed and intonation patterns of the original. They can then present their version in class and explain the successes and difficulties they had in getting the two versions to match each other.

20.7 Navigating, annotating and mining a recording

The closest we can come to a single application which can perform text-processing techniques on sound substance is with a programme called Audio Notetaker. This software allows the user to see – at a single view – images, references, text and sound substance. It was originally designed to be used by students listening to either live, or recorded, lectures. However, it is excellent software to prepare recordings for the kind of listening activities suggested in Chapter 19.

Figure 20.3 Screenshot of *Audio Notetaker*

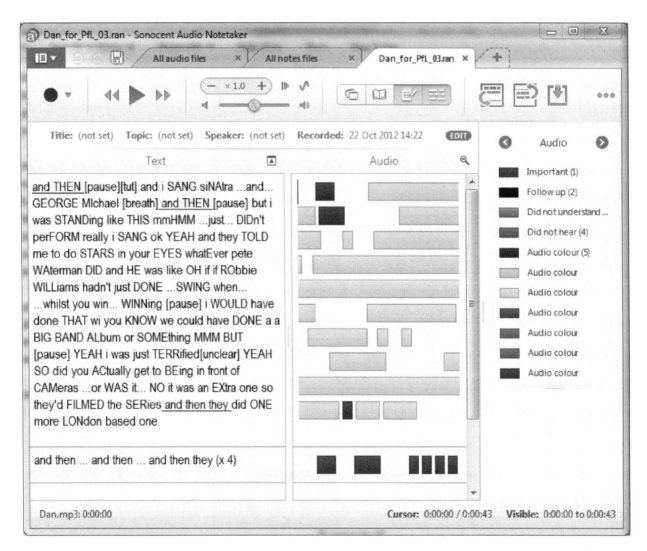

The main view has four panes and an editing column. In Figure 20.3, just two of the panes are shown: the text pane and the audio pane. The formatting column is also shown on the right-hand side. The audio pane consists of 'chunks' of sound substance, represented by rectangular bars. As you record or import a recording into Audio Notetaker, the software 'reads' the sound substance, and creates a series of rectangular chunks, which you can see growing as the recording is processed. Every time the software detects a pause, it ends the current chunk and starts a new one.

Once a recording is loaded, you can navigate with the click of a mouse, or by using the arrow keys, to any of the chunks in the audio pane. You can listen to each chunk as often as you wish, jump to any other chunk, edit and colour code them and annotate them.

In Figure 20.3 there are three instances of *and then* which are underlined in the text and represented by dark gray chunks (on screen, they are red) in the audio pane. You can then use the *Extract* button in the menu to extract, that is copy, the chunks that you have colour coded without affecting the original recording . The dark gray chunks are then automatically collected into a separate file. Using this *Extract* function, the instances of *and then* and *and then they* have been copied into the last row of this screen, which you can hear in Extract 20.3.

Extract 20.3: Dan *and then ... and then they*

```
|| and then || and then || and then they (x 4) ||
```

With Audio Notetaker you can divide up, annotate and code the recording and transcript very quickly. In fact it is so quick to do this that it can be used in real time in the classroom. For example, those parts of a listening comprehension recording that are identified as problematic during the class by students (as described in Chapter 19) can be accessed easily and listened to repeatedly.

Another useful feature is that the audio can be either slowed down, or speeded up, for playback. You can also record your own versions of the words of the recording directly into Audio Notetaker right next to the original words so that their soundshapes can be compared. This is a flexible, easy-to-use tool which helps teachers accommodate the moment-by-moment needs of students in the listening class by giving them direct experience of multiple soundshapes of the same word(s) and word clusters.

20.8   Producing versions at different speeds

It used to be the case that changing the speed of a recording meant that it would change in pitch. If you played an extract faster it would result in an unnatural chipmunk or helium-voiced high pitch; if you played it slower, it would result in an unnatural low growling pitch. Now the situation has changed and software can vary the speed of speech without changing pitch. Extract 20.4 shows a speech unit from Geoff, which we first heard in Chapter 7, going at three different speeds.

Extract 20.4 Geoff *this is ... in fact*

```
01 this is ONE i'm going to be looking at in slightly more DEtail in fact
```

```
02 this is ONE i'm going to be looking at in slightly more DEtail in fact
03 this is ONE i'm going to be looking at in slightly more DEtail in fact
```
Versions created by Amadeus.

Unit 01 gives the original, unit 02 is slowed by 50% and unit 03 is speeded up by 20%. As the speed is reduced the recording gets an increasing amount of echo, and as speed is increased (because the software has to cut out bits of the original signal) the recording sounds increasingly choppy and less like a smooth stream of sound.

The value of being able to change speed is twofold: at the slower pace students have a better chance of picking out the traces of words which are squeezed into very small shapes; and the faster pace gives students practice in handling the transience of speech (cf. Chapter 1.6).

20.9   Handling: comparing and deciding

Multi-touch devices such as the iPad enable learners to listen to a recording repeatedly, at will, speech unit-by-speech unit. Figure 20.4 shows a screenshot from an iPad application Cauldwell (2012).

Figure 20.4 Screenshot of rhythm exercises from *Cool Speech*

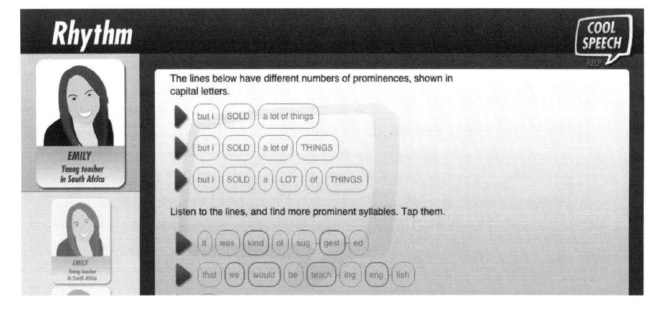

Students hear three rhythmic templates - a single, a double, and a triple-prominence speech unit featuring the same seven words 'but i sold a lot of things'. They play each unit in the template as often as they need to in order to get the different rhythms clear and distinct in their heads. After this they listen to a pre-selected stretch of spontaneous speech unit-by-unit and decide which of the templates (single, double, triple) is the best match for each successive speech unit. They then have to decide where the prominent syllables are. The task ends with them tapping what they believe to be the prominent syllables on the screen and then checking their answers. If they are correct, the syllables get a green border, if incorrect, a red border.

The value of doing a task like this is that the students are paying attention to the rhythm of the sound substance without having to worry about identifying the words themselves. They are attending to properties of the sound substance, making judgements about it and then checking on the accuracy of their judgements. It is this kind of interaction with the moment-by-moment decisions that speakers make (in this case, prominences) - that constitutes hi-tech 'handling' of the sound substance.

20.10   Student projects: Sampling and dictations

Many students own some kind of portable device which they can use to record and edit sound, and they are likely to have expertise which can be used for project work.

Groups of students can be asked to focus on one recording each and to collect together those parts of the recording which are of particular interest and/or difficulty. For example, they may choose to focus on words of high frequency spoken very fast, or an accent, or content words said in different ways. Alternatively they may choose to collect all the instances of drafting phenomena such as *um* and *uh* or *you know* and *like* (cf. Chapter 6). They then sample them – 'sampling' in this sense means choosing short digital extracts of sound and copying and pasting them into attractive, entertaining rhythmic patterns.

The results of the work can be made into presentations delivered to the whole class, or placed in a part of the classroom associated with the jungle (cf. Chapter 17). If your teaching circumstances allow, you can set up a listening station with headphones attached to a playback machine. Next to the listening station there can be posters or a page of commentary and illustrations describing, in both analytic and imaginative ways, the edited recording. The commentary might include statements about non-verbal sounds the fast speech reminds them of, or what words in their mother tongue the sounds remind them of. They can also create pictures to represent their experience of the features of speech. If the group contains a budding musician, rap artist or DJ, then that person could sample the recording and produce a highly rhythmic set of repetitions of a particular feature of speech, including slowing down and speeding up. The point is to get students to savour and handle the sound substance of spontaneous speech in playful ways which will make them familiar and comfortable with it.

Such manipulation of soundfiles can be used with the more traditional format of the dictation. The class can be divided into groups and each group assigned a recording, a CD-player, or some other means of playing the recording, and a transcript to work with. Preferably each recording should be one they have listened to before, and therefore have some familiarity with. The teacher asks them to listen to the recording closely to identify an extract of ten seconds or so to use as a dictation for one of the other groups. The segment should be difficult and deliberately chosen so that the other group is likely to have trouble decoding it. The nature of the difficulties should be related to the sound substance of the language, not grammar, nor spelling or vocabulary. The focus should be on fast speeds, lack of prominent syllables, difficult-to-hear negatives, weak forms, fixed phrases, etc.

After the dictation extracts have been selected, students then deliver the dictation to other groups – just as a teacher would – and, when the time comes to give the answers, the transcript relating to the dictation should be shown. There is then a discussion. The dictation makers take it in turn to explain why they chose their extract and then the dictation takers explain the difficulties and successes they had.

20.11 Conclusion

Hi-tech equipment and software give teachers and students the ability to create learning materials that experts have called for, and that research shows is valuable, but which hitherto has been impossible to create or assemble. For example, Field (2008: 166) suggests that it is 'a primary requirement' for learners to hear the same words in a wide range of contexts and voices. And trace theory (Shockey, 1983: 70) states that people only become efficient listeners by having large numbers of different traces (in our terms, soundshapes) of words and phrases in their mental store with which they recognise words as they are encountered in real time. We have seen in Chapter 18 that it is possible for teachers and students as vocal gymnasts to create variations of the soundshapes of words. In Chapter 19 we have seen how students can savour, handle, and interact with the sound substance in the traditional listening comprehension lesson. In this chapter we have seen how hi-tech solutions can be used to achieve the same results, by providing exciting new ways of visualising, accessing, editing and manipulating the sound substance in pursuit of a listening goal.

20.12   Further reading

One important source of scholarly articles is the online journal *Language Learning and Technology* http://llt.msu.edu. It is not, however, a journal specialising in listening technology. The Speech in Action website at http://www.speechinaction.com is also a source of information about developments in hi-tech approaches.

20.13   Learning and teaching activities

Activity 20.1: Learning

Download a trial version of Audio Notetaker (at the time of writing, you get 30 days free trial) and import a recording of a language that you either have learned, or are learning at the moment, in which you are not yet an expert listener. Find parts of the recording that go too fast for you and colour code them red. Use the speed controller to reduce the speed of playback and then listen again. Record your own versions of the extracts you have identified in both careful, and faster, versions. Discuss whether or not such work can help with your own language learning with a friend, colleague or fellow teacher. Summarise your thoughts, and the gist of your discussions, in your notebook.

Activity 20.2: Experiment in teaching

Choose one of the exercises suggested in this chapter and try it out in the classroom. Report on your students' reactions to a friend, colleague or fellow teacher. Summarise your thoughts and experiences in your notebook.

References for Part 4

Amadeus Pro (2011) *Amadeus*. [Digital audio editor]. Kenilworth: Hairersoft. http://www.hairersoft.com/pro.html

Anderson, A., and Lynch, T. (1988) *Listening*. Oxford: Oxford University Press.

Audacity (2000-2012) [Digital audio editor]. http://audacity.sourceforge.net/

Audio Notetaker (2012) Audio Notetaker 3.0. Chepstow: Sonocent. http://www.audionotetaker.com/

Brazil, D. (1994) *Pronunciation for Advanced Learners of English*. Cambridge: Cambridge University Press.

Buck, G. (1995) How to become a good listening teacher. In Mendelsohn, D. J. and Rubin, J. (eds.) *A Guide for the Teaching of Second Language Listening*, 113–131. San Diego, CA: Dominie Press.

Cauldwell, R. (2002) Grasping the nettle: The importance of perception work in listening comprehension. http://www.developingteachers.com/articles_tchtraining/perception1_richard.htm

Cauldwell, R. (2012) *Cool Speech: Hot listening, Cool Pronunciation*. [iPad application]. Birmingham: Speech in Action.

Cunningham, S., and Moor, P. (2005) *New Cutting Edge Intermediate*. Harlow: Pearson Education.

Field, J. (1998) The changing face of listening. *English Teaching Professional*, 6, 12-14.

Field, J. (2003) Promoting perception: Lexical segmentation in L2 listening. *ELT Journal*, 57/4, 325-334.

Field, J. (2008) *Listening in the Language Classroom*. Cambridge: Cambridge University Press.

Field, J. (2008a) Bricks or mortar: Which parts of the input does a second language listener rely on? *TESOL Quarterly*, 42/3, 411-432.

Field, J. (2009) More listening or better listeners? *English Teaching Professional*, 61, 12-14.

Harmer, J. (2001) *The Practice of English Language Teaching*, [3rd edition]. Harlow: Longman.

Hulstijn, J. L. (2003) Connectionist models of language processing and the training of listening skills with the aid of multimedia software. *Computer Assisted Language Learning*, 16, 413-425.

Longman Dictionary of Contemporary English. (2012) [iPhone app, iPad app]. Harlow: Longman.

Mendelsohn, D. J. (1998) Teaching listening. *Annual Review of Applied Linguistics*, 18, 81-101.

Roach, P., Setter, J., and J. (eds.) (2011) *Cambridge English Pronouncing Dictionary*. Cambridge: Cambridge University Press.

Rost, M. (2001) Listening. In Carter, R. and Nunan, D. (eds.) *The Cambridge Guide to Teaching English to Speakers of Other Languages*. Cambridge: Cambridge University Press.

Rost, M. (2011) *Teaching and Researching Listening*. [2nd edition]. Harlow: Longman.

Scrivener, J. (2005) *Learning Teaching: A Guidebook for English Language Teachers*, [2nd edition]. Oxford: Macmillan.

Shockey, L. (2003) *Sound Patterns of Spoken English*. Oxford: Blackwell.

Thorn, S. (2009) Mining listening texts. *Modern English Teacher*, 19/2, 5-13

Thorn, S. (2011-12) *Real Lives, Real Listening*. [Series]. London: The Listening Business.

Thornbury, S. (2006) An A-Z of ELT. Oxford: Macmillan.

Underhill, A. (2005) *Sound Foundations: Living Phonology*, [2nd edition]. Oxford: Macmillan Education.

Vandergrift, L. (2006) Listening to learn or learning to listen. *Annual Review of Applied Linguistics*, 24, 3-25.

Wells, J. C. (2008) *Longman Pronunciation Dictionary*. Harlow: Pearson Education.

White, G. (1987) *The teaching of listening comprehension to learners of English as a foreign language: A survey*. [M Litt dissertation]. University of Edinburgh.

Wilson, J.J. (2008) *How to Teach Listening*. Harlow: Pearson Education.

Appendix 1 Two models of speech

Careful Speech Rule-governed and tidy	Spontaneous Speech Unruly and messy	Chapter
The greenhouse and the garden	The jungle	17.3
Drafting phenomena do not occur	Drafting phenomena occur	6
Words have soundshapes close to the citation form	Words have soundshapes that may be very different from the citation form	8 & 9
Steady speeds	Extreme speeds at times	7
Pauses at phrase & clause boundaries	Pauses anywhere	6
Word stress, word order & sentence structure are the main shapers of the sound substance	Speakers are the main shapers of the sound substance	Part 1
We can predict where prominences, stresses and weak forms will occur	We cannot predict where prominences, stresses and weak forms will occur	Part 2
English is stress-timed	English is not stress-timed	10
People speak in clauses and phrases	People speak in rhythmic bursts	Part 1
Function words have a few weak forms	Function words have many weak forms	8
Function words are rarely prominent	Function words are often prominent	6
Content words have one or two soundshapes	Content words have many soundshapes	9
Content words receive prominences on their stressed syllables	Content words may or may not receive prominences on their stressed syllables	9
Nuclear stress falls on the last lexical item in the sentence	A 'sentence' is not a helpful concept. Speakers choose where the tonic prominence (not nuclear stress) goes	4
Connected speech rules (assimilation, elision, linking) adequately explain changes at syllable and word-boundaries	Connected speech rules do not adequately explain the changes that can happen when word meets word	8 & 9
Pairs such as *my train* and *might rain* are clearly distinguished	Pairs such as *my train* and *might rain* sound identical	8 &9
Differences which are important in grammar are audible	**Differences which are important in grammar may be inaudible**	Part 2
Different tenses sound different: *she's sold – she sold* *they'd bought it – they bought it*	Different tenses may sound identical: *she sold – she sold* *they bought it – they bought it*	Part 2

Negative morphemes are clearly heard: very legal – very illegal	Negative morphemes may often be inaudible: *verrilegal – verrilegal*	8
Tones carry meaning	**Tones co-occur with meaning**	15
Rising tones on *yes-no* questions sound 'polite'	Rising tones on *yes-no* questions can co-occur with any meaning	15
Falling tones on *yes-no* questions and requests sound impolite	Falling tones on *yes-no* questions can co-occur with any meaning	15
Wh-questions start high and then fall	*Wh*-questions can have any contour	15
Yes-no questions start high and end with a fall-rise	*Yes-no* questions can have any contour and tone	15
Listing intonation consists of rising tones ending with a falling tone	Listing intonation can have any sequence of tones.	15
There are no level tones	There are many level tones	5, 6

Appendix 2   Calculating the speed of speech

This appendix explains how to calculate the speed of speech of a short extract of a recording. First, we will look at how to calculate the speaking rate (cf. Chapter 7).

Calculating speaking rate

First we need to choose an extract and transcribe it into speech units, then we count the number of words and syllables in each unit. Table 1 shows an extract for which this has already been done.

Appendix 2 Table 1 Extract A.2.1 Corony *i was ... popular*

	words	syllables
01 ||... i WAS ... ||	2	2
02 || quite sucCESSful ||	2	4
03 || i i didn't MAKE an awful lot of MOney ||	9	12
04 || in the FIRST couple of YEARS ||	6	7
05 || ERM ||	1	1
06 || but i SOLD a lot of things ||	7	7
07 || it was OBviously very POpular ||	5	11
Totals	32	44

Counting words and syllables is not always completely straightforward: we have to make decisions about what constitutes a word, and how many syllables each of them contains. So in computing the figures in Table 1, the following decisions were made:

- in unit 03 we count *i i* as two words
- in unit 05 we count *erm* as a word
- in unit 07 we count four syllables in *ob.vi.ous.ly*. We could have counted it (but did not) as having three syllables, because it is often pronounced with the second and third syllables compressed into one.

Phonology for Listening

After counting up the words and syllables for each unit we get the figures shown in the columns on the right-hand side of the table.

With these figures we can calculate the syllable-to-word ratio:

- 44 syllables, divided by 32 words gives us a ratio of 1.375

(We saw the importance of this ratio in Chapter 7.4.)

We then measure the duration of the extract. This can be done in a number of ways. One of the easiest is to import it into a digital audio editor such as Audacity, and then use the cursor to select the extract at the moment at which it starts, dragging across to the moment when it ends: this will automatically indicate the duration at the bottom of the screen. This extract lasts 7.45 seconds.

To get the speaking rate in words per minute (including pauses) we do the following calculations.

- We divide the duration by the number of words: thus 7.45 divided by 32 = 0.233. This is the average duration of the words in this extract.
- We take the number of seconds in a minute – 60 – and divide by 0.233, which gives us 257. This gives us the speaking rate, in words per minute, for this extract. It is good practice to round this down to 250 wpm.

To calculate the speed of this extract in syllables per second, we then follow a similar procedure.

- We divide the duration of the extract by the number of syllables: thus 7.45 divided by 44 = 0.169. This is the average duration of the syllables in this extract.
- We divide one second by this figure: thus one divided by 0.169 = 5.917 which is the speed in syllables per second for this extract. It is normal practice to give this speed to just one decimal place, thus 5.9.

Articulation rate

If we want to calculate the articulation rate, then we need to remove the pauses from the calculation. There are two pauses after units 01 and after 04 totalling 0.59 seconds.

- We subtract the duration of the pauses from the total duration, thus 7.45 minus 0.59 = 6.86 seconds, which is the new duration for articulation rate.

For words per minute, we divide the new duration – 6.86 – by the number of words:

- 6.86 divided by 32 = 0.214. This is the average duration for the words in this extract.
- We divide 60 seconds by this figure: 60 divided by 0.214 = 280 words per minute.

For syllables per second, we divide the new duration – 6.86 – by the number of syllables:

- 6.86 divided by 44 = 0.156. This is the average duration of the syllables in this extract.
- We divide one second by this figure: 1 divided by 0.156 = 6.4 syllables per second.

Appendix 3 Word clusters of three or more words

Below is a list of examples of three-word and some four-word clusters of function words and other frequent forms which are commonly squeezed together into short bursts spontaneous speech.

a couple of	i am in my	quite a bit of
a lot of	i don't think	so that you can
and it was a	i have to say	so i was
and that was the	i was at	so that you'd
and so they were	i got a	that could be
and they are	i had a	that you can
and it is	i mean it's	that i was
and so it	i want to	the sort of
and at the	i'd been doing at	there was an
and like this	i'm going to be	they've had some
and i was	if you did	to get to the
because i was	if i was	to have a
because they're all	in a bit more	to get the
because i was	in our own	well on the
but they are	is of course	when they have
but you couldn't	it was the	where i was a
but it is	it was you know	which is a
but it was	it had a	which was at
but if you	it was a	who is the
did you have a	it was just	you got to the
do you think	of the very	

The ten word clusters beginning with the first person pronoun *I* at the top of the second column are given in lower case. This is to show that *I* is likely to be non-prominent.

Appendix 4   Creating an obscure acoustic blur

This appendix contains guidelines to help you create patches of 'obscure acoustic blur' (cf. Chapter 16.1) to be used in the learning activities described in Chapters 18 and 19. They give advice on how to reduce citation forms to soundshapes which they might have when they are non-prominent and spoken fast in the squeeze zones of speech units (cf. Chapter 3). The goal is *to make students better at decoding speech*, by helping them become familiar and comfortable with the squeezed soundshapes that words have in spontaneous speech.

These guidelines go beyond the normal list of connected speech rules of assimilation, elision and linking. They may therefore seem to be instructions for *how to be incorrect* and *how to create communication breakdowns*. However, I emphasise that our goal is *not* correct pronunciation. Instead, it is *to help learners with listening outside the classroom, in the real – or virtual – world*. The notion of 'correct pronunciation' does not apply to these guidelines.

The suggestions for the squeezed versions should be regarded as being at the *maximally squeezed* end of a *maximally-clear/maximally-squeezed* continuum. At one end of the continuum is the citation form e.g. *able*, at the other end is a squeezed form e.g. *ale*. We will use a right-pointing arrow '>' to mean 'the pronunciation of this word is heading in this direction'. Thus with *able > ale* the arrow means that the word *able* has a variety of soundshapes between the citation form at the *maximally-clear* end of the continuum and *ale* at the *maximally-squeezed* end of the continuum. In between there will be many versions, in which the realisation of the consonant |b| gradually diminishes until we get to *ale*. It may be helpful to consider the maximally squeezed soundshape (in this case *ale*) as *something the squeezed shapes seem to be heading towards*.

Each row in the following table lists only one type of squeezing, but words often undergo different changes simultaneously. For example *able* may undergo the processes of guidelines 5, 6 and 19 simultaneously, which would result in a soundshape close to |eʊ|. The right-hand column gives examples of speech units in which the words discussed in the other columns occur non-prominently.

To summarise, these guidelines are:

- for creating the 'obscure acoustic blur' of rapid casual speech
- for creating fast, compressed bursts of the stream of speech
- *not* for correct pronunciation – they help create vocal gymnastic exercises for listening
- for non-prominent syllables in squeeze zones before and between prominences
- not rules – notions of correctness do not apply.

	Guidelines	Non-prominent soundshapes	Example speech units
1	Make 'past tense' |t| and |d| inaudible in front of both consonants and vowels	realise**d she** > reali**se she** realise**d it** was > reali**se it** was	|| HE realise she was GONE || || I realise it was HER ||
2	Remove final |t| and |d| before consonants and vowels	le**ft** bank > le**ff** bank le**ft** open > le**ff** open again**st** it > again **s**it kin**d** of > ky**ne uv**	|| it's ON the leff bank NOW || || it WAS leff open aGAIN || || HE'S again sit NOW || || HE'S kyne of NICE ||
3	Make the final |t| of *that* and *at* into glottal stops before consonants and vowels	tha**t** must > |ðæʔ| muss a**t** our > |æʔ| our a**t** about > |æʔ| about	|| i'm SURE tha'muss HURT || || SHE'S a'our house NOW || || i'll be THERE a'about TEN ||
4	Remove the initial consonant |ð| of *that*, *this*, *the* after both consonants and vowels	reali**se that** > realiza**t** and **then** > annen in **the** > in**ner** for **this** > for **iss** see **that** > see **ut**	|| I realizat i'd LEFT it || || he CAME annen WENT || || i SAW them inner GARden || || i've PLANS foriss EVEning || || can YOU see ut it's GOOD ||
5	Make every diphthong a monophthong based on its first element	**rea**lise > **rill** eyes my **time** > ma **tam** **boy**'s a > **bore**'s a **a**ble > **e**bble **ou**t of > **a**tta **sou**th > **saa**th	|| I rill eyes it's LOST || || he SAID ma tam's FINished || || she SAID the bore's a FOOL || || he's NOT ebble to DO that || || HE'S atta LUCK || || in NORTH and saath LONdon ||
6	Avoid full closure for the stop consonants |p,t,b,d|	**p**urse > **f**urss cut it > cu**rr**it |kʊrɪt| a lot of > a lo**rr**uv pro**d**uce > pro-**use** mi**dd**le > mi**ll** a**b**le > a**le** to**t**al > to**ll**	|| i LEFT my furss at HOME || || it's BETter to currit OPen || || he SPOKE a lorruv SENSE || || in ORder to pro-use COFFee || || NEAR the mill of the PAGE || || he's NOT ale to COME || || it's NOT the toll COST ||
7	Change |θ| in *think* to |h|	**th**ink > **h**ink	|| the ANswer i hink is NO ||
8	Make final |z| sound similar to |s|	eye**s** > i**ce** doe**s** > du**ss**	|| she ONly had ice for HIM || || the WAY it duss THAT ||

Phonology for Listening

	Guidelines	Non-prominent soundshapes	Example speech units
9	Simplify clusters by removing one or two elements.	first call > furs call first of all > furs of all keeps on > kees on	|| my VEry furs CALL || || furs of all HE was LATE || || he JUST kees on GOing ||
10	Drop |k| in *extra*, *expected*	extra > estra expected > espected	|| it's ONE estra COpy || || DON'T espect him SOON ||
11	Drop |k| and |t| from *next*	next time > ness time	|| we'll DO it ness TIME ||
12	Omit the initial segment of the first word in a speech unit	if you've a > few vuh	|| few vuh MINute to SPARE ||
13	Make negative morphemes close to inaudible.	illegal > legal	|| OTHer legal DRUGS ||
14	Remove weak middle syllables from three syllable words	cont.**ra**.ry > cont.ry diff.**i**.cult > diff.cult fin.**a**.lly > fine.ly	|| it ISn't contry to THAT || || it WAS a diffcul TIME || ||and THEN finely THIS one ||
15	Drop weak syllables from the edges of words	year **a**go > year go **a**nother > noth |nʌð|	|| a YEAR go that i WENT || || WAS there noth QUESTION ||
16	Take care to mess up *have* clusters	you **have** a > yavva you are **having** > yavving to **have** a > tavva	|| i SEE yavva NEW one || || TELL him yavving a MEAL || || it's TIME tavva CHAT ||
17	Don't repeat a segments which are next to each other, and similar	ye**ar a**head> ye**ar** head	|| PLAN the year head NOW ||
18	Make two words into one	**too ear**ly > **twir**ly go over > gover |gəʊvə|	|| it's FAR twirly to SAY || || i'm GOing to gover NOW ||
19	Make |ɫ| vowel-like	feel > fee-oo |fiːʊ| (sounds close to **phew**)	|| DON'T fee-oo so BAD||

Glossary

accent	The sum of differences in the sounds in speech (words and intonation) which sets one group of speakers apart from another group, closely associated with a country, a region, or social group.
accent reduction	The process of attempting to change an L2, regional, or non-standard accent into a standard accent such as RP or General American.
acoustic blur	The continuous stream of speech which is difficult, if not impossible, to transcribe as a sequence of separate phonetic symbols.
acted speech	Speech created for ELT textbooks by actors who are working from a script.
activity	An observable behaviour – a 'doing'. For example an observer sitting at the back of the class might say 'they are doing a listening activity'.
allophone	One of a range of sounds that can count as the realisation of a phoneme, e.g. velar-l |ɫ| is an allophone of the phoneme |l|.
alveolar tap	The consonant sound – symbol |ɾ| – common in American English, which makes *writer* sound close to *rider*.
ambient noise	The noise from the environment in which a recording is made – it includes the echoes that the shape of a room may create, or the background noise of a street or a shopping arcade.
articulation rate	A measure of the speed at which a speaker produces a continuous series of sounds. It typically excludes silent pauses and it may additionally exclude drafting phenomena.
assimilation	The change of a speech sound to make it more like the sounds around it – e.g. *ten people* sounds close to *tem people,* where the 'n' of 'ten' turns into 'm' because of the following 'p'.
attitude	A feeling that you have towards a person, place, thing or abstraction.
bilabial	A speech sound made with two lips e.g. the consonant in *pip*.
bi-accentedness	The situation where a speaker uses (quite naturally, without affectation) different accents with different groups of people, in different contexts.

blur gap	The gap between the L1 speaker's perception that full words (e.g. 'where there were') were spoken and the acoustic fact that only very small traces (e.g. [we.ðe.wə] *weatherwuh*) were actually present in the sound substance.
broad accent	A version of an accent in which the features are at their most different from those of the standard accent.
Canadian raising	The feature of the Canadian accent which is caricatured by people who say *aboot* instead of *about* or *anyhoo* instead of *anyhow*.
careful speech model	A model of speech based on the guidelines for pronunciation and clear careful speech that appear in most language teaching materials. It is based on standard accents, the citation form and rules about speaking isolated sentences. These rules include 'the main stress goes on the last lexical item in a sentence' and 'the intonation of yes-no questions rises'. Such rules are inappropriate for spontaneous speech.
centring diphthong	A diphthong which has |ə| as the second element., e.g. |eə| in *there*.
citation form	The maximally-clear pronunciation of a word in isolation, in which the segments, syllables and stress patterns are clearly heard.
clause	A grammatical unit consisting of a subject and a verb – with the optional addition of an object, complement or adverbial.
collocate	A word which is reasonably likely to occur next to another word.
comprehensibility	The listener's perception of how easy or difficult it is to understand another person's speech.
connected speech	A concept from the careful speech model, which explains how word boundaries change when words occur together in the stream of speech.
content words	Words which carry the meaning of the sentence, e.g. nouns, verbs, adjectives.
contours	The sound substance's equivalent of mountain peaks (high and not so high), valleys (deep and not so deep) and slopes (steep and shallow).
contrastive stress	A concept from the *careful speech model:* an unexpected stress placement.
conventional listening lesson	A lesson which includes listening comprehension exercise with pre-, while-, and post-listening tasks; making the learners feel good about themselves, activating schemata, pre-teaching vocabulary, encouraging prediction and reviewing the students' answers to questions.

convergence	The process by which people, who start interacting with each other in two different accents, subconsciously change their accents so that they resemble each other in some features.
creak	A rasping, slow vibration/noise which accompanies the speech of some people, it is becoming common in the speech of younger people.
cut-glass accent	An RP accent found in British English which sounds strongly upper class.
decoding	The part of listening that involves recognising the words that occur in the sound substance of speech.
decoding gap	The gap between the teacher's and the students' perceptions of what the sound substance of a recording contains.
descriptive model	An explanation of how speech works which is based on the evidence of how speakers use speech in everyday circumstances. It is often contrasted with a 'prescriptive model' – a simplified version based on rules of careful speech.
diphthong	A speech sound that contains two vowel sounds – together making one phoneme – which glide from one to the other, e.g. $|aɪ|$ in *bike* $|baɪk|$.
discoursal meaning	The meaning of tones which concern to the relationship between speaker and hearer, and what the speaker assumes is new information which *needs to be told* (with falling tone) or old information which needs to be referred to (with rising tone).
discourse	A stretch of continuous language longer than a sentence.
discourse marker	A word that helps with the organisation or planning of speech.
disfluencies	A pejorative linguistic term used to refer to spontaneous speech phenomena such as pauses, hesitations and restarts.
distinct accent	A strong version of an accent in which the features are quite different from those of the standard accent.
drafting phenomena	A collective terms for silent pauses, filled pauses, stepping stones, repetitions, restarts and reformulations. These phenomena remain in the sound substance of spontaneous speech, whereas they are edited out of prepared speeches and other planned writing.
ELF	see English as Lingua Franca

Phonology for Listening

elided	A sound which is elided is one that is omitted or dropped e.g. $\|t\|$ in 'just seven' $\|dʒʌs sevən\|$.
elision	The process by which a sound, syllable or word becomes omitted or dropped.
emotion	Strong feelings such as 'happiness' or 'anger'.
emulation model	A prestige model of speech or language which acts as a guide – something to copy and imitate – for learning 'the best English' (or any other language).
English as Lingua Franca (ELF)	A perspective on the global, social, and political status of the English language which recognises that English is no longer the property of its native speakers, and that many if not most interactions in English take place between L2 speakers without any L1 speakers present.
epenthesis, epenthetic	The process by which a sound is inserted – e.g. $\|r\|$ in 'law and order' which can sound close to 'law rand order'.
Estuary English	An accent of English, with some features of the Cockney accent of the East End of London which is widely used amongst younger people. Originally used to refer the accents of people living in the Thames Estuary region, this accent has spread to many areas of the UK, thanks to the influence of programmes such as the BBC's EastEnders.
filled pauses	Non-word vocal noises which are used to give the speaker planning time. They are spelled in different ways such as *erm, er, um, uh, ah* and *ahm*. Their use is often deplored, but they are a normal feature of spontaneous speech.
five-part pattern	A table with five columns, each row containing a double-prominence speech unit, showing the squeeze zones – for explanatory and teaching purposes.
frequent forms	Words which are the statistically most likely to appear in spontaneous speech: e.g. *I, you, the*, etc.
function words	Words with a grammatical role, e.g. articles, pronouns, conjunctions.
General American (GenAm)	The accent of American English which is represented in general and pronunciation dictionaries and used as a model for teaching English
goal	A purpose for learning – a learning target which students work towards.
handling	A metaphor which uses the vocabulary of the sense of touch to help teachers and learners get a feel for ways in which the sound substance of speech can be experimented with and learned from.

identity	A person's sense of themselves as an individual in relation to other individuals and groups whose values give them a sense of belonging and self-worth.
intelligibility	The degree of a listener's understanding of an utterance.
interval	A linguistic term used to describe the gap in time between two events (e.g. stresses or prominences) in speech.
intonation	The overall shape of a stretch of speech as created by a speaker's use of prominence, non-prominence, key and tone.
isochronous rhythm	A rhythm which is perceived to be a sequence of events (e.g. the occurrence of a stress or a syllable) in equal timing, or 'on the beat'.
isochrony	The equal timing of intervals between stresses or prominences.
key	The three choices of pitch height - high, mid and low - which a speaker can select for any prominence.
kinesics	The study of how movements of the face and the body (popularly known as 'body language') contribute to communication.
L1 (English) speaker	A speaker of English for whom it is their native, first or mother tongue.
L2 (English) speaker	A speaker of English for whom it is their second, or auxiliary language or lingua franca.
lenition	The softening, or weakening of a consonant, e.g. the 'soft-t' of Irish *let*.
lexical segmentation	The process of identifying boundaries between words in the stream of speech and thereby allowing the division of the stream of speech into individual words.
lexical stress	The relative emphasis that is given to syllables of a word – e.g. *pho.to.graph.er* has lexical stress on its second syllable *-to-*.
Lingua Franca Phonological Core	A pronunciation syllabus which only contains items which are essential for international intelligibility. This syllabus omits some of the items that would otherwise be regarded as 'required': e.g. the pronunciation of $|\eth|$ and $|\theta|$.
linking	A connected speech process in which words are joined together as if they are a continuous sequence of syllables, e.g. *looked in* sounds like *look tin*.
moderate accent	A version of an accent in which the features are not very different from those of the standard accent.

Phonology for Listening

mondegreen	A mishearing of one word, or group of words, as another word: e.g. *back to see* being heard as *Battersea*.
nasal	A speech sound which is produced with an airflow through the nose.
nasalisation	The adding of an airflow through the passages of the nose in the production of a speech sound which is not normally nasal.
native speaker	A person who has learned a particular language from birth, or from very early in life, and for whom it remains their first language.
no audible release	The absence, in the sound substance, of the final part of a stop consonant such as |p|. This occurs when two consonants overlap and the preparation for the second consonant masks the end of the first one.
non-finite clauses	A clause with a non-finite verb, with no subject, and no tense.
non-prominent syllables	The syllables in a speech unit which a speaker chooses not to highlight –shown in transcriptions in lower case letters, e.g. *where there were* in `|| where there were STREET LIGHTS ||`
non-rhotic accent	An accent in which the |r| at the end of words such as *car*, and within words such as *cards*, is not pronounced.
normal settings	The parameters of volume, clarity, etc. which are the norm for a particular person in a particular context.
normalisation	The process by which a listener 'tunes in' to the normal settings of a person's voice.
noticeability threshold	The point at which a feature of someone's speech (such as *you know* or *um*) becomes so frequent or loud, etc., as to be distracting for the listener.
noun group	A group of words that function as a single noun.
nuclear stress	The strongest stress in a sentence, usually on the last content word.
osmosis	A model of learning which involves acquisition through direct contact, or practice, and little or no teaching.
paralinguistic systems	Vocal effects such as whispering, laughing or sobbing.
pause for effect	A strategic pause used by the speaker as a deliberate choice to delay uttering a word or phrase in order to maximise the effect of saying that word or phrase.

perceived syllable timing	The rhythm of L2-speaker (or non-standard L1-speaker) speech in which there is noticeably less vowel reduction than in L1 standard speaker speech.
phonetic indeterminacy	A situation in which it is impossible to decide whether one phonetic event or another has occurred, for example whether the speaker said *a* or *the*.
phonology	The study of how languages make systematic use of sounds of the voice.
phrasal stress	The concept of word-stress extended to a phrase, so that *a lot of things* has two unstressed syllables (on *a* and *of*) a secondary stress on *lot* – and a primary stress on *things*.
plasticity	The capacity to change shape. Words are 'plastic' – they vary in shape as they experience the forces of spontaneous speech.
pre-pausal lengthening	The lengthening of syllables as speech slows down before a pause.
prepositional phrase	A group of words which begin with a preposition.
prestige accent	An accent which is highly regarded by a large number of social groups.
primary stress	The syllable of a citation form that has the strongest stress: e.g. the fourth syllable of *association* |əˌsəʊ.siˈeɪ.ʃən|.
principle of best fit	When faced with uncertainty, the transcriber creates two transcriptions and selects the version which is the closest to the recorded evidence.
principle of the listener's plight	When faced with uncertainty, the transcriber creates two transcriptions and selects the version which will be of most help in teaching.
prominence prominent syllable	A syllable which has been highlighted by a speaker in that it is louder, longer, clearer or at a different pitch so that it stands out in relation to neighbouring non-prominent syllables.
prosodic systems	Vocal effects such as tenseness, acceleration, and drawling.
prosodic environment	The total sound-substance context in which a word or syllable occurs: including location in a speech unit, the overall volume, speed, and other vocal effects (e.g. tenseness, laughter).
prosody prosodic features	A collective term for the variations in pitch, loudness, tempo, rhythm and other features of the sound substance of speech.

Phonology for Listening

recasting	Starting an utterance, stopping after a few words or syllables before the utterance is complete, and then beginning again.
Received Pronunciation (RP)	The accent of British English as represented in pronunciation dictionaries such as Cambridge English Pronouncing Dictionary and the Longman Pronunciation Dictionary.
reference model	The collection of citation forms which make up an accent of English (such as Received Pronunciation or General American), which are described in dictionaries and which are used in the teaching of pronunciation
reformulation	Saying something that you have just said using different words.
regional accent	An accent which is associated with a particular geographical area such as a particular country or region.
response token	A word or short phrase such as *Mmm*, *Oh*, *Really*, which shows that the listener is paying attention to what the speaker is saying.
restarting	Starting an utterance, stopping after a few words or syllables before the utterance is complete, and then beginning again.
rhotic accent	An accent in which the |r| at the end of words such as *car*, and within words such as *cards*, is pronounced.
rhythm	A general term used to refer to the relationship between a given set of linguistic events (stresses, syllables, prominences) and a regular timed beat.
rhythmically smallest speech unit	A speech unit which has the same number of syllables and prominences.
rhythmically complete speech unit	A speech unit in which all parts have at least one syllable, for example a double-prominence speech unit which has five parts, with all five parts containing at least one syllable.
RP	See Received Pronunciation.
savouring	A metaphor which uses the vocabulary of the sense of taste to help teachers and learners think of ways in which the sound substance of speech can be experimented with and learned from.
schema/schemata	A framework of social or cultural ideas or concepts which brings to mind a scene or a standard set of behaviours.

secondary stress	The syllable of a citation form that has the second strongest stress: e.g. the second syllable of *association* |əˌsəʊ.siˈeɪ.ʃən|.
segmental phonology	A branch of phonology that focuses on the phonemes (vowels and consonants) of speech.
segmentation	The division of speech into its component words or syllables.
sentence stress	The sequence of stresses in a sentence, ending in a main stress 'on the last lexical item' of a sentence. This is a concept from the careful speech model.
sentence stress	The placement of the main stress in a sentence.
silent pauses	A gap in the sound substance of speech of 0.2 seconds or more.
slight accent	A version of an accent in which the features are only slightly different from those of the standard accent.
soft focus listening	A technique where you stop listening for meaning and instead direct your attention to the sound substance of speech: its rhythms, its different levels of volume, different speeds, different contours and levels of clarity.
softener	A phrase such as *kind of* which signals that speakers do not intend their words to be taken literally: they want them to be understood to be imprecise, or vague.
sound substance	The sound substance is the acoustic blur of the stream of speech which exits the mouth of the speaker, travels through space, and enters the ear of the listener. It is the substance that a computer program or a recording device captures.
soundshape	The acoustic shape of a word. This would traditionally be the citation form of a word. However, all words have a variety of soundshapes, even in the speech of one speaker.
speaker roles	The speaker refers to her/himself as *I* and refers to the listener as *you*: the *I* and *you* are thus speaker roles.
speaking rate	A measure of the speed of speech which includes the time taken by silent pauses and other drafting phenomena in the calculation.
speech unit	A speaker-defined rhythmic chunk of speech involving an alternation of prominent and non-prominent syllables.
spontaneous speech	Unscripted, unprepared speech which is constructed moment-by-moment in real time.

Phonology for Listening

squeeze zone	A part of a speech unit – either in front of or between prominences – where non-prominent words are squeezed and reshaped into bursts of the stream of speech.
standard accent	An accent which is generally regarded as the one to be represented in a general dictionary or pronunciation dictionary.
stepping stones	Words which speakers lengthen (usually with level tone) in order to buy themselves time to plan what to say next.
stigmatised accent	An accent which excites a great amount of negative and prejudiced reactions from a wide range of individuals and groups.
stream of speech	The flowing together of words spoken aloud, as opposed to the separate word-by-word experience of the written language. Any speech, whether scripted or unscripted, prepared or unprepared, is experienced as a stream unless the speaker makes a deliberate effort to speak it word-by-word.
stress-shift	Long words such as *observation* have both primary and secondary stress. Stress-shift occurs when the secondary stress is prominent and the primary stress is non-prominent.
stress-timing activities	Pedagogic activities which practise the relationship between prominent and non-prominent syllables, particularly the effects of squeezing on the soundshapes of words.
stress-timing theory	One half of the hypothesis that languages are of two types: stress-timed and syllable-timed. In stress-timed languages, stresses are thought to occur at equal intervals of time. It is also believed that the syllables in the intervals between the stresses become shortened. This is a refuted hypothesis.
stressed syllable	A property of a word in its citation form – a syllable which is shown in the dictionary to stand out from unstressed syllables by being louder longer or at a different pitch.
strong accent	A version of an accent in which the features are very different from those of the standard accent.
suprasegmental phonology	A branch of phonology that focuses on units of the stream of speech which are larger than single segments.
syllabic consonant	A consonant such as |n| or |l| that occurs as a syllable without a vowel (normally syllables have vowels) – e.g. *button* |bʌtn̩|.

syllable isochrony	The concept that syllables occur at equal intervals of time, at a rhythm to which it is possible to tap along with a pencil using equal beats. A discredited part of the stress-timing/syllable-timing theory.
syllable-timing theory	One half of the hypothesis that languages are of two types: syllable-timed and stress-timed. In syllable-timed languages syllables are thought to occur at equal intervals of time. It is also believed that the intervals between the stresses change in length to accommodate the weaker syllables.
syntactic boundaries	The boundaries between the components of a sentence.
syntax	The rules which govern the way words combine into clauses and sentences.
thick accent	A strong version of an accent in which the features are very different from those of the standard accent.
tone	The choice of one of five pitch movements (fall, fall-rise, level, rise, rise-fall) which occur on the last prominence in a speech unit.
tone groups	A term equivalent to *speech units* – used by Halliday and others.
tone units	A term equivalent to *tone units* – used by Crystal and others.
tonic prominence	The prominence on which the tone starts, which is always the final prominence in a speech unit.
tonic syllable	The syllable where the tone (fall, rise, level, etc.) starts.
turn	A contribution that a speaker makes to a conversation, it ends when another speaker takes over.
uptalk	A feature of speech in which rising tones occur where falling tones would normally be expected.
verb group	A group of words that function as a single verb.
vocal effects	The full range of effects that the vocal apparatus (lungs and vocal tract) can produce. These include tone (cf. Chapter 4), and all the terms of the prosodic and paralinguistic systems, e.g. tense, creak, sob, etc.
vocal range	A person's vocal range is that part of their total vocal capacity which they are currently using. The vocal range drifts up and down according to physiological, social and contextual factors and is not fixed.
vocalised pauses	A pause in speech which is filled by *erm, er,* etc.

weak forms	The soundshapes of non-prominent function words – they are much shorter than the citation form, and with reduced vowels.
window on speech framework	A collective term for the descriptive framework of five types of speech unit, five tones and three types of key which are presented in Part 1. It is a 'window' because it is a tool for observing the stream of speech.
word clusters	Groups of words that commonly occur together, e.g. *there were a.*
word stress	The relative emphasis that is given to syllables of the citation form of a word – e.g. of the five syllables of *association* $\vert\text{ə,səʊ.si'eɪ.ʃən}\vert$ the fourth has primary stress, the second has secondary stress, and the others are unstressed.
Ying moments	Moments in spontaneous speech when words are squeezed into new and unfamiliar soundshapes which are a likely source of decoding problems.
Ying's dilemma	The situation where you believe you know a word (it is in your active vocabulary) but you cannot recognise it when it occurs in speech.
yod	The name of the symbol that for the sound $\vert\text{j}\vert$ at the beginning of *yes* $\vert\text{jes}\vert$ and the second sound of British English *new* $\vert\text{njuː}\vert$.
yod coalescence	The process by which the first two consonants of *Tuesday* – $\vert\text{t}\vert$ and $\vert\text{j}\vert$ (yod) become a single consonant like the $\vert\text{tʃ}\vert$ in *church*.

Made in the USA
Charleston, SC
05 March 2016